AF773175

The Law of Beauty

This book examines the longstanding, yet ambiguous and deeply complex, relationship between law and aesthetics.

Despite numerous studies dedicated to the topic, the relationship between aesthetics and law tends to be interpreted as one between two approaches, two thematic horizons, two disciplines, or two distinct semantic universes. Conversely, the book argues that legal phenomena cannot be properly understood without grasping the relevance of aesthetics within the experience of law itself, nor the intrinsically political and regulatory character of aesthetic experience, considering how it shapes our social world by affecting people as sensate bodies. The book examines a series of current issues that arise from the ambiguous relationship between law and aesthetics, such as the legal status of aesthetic objects, the aesthetic analysis of legal texts, the conflicts between aesthetics and legal principles, as well as the legal relevance of ugliness. It is only by taking into account the inextricable nexus between aesthetics and aesthesis, that is, both the epistemological level and the question of how people see, hear, and feel, that we can understand these issues.

This book will appeal to scholars and students in legal theory and philosophers with interests in law and aesthetics.

Fabio Macioce is Professor at LUMSA University, Rome, Italy.

The Law of Beauty

The Troubled Relationship Between Law and Aesthetics

Fabio Macioce

Routledge
Taylor & Francis Group
a GlassHouse Book

First published 2026
by Routledge
4 Park Square, Milton Park, Abingdon, Oxon OX14 4RN

and by Routledge
605 Third Avenue, New York, NY 10158

A GlassHouse book

Routledge is an imprint of the Taylor & Francis Group, an informa business

© 2026 Fabio Macioce

The right of Fabio Macioce to be identified as author of this work has been asserted in accordance with sections 77 and 78 of the Copyright, Designs and Patents Act 1988.

All rights reserved. No part of this book may be reprinted or reproduced or utilised in any form or by any electronic, mechanical, or other means, now known or hereafter invented, including photocopying and recording, or in any information storage or retrieval system, without permission in writing from the publishers.

Trademark notice: Product or corporate names may be trademarks or registered trademarks, and are used only for identification and explanation without intent to infringe.

British Library Cataloguing-in-Publication Data
A catalogue record for this book is available from the British Library

Library of Congress Cataloging-in-Publication Data
Names: Macioce, Fabio author
Title: The law of beauty : the troubled relationship between law and aesthetics / Fabio Macioce.
Description: Abingdon, Oxon [UK] ; New York, NY : Routledge, 2025. | Includes bibliographical references and index.
Identifiers: LCCN 2025008458 (print) | LCCN 2025008459 (ebook) | ISBN 9781032964348 hardback | ISBN 9781032964362 paperback | ISBN 9781003589426 ebook
Subjects: LCSH: Law and aesthetics | Law—Philosophy | Aesthetics
Classification: LCC K487.A3 M33 2025 (print) | LCC K487.A3 (ebook) | DDC 340/.1—dc23/eng/20250307
LC record available at https://lccn.loc.gov/2025008458
LC ebook record available at https://lccn.loc.gov/2025008459

ISBN: 978-1-032-96434-8 (hbk)
ISBN: 978-1-032-96436-2 (pbk)
ISBN: 978-1-003-58942-6 (ebk)

DOI: 10.4324/9781003589426

Typeset in Sabon
by Apex CoVantage, LLC

To my wife, who brings joy and beauty into our lives.

Contents

Chapter 1

Introduction

Law and imagination

The relationship between aesthetics and law, or between aesthetics and ethics, has long attracted the attention of scholars.[1] It is possible, on the one hand, to analyse the relationship between aesthetics and law as if they were two distinct objects that we can compare or relate to each other in various ways. However, this approach only captures one aspect of the issue: law and aesthetics have a deeper conjunction, such that aesthetics is part of legal experience and law is part of aesthetic experience.[2] Therefore, on the other hand, it is also possible to analyse law from an aesthetic perspective, and discuss not only its formal, symbolic, and visual aspects but also the impact it has on those who experience it as an aesthetic object, something that is *staged*. When both these perspectives are given due consideration, and merged, the characteristics, contradictions, and tensions of this matter are better understood.

Indeed, the relationship between aesthetics and law can certainly be interpreted as one between two approaches, two thematic horizons, two disciplines, or two distinct semantic universes. At the same time, one cannot properly understand legal phenomena without grasping the relevance of aesthetics within the experience of law itself, that is, within the way norms are produced, drafted, applied, or interpreted; nor is it possible to overlook the normative dimension and intrinsically regulatory character of aesthetic experience, as well as the social role of the parameters (i.e., norms) of beauty and ugliness, and so on. As it has been demonstrated by the analyses of Goodrich, Douzinas, Manderson, Matthews, and many others,[3] aesthetics

1 For a recent overview, see Kamil Zeidler and Joanna Kamień, eds., *Aesthetics of Law. From Methodology to Manifestations* (Springer Nature, 2024).

2 Jacques Rancière, *Aisthesis: Scenes from the Aesthetic Regime of Art*, trans. Zakir Paul (Verso, 2013).

3 Peter Goodrich, "Signs Taken for Wonders," *Law and Social Inquiry* 23 (1998): 707; Peter Goodrich, *Oedipus Lex: Psychoanalysis, History, Law* (Berkeley: University of California

DOI: 10.4324/9781003589426-1

is a kind of human experience internal to law (and not only law). Both of these approaches must be held together if we are to understand how law and aesthetics intertwine and shape each other.

The awareness of the need to hold these approaches together is not obvious. An empirical confirmation of this can be found in the observation of the limited presence of legal aesthetics in university curricula: although courses in law and literature or legal aesthetics are now widespread, they remain related to specific interests rather than a necessary epistemological approach. Of course, one can legitimately isolate law and aesthetics, and consider them as two distinct fields, or two semantic frameworks, each with its own rules and different operating mechanisms. From this perspective, many points of contact can be highlighted, as well as the differences, depending on the subjective perspective and different historical or social circumstances. Accordingly, it is possible to believe that the fields of ethics and law, and that of aesthetics, are mostly independent, and that if an educated lawyer may dabble in literature or fine arts, or have a passion for chamber music or opera, this will add nothing to his or her qualities as a legal professional. A good judge remains a good judge regardless of his or her capacity to appreciate a beautiful sunset, a fine play, an opera, or a poem.

Similarly, artists can be *'engagé'*, committed to using one's art to convey social messages, promote moral values, and struggle for justice; one can follow a tradition that Zola first, and Sartre later, made crucial in the twentieth century, according to which (at least) writers have chosen to "unveil the world" in order to enable the reader to take responsibility for it. Writers, for Sartre, have an essentially political role, because they force the reader to choose whether to leave society as it is or to change it. Art (prose writing, in particular) is a message that is addressed to free people and has freedom as its object.[4] And yet, an artist may very well perform none of these tasks, and the aesthetic value of what he or she does would in no way be impoverished or called into question: whether this separation between beauty and justice, or between artistic creation and commitment to the good, is a programmatic choice, or a historical stage in the process of evolution of the role of the intellectual,[5] the fact remains that the link between these dimensions is no longer considered necessary, but only possible.

Years ago, in a beautiful pamphlet on justice and beauty, Luigi Zoja argued that our societies (at least, those in the contemporary West) have embraced a functionalist culture in which ethics and aesthetics have been detached, relegating ethics to an entirely marginal and ancillary role. While ethics regulates

Press, 1995); Costas Douzinas and Ronnie Warrington, *Justice Miscarried: Ethics, Aesthetics, and the Law* (Hemel Hempstead: Harvester Wheatsheaf, 1994).

4 Jean Paul Sartre, *Qu'est-ce que la littérature?* (Paris: Gallimard, 1948), 70.

5 Elémire Zolla, *Eclissi dell'intellettuale* (Bompiani, 1959).

human life, producing norms to distinguish what is licit or illicit, what is correct and what is not, and what is right from what is wrong, aesthetics remains in a corner, invoked rather than practised: the aesthetic experience has eventually been degraded to mere entertainment.[6] Aesthetics has lost any moral task; it has been reduced to art, or to a kind of art that people no longer understand: it has become intellectualistic and academic, inaccessible, and far from people's everyday life, far from public places, from schools, or from places/houses of worship (which are often absolutely hideous), and is now hidden in museums and places intended for artistic enjoyment.

Nevertheless, it is also possible to find, in everyday experience, evidence of an opposite awareness, namely of the profound union between law and aesthetics. Allow me to take a very trivial example from everyday experience. Some years ago, invited as a guest at the Sanremo festival (a famous song competition between Italian singers: that is, an aesthetic experience, albeit questionable at times), the actor and director Roberto Benigni gave a sort of lecture on the Constitution. More precisely, he delivered an apology for the Italian Constitution, calling it – using a bit of rhetoric – the most "beautiful" in the world, without anyone being all that surprised.

I am not in a position to say, of course, whether the Italian Constitution is the most beautiful in the world, or not; I would perhaps be more cautious, not knowing all the constitutional Charters in force, and appreciating others as well, but I think it is interesting that no one was surprised by such a judgement. Certainly, it is a beautiful text: in the sense that it is well-written (especially in its original parts); it is worthy of admiration on the historical-political level, for the effort of mutual understanding made by the parties and political groups that drafted it; and it conveys a truly strong and pervasive idea of the common good. But it is also beautiful in a sense closer to what we mean when we appreciate a good movie: beyond specific, formal, or content-related aspects, the Constitution (like a good movie) is beautiful because it excites, strikes our imagination, speaks not only to our minds but touches our emotional sphere when we read it.

What the common sense highlights here is that the aesthetic experience is internal to legal phenomena and entities: is not strange that such a *fundamental* legal instrument, which is placed at the foundation of an entire legal system, is almost necessarily an emotionally dense and meaningful text. Indeed, this characteristic depends on its ambition to motivate action, stimulate collective action, and guide people's consciousness and political action, as well as the activity of legal professionals. To write a constitution as a text for bureaucrats would be to write it badly, for it would be reduced to its functional level and deprived of its symbolic value.

6 Luigi Zoja, *Giustizia e bellezza* (Bollati Boringhieri, 2007), 25.

As Castoriadis wrote,[7] law maintains an essential relationship with the *imaginary* institution of society, that is, with the capacity to create possible universes, and to translate them into symbolic systems.[8] The imaginary, rather than simply being the image of something, is a ceaseless and indeterminate creation of figures and forms in which the development of social life consists.[9] The historical reality – the world in which we live right here and now – is never integrally rational, for otherwise our doing, our ability to plan and imagine, would make no sense. We come up against an enormity of unacceptable things daily, which depend on the functioning of the society in which we live, and we need to make sense of our efforts, our struggles, and our daily commitment. We need to think that a different world is possible, and a different way of living is plausible. Therefore, the symbolic order of a society, its set of representations, orders, values, and principles, all of this is certainly something *given*, but it must be continually reconstructed and rethought. In other words, our reality is always at the centre of processes of modification and – to use Castoriadis' term – imagination: the imaginary is the place where we make things happen that are not yet present, or in which we make these things different from what they are.

Every constitution defines a symbolic universe, imagining and designing a social order which is different from the one history delivered to us. In European countries, for instance, constitutions delineate societies where some practices have value – solidarity, dignity, respect for equality – and others do not – fascism and racism. In this sense, precisely because they create frameworks of meaning, and because they draw societal orders before they are factually in place, they stand on a level that is not only normative but also creative, imaginative, and aesthetically comprehensible. To put it more explicitly: to think of a society based on gender equality in 1948, for instance, meant putting one's imagination to work, and doing so not merely for the sake of fiction but precisely to make it *happen*. It took decades for our societies to come closer to that imagined picture, and a considerable distance still separates us from it. Nevertheless, the power of envisioning a symbolic universe, and making it exist in the real world, is to make the legal and aesthetic dimensions truly meet.

7 Cornelius Castoriadis, *L 'institution imaginaire de la société* (Seuil, 1975/2021), K. Blamey, trans., *The Imaginary Institution of Society* (Polity Press, 1987).

8 The necessity of the symbolic dimension in law and legal systems is analysed thoroughly by Daniele Cananzi, *Estetica del diritto. Sul fondamento geologico del diritto (with an Introduction by Robert Jacob)* (Giappichelli, 2017).

9 Castoriadis, *L 'institution imaginaire de la société*, 3.

Law, beauty, or law and beauty: a complicated story

The aesthetic dimension is therefore understood – in this crucial respect – as intrinsic to law, and not only as a field of human experience with some contact points or similarities with law. However, depending on whether more emphasis has been placed on one or the other approach, and to the extent that the aesthetics-law plexus has been observed exclusively from one of the mentioned points of view, it might be difficult to draw an overall picture. As I have said, that between aesthetics and law is, at the same time, a relationship between two distinct entities (law *and* art, justice *and* beauty, etc.), and the experience of a mutual interpenetration.

Aesthetics not only refers to a specific philosophical domain mainly concerned with the rational understanding of beauty, following a Kantian tradition. Besides this, it refers – as Eagleton writes – to "the whole of our sensate life together",[10] that is, to affections and aversions, to bodies and senses, and to what takes root in the gaze and our biological insertion into the world. Therefore, besides the rational understanding of aesthetics, a second approach must be taken into account, that which the German philosopher Alexander Baumgarten linked to the conditions of sensory perception.[11] If one excludes this second approach (which some call *aesthesis*),[12] and limits oneself to observing the relationship between two distinct entities, contradictions and anomalies emerge.

I'm not arguing that these two approaches must always be kept together, but that they are both (equally) relevant and necessary for understanding law and its aesthetic dimension. For instance, we can examine how law and justice are represented within a range of cultural resources, taking law and aesthetics as separate domains, but if we isolate this point of view we cannot understand the importance of the multiple ways legal institutions use aesthetic means and languages, such as the emblems and icons of power. Similarly, if we only consider the relationship between aesthetics and law, and we do not study the ways in which people as sensate subjects are immersed in a social space, where the conditions of perception are shaped by law and power and vice versa, we cannot fully understand the reasons for some phenomena at the intersection of law and aesthetics. In some cases, a merely rational analysis is not sufficient: if political, moral, or affective aspects are at stake (i.e., relating to the sensations and perceptions of the beholder), any

10 Terry Eagleton, *The Ideology of the Aesthetic* (Blackwell, 1990), 13.

11 Alexander Baumgarten, *Reflections on Poetry*, trans. K Aschenbrenner and W. B. Holtner (Berkley: University of California Press, 1954).

12 Daniel Matthews and Illan rua Wall, "Legal Aesthesis: Affect, Space and Encounter," *Law, Culture and the Humanities* 19, no. 2 (2023): 186–90: "The specific contribution of legal aesthesis in this context is to attend to the work that law does in shaping the conditions of sensory perception, and the work that sensory perception does in shaping law's power."

rational discussion concerning our ideas of beauty and justice is misleading. As Matthews correctly writes, other factors are often at stake, such as "unarticulated anxieties, hopes, fears, loves and hates (that) mobilise subjects in ways that orthodox accounts of agency fail to describe".[13] In these cases, a consideration of *aesthesis* is necessary.

A recent case may be an example of how, in the relationship between law and aesthetics, emotional and affective factors are relevant, so that a legal issue can only be understood through an analysis of people's "affective relations within social space".[14] In the spring of 2022, Maestro Valery Gergiev, a well-known conductor, kicks off a series of performances of *The Queen of Spades*, at La Scala Theatre in Milan. *The Queen of Spades* is a beautiful, dramatic Russian opera composed by Tchaikovsky in 1890, based on a story by Pushkin. The aesthetic level, indeed, could not be higher: a great opera, a story by a great writer, a great orchestra, and one of the most celebrated conductors of our time. Everything is beautiful, and all is very Russian, except the orchestra. A dilemma arises because, after the first performance, Russia invades Ukraine, initiating the largest and most dramatic military conflict on European territory since World War II. Consequently, the mayor of Milan, a shareholder of La Scala, asks the conductor for a kind of abjuration, or more precisely, to officially distance himself from the decision of his country's government to invade Ukraine. Maestro Gergiev refuses to do so (the reasons for this choice are not known), and La Scala decides to terminate this collaboration. The resolution adopted by the Italian theatre was taken as a model: after a short time, other European theatres (Munich, Paris, Rotterdam) discontinued their collaborations with the Russian Maestro. Contracts involving artistic performances have been terminated or suspended, not for aesthetic reasons – the object of the performance being an artistic performance – but for political or generically ethical reasons. It is not considered acceptable for a pro-Russian artist, or at any rate a supporter of the Russian government's choices (who knows precisely to what extent), to direct a Russian opera, for which he was certainly qualified. And it is not acceptable because the Russia-Ukraine war goes against the principles European states recognise and value, not because his artistic performance was not aesthetically appreciable.

To further complicate the situation, Anna Netrebko, one of the most beautiful voices in contemporary opera and a Russian herself, intervenes in the *querelle* by putting her finger on the sore spot: although subjectively opposing the war (she openly spoke out against military intervention), she believes that it is not right to ask an artist to take sides against his or her country, *as*

13 Matthews and Wall, "Legal Aesthesis," 189.

14 Daniel Matthews, "Law and Aesthetics in the Anthropocene: From the Rights of Nature to the Aesthesis of Obligations," *Law, Culture and the Humanities* 19, no. 2 (2023): 227–47.

a matter of principle. An artist should be evaluated only from an aesthetic point of view, not on a political or moral level. And this is because – we could add – the plane of aesthetics must be separated from that of ethics and law, and the only relevant aspect for artistic performances must be specifically the aesthetic one. Politics, law, and ethics are dimensions that should have nothing to do with art, music, and beauty. Therefore, in opposition to La Scala's decision, Netrebko also chose to abandon her engagement to the disappointment of her admirers for her not taking part in the performances of Adriana Lecouvreur, scheduled in the same theatre.

Here, then, is one of the many possible stumbling blocks in the mono-focal analysis of the issue. If, in order to understand the relationship between law and aesthetics, we focus solely on the rational plane, on content, on the rational judgement on art and beauty, Anna Netrebko's arguments are perfectly sound. If, on the other hand, we consider the experience of subjects in social space, and how visual and sensate experiences overlap with power relations that orders people's perception of the world,[15] things might be different. Our access to the world is bodily and affectively mediated – as Davies suggests[16] – and this makes us more or less sensitive to facts, actions, and statements. Legal facts do not escape this mechanism: on the contrary, they are fully internal to it, both as screens interposed between the subject and the reality, thereby conditioning our understanding of it, and as objects of our sensations and affective perceptions.[17] Similar cases have happened several times, and none of them can be fully understood if one neglects one of the two dimensions mentioned (aesthetics and aesthesis). In the last century, for instance, the Furtwängler affair raised a similar question, and the decades-long refusal by Israeli orchestras to play Wagner was certainly not motivated by an aesthetic judgement so much as by his influence on the behaviour of the nazi leaders and by the reactions his music elicited among the Jews of Israel.

In the same way, the more specific relationship between justice and beauty (better: between what in different times and places was considered right, and what was considered beautiful) cannot be understood if either approach is left out: both justice and beauty have been the subject of rational understanding and analysis, on the one hand, and both are relevant in the perspective (aesthesis) of a bodily, affective, and sensuous experience of social life, on the other. Of course, the way of understanding the relationship between justice and beauty is changeable, but the content and consequences of this

15 This approach highlights the political relevance of the "sensible" and its sharing, with Rancière's words: see Jacques Rancière, *The Politics of Aesthetics* (London: Continuum, 2011).

16 Margaret Davies, *Law Unlimited: Materialism, Pluralism and Legal Theory* (Abingdon: Routledge, 2017), 72.

17 Costas Douzinas, "A Legal Phenomenology of Images," in *Law and Art: Justice and Aesthetics*, ed. Oren Ben-Dor (Abingdon: Routledge, 2011), 253.

relationship have also been conditioned by the intertwining of the two perspectives already mentioned.

Furthermore, aesthetics and law are in themselves ambivalent dimensions. For example, it is commonly believed (and not entirely wrong) that the aesthetic and ethical dimensions were, in the Greek culture, thought of as unitary or connected: yet this is not true for the whole of Greek thought, and this connection did not always have the same meaning. In other words, one cannot speak of a connection between justice and beauty in the Greek world as if justice and beauty were, in classical Greek philosophy, two unambiguous or clear-cut categories, and as if they corresponded perfectly to what we mean today by justice and beauty. The opposite, if anything, is true. Both beauty and justice, and more generally aesthetics, morality, and law, have been thought of in different ways throughout history both as single concepts and through their interrelations. None of these dimensions has a unified epistemological status historically, and each way of understanding law and aesthetics has resulted in a different relationship (or even an absence of relationship) between them.

We can easily realise how ambivalent and changing this relationship is if we consider the iconography of justice and one of the signs we most frequently associate with the image of justice: the blindfold.[18] While the representation of justice as a blindfolded woman is still very common today, it is interesting to point out the relevance of this iconographic element precisely from an aesthetic perspective.[19] In a sense, the blindfold over the eyes of justice could indicate an irrelevance of the aesthetic dimension, in the practice of such virtue. If justice is blindfolded, one of the main possibilities of access to the aesthetic dimension is barred. However, I argue that the presence of the blindfold on the eyes of justice is somehow related to the alternative between a rationalistic and an aesthesis-oriented approach. Of course, this is not the only factor that has led to such a significant variation in the iconography of justice, but I think this element is nonetheless relevant and useful in understanding it.

Throughout history, justice has not always been depicted with a blindfold over her eyes.[20] Indeed, in representations from Roman times, visible on coins from the reign of Tiberius, she is depicted as a woman with a sword in one hand, indicating state power, and scales in the other, this symbol probably

18 On the blindfold and its ambivalent and oscillating meaning, see Valérie Hayaert, "The Paradoxes of Lady Justice's Blindfold," in *The Art of Law. Artistic Representations and Iconography of Law and Justice in Context, from the Middle Ages to the First World War*, eds. Stefan Huygebaert et al. (Cham: Springer Nature, 2018), 201–21. See also Nancy I. Meyers, "Painting the Law," *Cardozo Arts & Entertainment Law Journal* 14, no. 2 (1996): 397–406.

19 The ambiguities internal to the images of Justice are well analysed by Dennis E. Curtis and Judith Resnik, "Images of Justice," *Yale Law Journal* 96, no. 8 (July 1987): 1727–72.

20 Franca Marcílio, "The Blindness of Justice: An Iconographic Dialogue between Art and Law," in *See*, eds. Andrea Pavoni et al. (University of Westminster Press, 2018), 159–96.

derived from the theme of weighing souls in the Egyptian Book of the Dead. But there is no blindfold in these images.[21] In actual fact, she will have no blindfold until roughly the fifteenth century. If we think of medieval depictions, foremost Giotto's painting in the Scrovegni Chapel in Padua – the marvellous series of the Virtues, from 1306 – we still find justice with its eyes wide open, careful to consider the specific cases and circumstances of the individual case, weighing the positions of the two disputants, placed on the plates of the scales she holds in her hands. She is justice as fairness, the justice that does not merely apply abstract rules but, flexible as the Lesbian rule, finds the right measure for each case.[22] It is Injustice, on the contrary, that keeps its eyes closed: in fact, Giotto depicts it as a sullen old man, with nails as long as claws, and tilted sideways, indifferent to the scenes of violence that take place at his feet. So, similarly, Justice is depicted by Pollaiolo, in a painting originally made for the Tribunale di Mercanzia in Florence, or by Raphael, in the Stanza della Segnatura in the Vatican: in both cases, Justice has a sword; in Pollaiolo's painting she holds a globe – another symbol of power – but no blindfold appears. Justice sees us very well; indeed she *must* see us because it is only through a careful gaze that she can grasp reality, the beauty of what needs to be preserved, as well as the characteristics of the case. In all these cases, the aesthetic approach to justice is well present: justice sees, feels, is moved, and has a physical and affective understanding of reality.

It was approximately the end of the fifteenth century when people began to put a blindfold over Justice's eyes. The first image showing such a new attribute is probably a wood engraving from 1494 depicting a madman covering Justice's eyes, an illustration from Sebastian Brant's *Narrenschiff* (*Ship of Fools*). Initially, the blindfold suggests that Justice has been deprived of her ability to understand reality and is therefore also unable to use her sword and see what is balanced on her scales.[23] The blindfold, in short, far from being a positive attribute of impartiality, is the act of a madman; it is an absurdity that prevents Justice from being herself. Only gradually, first in the German area and then in southern Europe, does a blindfolded Justice begin to acquire a positive value,[24] and the condition of not seeing becomes an appreciable trait rather than a sign of powerlessness. According to some, this change may have been influenced by the way the Synagogue was represented

21 Martin Jay, "Must Justice be Blind? The Challenge of Images to the Law," in *Refractions of Violence*, ed. M. Jay (Routledge, 2013), 97–112.
22 Thus Aristotle, *Nicomachean Ethics*, V, 14, 1137 b.
23 Jay, "Must justice be blind?" 66.
24 Adriano Prosperi, *La giustizia bendata. Percorsi storici di un'immagine* (Einaudi, 2009); Mario Sbriccoli, La benda della giustizia: iconografia, diritto e leggi penali dal Medioevo all'età moderna, in *Ordo iuris. Storia e forme dell'esperienza giuridica*, eds. M. Sbriccoli et al. (Milano: Giuffré, 2003), 41–95.

in medieval Christian iconography:[25] traditionally depicted with blindfolded eyes – and with a broken spear – to symbolize its resistance to divine light, it was contrasted negatively with the Church, depicted instead with its eyes open, as in the pair of statues on the southern door of Strasbourg Cathedral. This image, as mentioned, would be reversed when, as a result of the Reformation (with its objectively iconophobic traits), the idea of the biblical prohibition of images, which Augustine had famously linked to an "unbridled" lust for eyes, was accepted.

Here, then, the image of Justice also ends up changing, for a blindfolded Justice could consequently avoid the seductions that affect the soul through the eyes and gain the necessary detachment to deliver impartial verdicts. Justice, in short, blindfolds herself. And if Justice blindfolds herself, and can no longer see, it is very unlikely that she can still be linked to the aesthetic dimension, and to beauty, because beauty is the only idea, as Plato teaches us, that can be experienced with the senses. Justice, once she has blindfolded herself, can be rational, cold and austere, but she will no longer have emotions, feelings, and mercy: she will not be affected (she must not be affected) by what she feels; only her reason matters.

This way of thinking about justice is ancient, and already present in Roman culture. This is because it depends not only on a change in theological perspective but also on a greater or lesser devaluation of the *aesthesic* approach. Titus Livius, in the History of Rome, uses a very revealing term from this point of view. Justice is presented as *inexorabilis*, that is, literally as deaf and blind to prayer, unable to be moved and affected (in-exorabilis). She is deaf and blind, so as not to be conditioned in her judgement by what she hears or sees. In short, there are already present, well before the Reformation and the rationalist reading of Justice, representations that exalt her *severitas*, a trait related to the ability not to look and not to be moved. Thus, for example, in Aulus Gellius[26] we find the description of Justice that he attributes to the Stoic philosopher Chrysippus: she is said to be a virgin – writes Aulus Gellius – because this symbolises her uncontaminated character, her nothing to concede to the wicked, and the fact that neither indulgent speech, nor supplication or prayer, nor flattery, nor anything else of this kind touches her. Consequently, she is painted frowning, her face rigid, her gaze intense and terrible, to instill fear in the unjust, courage in the righteous, to the latter that face appears amiable, to others hostile. Here Justice sees us, of course, but she uses her gaze to instil fear, to frighten. Her eyes do not seem capable of capturing beauty, but readily capable of subduing and frightening.

25 Robert Jacob, *Images de la justice: essai sur l'iconographie judiciaire du Moyen Age à l'age classique* (Le léopard d'or, 1994), 234.
26 Aulus Gellius, *The Attic Nights*, XIV.4.

Beauty: experiencing justice, anticipating utopia

Evidence of the necessary contact between the two mentioned dimensions relates to the importance of the ideal factor (to put it that way) in law. This factor makes evident that between law and aesthetics there is not only a relationship but also a deeper conjunction; it sheds light on the necessary understanding of the aesthetic practices the law implements to order our social life, rather than simply looking at law and aesthetics (or art) as two separate dimensions we can compare and put together, with an inter-disciplinary approach. With the words of Douzinas, "by reconciling us to radical alterity and by introducing us to difference, the law helps the imagistic staging of the world for the subject".[27]

A long tradition of studies highlighted the relevance of visual elements and perceptions in the perspective of sovereignty, as well as in the scaffolding of the political imaginary.[28] Myths, ceremonies, images, visual or mass representations, both shape the ways people see and feel, and play a crucial role in the articulation of state power.[29] All these studies highlight that aesthetics is concerned when the ordering of social relationships is at stake, because it concerns the ways senses – and bodies – are affected and ordered. When we take sovereign power into consideration, the question of how and what people see, hear, and feel, as well as how these embodied subjects are affected by legal objects (the words of legal texts, judgements, and contracts), matters as much as their reasonableness or rationality.

In this vein, the role of the ideal in law can be understood precisely by placing it at the intersection of the rational and affective dimensions, and analysing it from both a descriptive and a normative standpoint.[30] Descriptively, the ideal dimension serves to steer interpretation and application. We interpret norms based on some ideal dimension that guides us in selecting among potential alternatives. For instance, according to Dworkin, appeals to the ideals of integrity, justice, fairness, and due process help guide the

27 Douzinas, "A Legal Phenomenology of Images," 256–57.

28 Among the many, Walter Benjamin, *Illuminations* (Pimlico, 1999); Terry Eagleton, *Holy Terror* (Oxford University Press, 2005); and Terry Eagleton, "Aesthetics and Politics in Edmund Burke," *History Workshop Journal* 28, no. 1 (1989): 53–62; Giorgio Agamben, *The Highest Poverty* (Stanford University Press, 2013); and Giorgio Agamben, *Opus Dei* (Stanford University Press, 2013); Desmond Manderson, "Here and Now: From Aestheticizing Politics to Politicising Art," in *Sensing the Nation's Law: Historical Inquiries into the Aesthetics of Democratic Legitimacy*, eds. Mark Antaki et al. (Springer, 2018).

29 See, for an overview, Benite Zvi Ben-Dor, Stefanos Geroulanos, and Nicole Jerr, eds., *The Scaffolding of Sovereignty: Global Aesthetic Perspectives on the History of a Concept* (Columbia University Press, 2017); for an analysis of how sovereignty shapes and order our (bodily) perception of the reality see Terry Eagleton, *Ideology of the Aesthetic* (Wiley-Blackwell, 1990), 13.

30 Wibren Van der Burg and Sanne Taekema, eds., *The Importance of Ideals: Debating Their Relevance in Law, Morality, and Politics*, no. 10 (Peter Lang, 2004).

interpreter's activity and confine interpretation outcomes within an axiological horizon recognised by a given community.[31] Alternatively, the ideal dimension acts as a necessary reference for understanding what law is and how it functions: in Fuller's view, for instance, the Rule of Law is conceptualised as an ideal, a sort of archetype toward which single social practices gravitate to varying degrees, thereby rendering them identifiable[32] and understandable. The Rule of Law, akin to other concepts, constitutes an 'idea' pertaining to the correct execution of social practices, thus enabling us to apprehend and comprehend the law. In other words, positive law is the realisation – perhaps imperfect – of an ideal, of a certain idea of society in which rules lose their arbitrary and merely voluntary character and become the place of cooperation between subjects, of fairness and reciprocity.[33]

On the normative level, the role of the ideal dimension is intertwined with that of justice, or at least with the function that a specific social, political, or economic model has in shaping legal systems, serving as a reference or rationale for the system itself. In this vein, the ideal dimension can manifest in various ways (as a critical standard, a developmental model, or a regulatory ideal), but it remains relevant to the legal experience. Of course, discerning the contents of such an ideal dimension proves challenging; the history of legal philosophy, after all, constitutes an ongoing endeavour to flesh out such an ideal, elucidating its scope and limitations. Nevertheless, it is through this ideal dimension that values, ideas, models, and aspirations from other spheres of practical life, such as morality, economics, religion, and society,[34] infiltrate law and orient the normative choices and the evolution of legal systems.

In both cases, the ideal dimension remains at the core of the legal experience. Human beings strive to actualise their expectations concerning ideals of freedom, equality, solidarity, efficiency, security, and so forth, thereby conditioning law, normative and interpretive choices, or political decisions. Law, in short, is conditioned by a 'demand' for justice, and by the need to realise the ideals underlying the system. While the expression of this need may assume various forms (social expectations, political ideologies, meta-positive values, or a set of historically determined and perhaps constitutionalised principles), it only underscores the fact that the life of legal systems and their historical structure necessarily require reference to the ideal dimension, and to the theme of justice. The ideal of a well-ordered and just society acts as a compass for individuals grappling with non-ideal situations and existing

31 Aldo Schiavello, "Il Rule of law secondo Ronald Dworkin. Qualche Osservazione Critica," in *Rule of Law. L'ideale della legalità*, eds. G. Pino and V. Villa (Il Mulino, 2016), 121–22.

32 Francesco Viola, *1900–2000. Una storia del diritto naturale* (Giappichelli, 2021), 155.

33 Lon L. Fuller, *The Morality of Law* (Yale University Press, 1969); Nigel E. Simmonds, *Law as a Moral Idea* (Oxford University Press, 2007), 52.

34 Viola, *1900–2000. Una storia del diritto naturale*, 159.

injustices, enabling them to come to terms with a society that, regrettably, is far from that ideal.[35] The ideal dimension functions as a *realistic utopia*: it is a model toward which the citizens of a real political community can strive while organising or reforming society's basic structures.

However, a purely rational account of these values, models, and ideals is not sufficient for the ordering of social relationship. Ideals must be perceived to be effective; they need to be touched, seen, and experienced to affect reality. I am not solely referring to the political and propagandistic utilisation of art and architecture, although such practices are well-known and frequent. Strolling through Rome, probably more so than in other European cities, not only enables us to appreciate artistic beauty across various eras and styles but also to encounter diverse political-legal projects, utopias or dystopias, and varying conceptions of the citizen-power relationship and power itself. From the Ara Pacis to the Imperial Fora, from Baroque churches to the Fascist rationalism of the Eur, imperial, ecclesiastical, and civil power have shaped the city's urban fabric and form, altering models, references, ideals, and translating them into forms and images. Alongside this celebratory and somewhat propagandistic function, aesthetic experience facilitates an "anticipatory illumination"[36] of the possibilities and ideals inspiring law, imbuing that utopian reference, inevitable and necessary within legal orders, with tangibility. Indeed, aesthetic experience can perform an anticipatory function by allowing individuals to experience possibilities, needs, and goals not yet realised, but which they strive for through legal and political structures.

We need to believe in the possibility of justice, to manage our lives accordingly. Any aspiration, however noble (toward equality, solidarity, justice, fairness, efficiency, the common good, etc.), must effect social change and do so not merely as an end goal but here and now. Therefore, any proposed (or imposed) ideal orientation for the rules governing our civic life cannot merely be proposed as an argument, or a daydream; it must be somehow brought forward to the present, made accessible to our concrete experience. This is what aesthetic experience can offer: the ability to give concreteness to utopia.[37] This is the place where rationality and affective bodily experience overlap.

Not every aesthetic experience serves this function, of course, but it can. It can facilitate an intrusion of imagination into experience, thereby activating individuals' capacity to critically reject an inhibiting reality or realise a

35 John Rawls, *The Law of Peoples: With "The Idea of Public Reason Revisited"* (Harvard University Press, 1999), 12.

36 Ernst Bloch, "The Artistic Illusion as the Visible Anticipatory Illumination," in *The Utopian Function of Art and Literature*, ed. Ernst Bloch (MIT Press, 1988), 145.

37 In a similar vein, Clammer argues that art is one of society's generative aspects, rather than a mere epiphenomenon: John Clammer, *Vision and Society: Towards a Sociology and Anthropology from Art* (Routledge, 2014).

different reality. Through aesthetic experience, one can anticipate the future to explore human potentialities, maintain the need for justice (or happiness, or solidarity, or power, etc.), and anticipate what has not yet happened but might yet be, by means of which the law is a kind of promise.[38] According to Bloch, aesthetic experience allows for an anticipatory illumination, an opening toward the possibilities of modifying society, power, and legal relations so that we may construct that ideal condition of which we all have a vague perception but have never truly seen or experienced.[39]

We can certainly dream of a world without injustice, for example, or governed by reason and marked by relationships of solidarity and equality; but if we want to build it and begin to organise our relationships based on these ideals, we need to experience them, at least a little. We need to anticipate the world that will be, just as we need, with a computer rendering, to anticipate the experience of living in a certain place, in a certain house, more than we would be able to through a mere description or a blueprint on paper. Aesthetic experience is not mere semblance but is a *pre-appearance* of reality, specifically representable in an aesthetically immanent sense.[40] Art, Bloch continues, is a laboratory and manifestation of "performed possibilities"; precisely, it is an anticipation, which it is up to us to realise historically if we can and will.

After all, it is precisely in this possibility of representing the ideal that the hatred of images originates, that iconoclastic fury that periodically blinds human beings. It may arise from the rejection, as a matter of principle, of any representability of the ideal and the absolute, perhaps out of a fear of confusion between the representative and what is represented. Examples include the Fourth Commandment ("Thou shalt not make unto thee any effigy or image of that which is up there in heaven, nor down here on earth, nor in the waters under the earth") and rationalist devaluations of art as mere appearance, or the Platonic idea of art as mere imitation. Paradoxically, however, iconoclasm can also arise from the opposite notion: namely, from the recognition of art's anticipatory function and its ability to give substance to the ideal, albeit when contested as the ideal reference of a work of art. An example is found in recent anti-racist critiques that have targeted statues of figures like Columbus in the U.S. or Churchill and Queen Victoria in the U.K., not

38 On art, beauty, and social transformation see John Clammer, *Cultural Rights and Justice: Sustainable Development, the Arts and the Body* (Springer, 2018), 94 ff.; Gert Ueding, ed., *Literatur ist Utopie* (Suhrkamp, 1978).

39 Jack Zipes, "Introduction: Toward a Realization of Anticipatory Illumination," in *The Utopian Function of Art and Literature: Selected Essays*, ed. Ernst Bloch (MIT Press, 1989), xxxii.

40 Bloch, *The Principle of Hope*, 699 ff., 794 ff. See also Salomon Terreblanche, "Towards a Humanistic Narrative about Arts on Emmanuel Levinas and Ernst Bloch," *Acta Academica* 39, no. 1 (2007): 1–33.

out of a desire to vandalise the statues themselves or the people they depict (all long deceased), but out of opposition to the ideals these statues represent, allowing racist ideology or geopolitical visions of slavery to be visible and confronted. Destroying or defacing these statues rejects their anticipatory function; people reject a racist society and thus do not want a representation of that racist ideal, refusing to experience it even in images.

The analyses proposed in this book aim to discuss this idea. The relationship between law and aesthetics, as well as that between justice and beauty, is enduring, yet simultaneously ambiguous and complex. While the classical ideal of a profound union between ethical and aesthetic dimensions remains central in Western culture, the outcomes of this union do not always align with our expectations: as we will discuss in this book, the exaltation of beauty, *even* from moral, legal, and social perspectives, can lead to the exclusion of what is deemed not beautiful and of individuals deemed to be somehow marked by ugliness. However, the complexity of this question goes beyond its ambivalence, but derives from the duplicity of planes on which it stands. As I said, it is a relationship that can be understood on the epistemological level, as a relationship between concepts, and between separate dimensions that it is up to reason to compare and put together. At the same time, there is a deeper relationship between these two dimensions, both concerning our bodily sense perception, and the question of how we see, hear, and feel. Such a focus on *aesthesis* within the study of law and aesthetics highlights the relevance of people's anxieties, hopes, and fears, how they mobilise people, and how these elements order (and are implemented to order) our social space.

It is only by taking into account this inextricable duplicity that we can discuss issues such as the legitimacy of the aesthetic analysis of law (Can law be beautiful? Do we care if it is? If we say that our Constitution is beautiful, are we making a meaningful statement?). Similarly, if it is true that law has a meaningful relationship with aesthetics, it is necessary to inquire how and where the law engages with beauty (Does it protect it? Does it enhance it? And how is that possible if we do not agree on what beauty is?). In the same vein conflicts between beauty and law can be analysed: for instance, it might be possible to understand these conflicts as consequences of a radical separation between the rational plane and that of sensory perception. Only by considering both these planes, and not absolutising any of them, can we deal with questions concerning aesthetic experiences that – for various reasons – are inextricably linked to content and values rejected by the law.

All these questions, and many more, elucidate why the relationship between law and beauty is far from linear and clear. Like any enduring relationship, it has its dark aspects, its ambiguities, its gaps, and above all, it is a relationship that evolves over time. One caveat must be stressed: this book is not a historical treatise, of course, but references to changing times and sensibilities will be frequent. However, it is crucial to remember that the relationship between law and beauty is relative to a specific time and place because both law and beauty are historically determined. I do not mean to suggest that they lack objective consistency, but only that the historical dimension is fundamental to understanding their essence and manifestation. In short, it is a complicated story: a long-lasting, fundamental, at times even ambivalent and conflicting story.

Chapter 2

Justice and beauty

The classical unity

The need to hold together the conceptual analysis of the relationship between aesthetics and law, on the one hand, and the sensory perception of law, on the other (i.e., to hold aesthetics and aesthesis together), is particularly evident in the analysis of the relationship between justice and beauty. This is, as is well-known, an ancient issue, complicated by the fact that both terms have historically variable epistemological status. It is not my intention, in these pages, to outline a theory of the relationship between beauty and justice: rather, the purpose is to show how only if we hold together the conceptual and rational plane, on the one hand, and the consideration of perception and sensibility, on the other, can we understand some otherwise contradictory aspects in this long history.

A simplifying interpretation of the classical epic, often reinforced by the representations of Hollywood cinematography, strengthened the idea that in the classical world the relationship between ethics and aesthetics (expressed by the concept of *kalokagathìa*) was straightforward and linear. The simplistic idea of a mysterious and fascinating unity between the realms of beauty and moral goodness has been reinforced by the portrayal of contemporary heroes and characters of action movies – all of whom are beautiful, handsome, examples of courage and virtue, contemptuous of danger and fascinating, capable of actions bordering on the heroic. Exceptions are possible, of course, but moral virtues go hand in hand, in large measure, with beauty, from Achilles to James Bond and Lara Croft.

In the opposite way, vice, negativity, and immorality are often represented through physical ugliness, deformity, or aesthetic degradation. It is not only Hollywood imagery that confirms this idea. If we consider Thersites and Homer's description of him, we find one of the earliest representations of this reversed *kalokagathìa*, that is, the affirmation of a link between ugliness and cowardice or immorality. This idea, too, will have a long literary fortune and – as we will discuss in the last chapter – will be the reason for a marginalising and discriminatory

DOI: 10.4324/9781003589426-2

aesthetic understanding, whose effects are still relevant and pernicious.[1] Homer writes:

> Now the others sate them down and were stayed in their places, only there still kept chattering on Thersites of measureless speech, whose mind was full of great store of disorderly words, wherewith to utter revilings against the kings, idly, and in no orderly wise, but whatsoever he deemed would raise a laugh among the Argives. Evil-favoured was he beyond all men that came to Ilios: he was bandy-legged and lame in the one foot, and his two shoulders were rounded, stooping together over his chest, and above them his head was warped, and a scant stubble grew thereon. Hateful was he to Achilles above all, and to Odysseus, for it was they twain that he was wont to revile; but now again with shrill cries he uttered abuse against goodly Agamemnon. With him were the Achaeans exceeding wroth, and had indignation in their hearts.[2]

As I have already said, this correspondence between beauty and justice is a simplification, but is not entirely unknown to the classical world: indeed, statues of Greek heroes exalt their physical beauty at least as much as they celebrate their moral virtue. However, the relationship between beauty and virtue – and, among all virtues, justice – is much more complicated than that, being related more to something to be perceived, constructed, and accomplished, than to something to be observed and celebrated. The very idea of justice, for example, and even more so the idea of beauty, is in Platonic or Aristotelian texts far removed from contemporary Hollywood's reductions. Moreover, neither is the idea of justice placed in a privileged and exclusive relationship with the sphere of law, nor is the idea of beauty limited to the aesthetic sphere.

Accordingly, when we interpret the concept of *kalokagathìa*, it is important to be wary of a reduction of *kalòn* to what is 'beautiful'. The *kalòn* can certainly be close to what we understand as being beautiful, but it is first and foremost what attracts the gaze, arouses admiration and applause, gratifies sight and senses, and impels us to continue to look and act. The *kalòn* belongs to the aesthesis, what involves sensory and emotional responses, more than our theoretical understanding of concepts and definitions. A body can be beautiful, but so can a relationship between lovers, the proportion and symmetry we observe in a sculpture, a rhetorician's speech, and the rhythm of a poem, because all of them affect our senses and concern our perceptions. And

1 Ingomar Weiler, "Inverted kalokagathia," *Slavery & Abolition* 23, no. 2 (2002): 9–28.
2 Homer, *Iliad, Book II, Verses 212–223*, English trans. Augustus T. Murray (Harvard University Press, 1924).

even war, however terrible and deadly it might be, can be beautiful, as well as the exercise of military virtue, all things which we today tend to appreciate or despise politically, but which we no longer judge in aesthetic terms.[3]

In this sense, the *kalokagathìa* does not express the union between two elements – beauty and goodness – that are autonomous in themselves, but it highlights in a "visible" way a relationship of reciprocal belonging. The Homeric hero – Achilles, for example – is not valorous *and* handsome, as we might say of any James Bond or Marvel hero, but he is handsome *because* he is valorous: his beauty depends on and is one with the admiration that his deeds arouse. This idea, this deep and radical union between appreciation of beauty and admiration for virtue, emerges everywhere in classical culture: in lyric, epic, sculpture, and philosophy. Sappho, in a splendid lyric, writes this in splendid, limpid, and precise terms: "Some say an army of horsemen, some of footsoldiers, some of ships, is the fairest thing on the black earth, but I say it is what one loves."[4] Thucydides, in the Peloponnesian War, gives us another example of this inextricable relationship between *tò kalòn* and *tò agathòn*: he reports Pericles' *lògos epitàphios*, the speech Pericles addressed to the city (and, in particular, to the soldiers and families of the fallen), in which he stresses the peculiar value of Athens, the superiority of Athenian values and civilization over that of other poleis. In this speech, in which the strength and laws of Athens are extolled, Pericles points to a special quality of the Athenian people, the one that makes them truly peculiar and admirable: Athenians, says Pericles, love knowledge without softness, and love beauty when it is oriented to a good end: that is when it is precisely connected with truth and goodness.

The concept of *kalokagathìa*, in other words, conveys both the rational consideration of the moral value of actions and the admiration that these actions arouse. For this reason, we cannot understand it if we isolate the sensory perception from the theoretical analysis. Both are relevant, and both convey the excellence of what we admire. If we think of the Homeric Achilles, we should not be misled by the Hollywood understanding of this hero, played by the handsome Brad Pitt; Achilles was beautiful not because he was particularly attractive in an aesthetic sense, but because on the battlefield he displayed, in a truly splendid way, the fullness of virtues (courage, temperance, daring, strength, etc.), thereby arousing emotion and admiration in the beholder. And that is why war itself can be beautiful, contrary to what we think today: war was, for the Greeks, the site where the value of the human being emerged; it was the ground from which the moral and intellectual

3 For an overview of the multiple aspects of *kalòn*, see David Konstan, *Beauty: The Fortunes of an Ancient Greek Idea* (Oxford University Press, 2014).

4 ἔγω δὲ κῆν' ὄττω τις ἔραται.

qualities of the human being, their virtues, were made perceptible, therefore deserving of praise and admiration above all else.

A seemingly perfect relationship

If we take two of the most beautiful and well-known Greek sculptures, the *Doriphorus* and the *Discobolus*, we may admire a plastic representation of *kalokagathìa*. In both sculptures, Polyclitus and Myron depict two pentathletes, that is, two athletes engaged in one of the five disciplines that formed the ancient pentathlon (running, jumping, javelin throwing, discus throwing, wrestling). Aristotle himself offers us a meaningful description of these athletes:

> Beauty is different for each time of life. It is a youth's beauty that his body should be serviceable for the toils of the race and for feats of strength, while he is also pleasant to look upon – so that the practices of the pentathlum are most beautiful, being formed at once for strength and for speed. . . . Athletic excellence of body results from size, strength, and swiftness; for the swift man is strong. He who can throw his legs in a certain way and move them quick and far, is fit for running; he who can compress and hold, for wrestling; he who can drive with a blow, for boxing; he who can do both the last, for the pancratium; he who can do all, for the pentathlum.[5]

I have said that these sculptures offer us a plastic portrayal of the (seemingly) connection between beauty and justice, or more precisely between *kalòn* and *agathòn*. However, as is often the case, what may initially appear clear and linear turns out to be full of nuances, imperfections, and roughness, when observed from a lesser distance. So it is with the relationship between these two dimensions.

Plato

To see these nuances and variations, it is convenient to take Plato, as our first point of observation. If we read his works, we can understand that the relationship between *kalòn* and *agathòn* does not have to do with beauty and justice, at least as we understand them today. First of all, the *kalòn* in Plato (but also in Aristotle) does not have to do with a purely aesthetic dimension, the formal and objective expression of beauty, but it indicates a trait of people, of their actions and character. It labels something that is certainly

5 Aristotle, *Rhetoric*, 1361b1 ff., Reeve, C. D. Catherine, trans., *Aristotle, Rhetoric, Translation with Introduction and Notes* (Hackett Publishing, 2018).

an object of observation and admiration but does not refer primarily to an artistic object or artefact. Even when the term *kalòn* is used to qualify these objects, what is really at stake is their usability, or the expertise of those who crafted them, rather than the objects in themselves.[6] Second, the word *kalòn* has a much broader sense than 'beautiful', and it merges what we define as beautiful and what we would define as 'good'. This is not because the same term can be used for different things and in different contexts: on the contrary, this is possible precisely because the concept of *kalòn* concerns what is morally good as much as what attracts the eye, arouses admiration, and is pleasing to the eye.[7] The *kalòn* is at the intersection of theoresis and sensation, rational aesthetics and *aesthesis*.

Of course, when we refer to Plato, we cannot but recall the harshness with which he dismisses art as an expression of beauty. Painters, poets, and sculptors, in Plato's eyes, are pseudo-creators,[8] people who produce artefacts of little moral value, even if Plato's writings often display (and exploit) an ambiguity between composition and performance, concerning the question of *mimesis*.[9] And this is not because their products are aesthetically unappreciable: even where they are artistic masterpieces – to use a term close to our culture – they are still something that distances us from Truth, being a mere appearance. Even Homer, for Plato, is an "imitator" of images of virtue and all the other objects on which he works,[10] because like any creator he produces images of images, representations of a reality that is itself an image of Truth and Ideas. Just as good or courageous deeds are an image of the idea of Goodness or Courage, a description of heroic and good deeds is but a second-rate representation, an image of an image. And according to Plato, poetry (we might add, any artistic creation) appeals to the less noble part of the human soul and awakens it, stimulates it, and makes it prey to the passions and feelings, to the point of suffocating our rational part.[11] Artists delude us, in short, because instead of making us see the Truth, they lead us away from it, and bind us to appearances and to what is merely an image of the Truth but is not the Truth. And they stun us through their works, arousing our passions and feelings; we are moved and exalted cheered and pulled

6 Aryeh Kosman, "Beauty and the Good: Situating the Kalon," *Classical Philology* 105, no. 4 (2010): 342.

7 Rachel Barney, "Notes on Plato on the Kalon and the Good," *Classical Philology* 105, no. 4 (2010): 363–77.

8 Giovanni Reale, *Platone. Alla ricerca della sapienza antica* (Rizzoli, 1998), 46.

9 For an excellent analysis of the literature concerning this issue, see Ramona Naddaff, *Exiling the Poets: The Production of Censorship in Plato's Republic* (University of Chicago Press, 2002), 136; see also Stephen Halliwell, *The Aesthetics of Mimesis: Ancient Texts and Modern Problems* (Princeton University Press, 2002).

10 Plato, *Republic*, X 600 and ff.

11 Plato, *Republic*, 605 a-c.

down, and therefore, in the end, they deprive reason of its capacity to govern our lives.

However, we should hold together the rational plane of aesthetic analysis and the plane of sensation: they both have to be considered and make Platonic thought complex and multifaceted. Plato, in the Republic, confesses his love for poetry (and after all, he will always be a poet, the author of aesthetically beautiful as well as philosophically immense dialogues), and that he has abandoned it only with difficulty. Above all, he recognises that in poetic creation there is a "divine force,": poetry has the power to become the place where the gods, by taking away one's wits, can inspire and communicate. And so, in the *Phaedrus*, through the mouth of Socrates, Plato goes so far as to affirm the superiority of the *manìa* over restraint and self-control, arguing that the greatest and best things come to human beings from it: "the greatest blessings come by way of madness, indeed of madness that is heaven-sent".[12] It is, as mentioned, a divine fury, an inspired *manìa*, which Plato links to Apollo[13] – against an interpretative tradition that linked ecstatic and prophetic fury exclusively to Dionysus, at least since Nietzsche.[14] Indeed, at Delphi Apollo revealed himself through enthusiasm, understood in the literal sense that the Pythia became *entheos*, that is, received the god within herself by allowing him to speak through her mouth and losing the use of reason:

> The prophetess at Delphi and the priestesses at Dodona when they have been mad have conferred many splendid benefits upon Greece both in private and in public affairs, but few or none when they have been in their right minds (σωφρονοῦσα).[15]

Art, and poetry, are thus not only the site of deception and surrender to knowledge and truth: they can also be an opportunity to step outside of oneself that allows the wise, and the initiated, a cognitive liberation, a liberation from the constraints that limit the possibility of seeing, and that enable him/her to see "the things that were, and that were to be, and that had been before," as Homer says, rising above the contradictions within which the knowledge of the ordinary person is closed and limited.[16]

In the earlier passage, Plato understands beauty (and art) from a theoretical perspective: for him, there, the problem is precisely that of the (conceptual)

12 Plato, *Phaedrus, 244 a*, trans. Reginald Hackfort (Cambridge University Press, 1952).
13 Eric R. Dodds, *The Greeks and the Irrational* (University of California Press, 1951), 215 ff.
14 Friedrich Nietzsche, *The Birth of Tragedy and Other Writings* (Cambridge University Press, 1999), 26 ff.; see also E. Rohde, *Psyche* (Laterza, 1970/2018), 355, 389 ff.
15 Plato, *Phaedrus*, 144 b.
16 Homer, *Iliad* I, 70.

relationship between the aesthetic and epistemic dimensions, between our aesthetic perception and our understanding of truth and goodness. And yet, at the same time, Plato is well aware that the aesthetic dimension is not exhausted on the conceptual level. Crucial, in Plato's perspective, is precisely an *aesthesic* perspective, that is, the sensorial involvement and emotional responses of the beholder.

It is only by taking this different perspective into account that we can understand an apparently contradictory aspect of Plato's thought, in which he recognises poetry and art as having a positive ethical and political value. Such a value is somehow similar to the anticipatory function of aesthetic experience that I discussed earlier: according to Plato, art can perform this anticipatory and pedagogical function at least for young people, that is, those minds that have yet to receive an orientation and education to justice. Every community has, according to Plato, the goal of forming new generations according to a "footprint," and tales and myths serve precisely this purpose: "We will desire mothers and nurses to tell their children the authorised ones only. Let them fashion the mind with such tales, even more fondly than they mould the body with their hands".[17] What is at stake, here, is not the opportunity of a political use of art. What matters is that for Plato both the conceptual and sensorial sides of aesthetics matter: tales and myths convey concepts and precepts, but at the same time they stimulate senses and arouse emotion.

In other words, the devaluation of art and aesthetic representation must be understood from a theoretic point of view: however, the plexus ethics-aesthetics cannot be limited, for Plato, to a mere conceptual appreciation of works of art. Rather, it occurs in the *erotic* sphere, in a dimension that is built on the desire for Beauty and, through it, on the search for what we are lacking. Eros, in Plato, is a mediating god that connects opposites: he is the son of *Penìa* – goddess of poverty and lack – and *Pòros*, the bold and hunter god, the personification of ingenuity and the ability to procure what is lacking. Eros, as the force that drives us toward what we desire (and the more we desire something the greater the distance that separates us), because it is what moves our search for beauty and goodness: and through the enjoyment of beauty, Eros is what drives us to desire and seek what is right. In the Phaedrus and the Symposium Plato guides us through this relationship between beauty and truth, mediated by the erotic drive.

Beauty, unique among all ideas, has the privilege of being perceivable by the senses, that is, not only with thought but also through contemplation of its expressions. While "Justice and Temperance do not shine out through their images down here, and neither do the other objects of the soul's admiration",

17 Plato, *Republic*, II 377 b.

beauty can be grasped even here, in this way of appearances and weak images of the Ideas:

> for sight, for us, is the keenest of the sensations we receive through the body. But with it we do not see Wisdom . . . only Beauty received this fate, to be that which is most manifest and most lovable.[18]

Eros, then, impels us to desire the beauty we see, and first of all that beauty we perceive *in bodies*, to search for that Beauty (the Idea of Beauty) which is displayed in all beautiful bodies, and which makes them desirable. Eros is an impulse toward the *Kalòn*, toward the body of a beautiful boy – the place where, first and foremost, Beauty is made visible – and it arouses the desire for such beauty.

At the same time, Eros is not only born of lack (inheritance from his mother, Penia) but is also capable of abundance and fullness (thanks to Pòros, the father). Therefore, within the erotic desire for beauty, there is not only lack, emptiness, and the search for completion but also a desire for fullness, an impulse to generate: we desire to generate and give birth in beauty.[19] The movement that Eros impels us to make, and that makes us desire the Beauty we perceive in bodies, first of all, and then in the soul, and then again in the contemplation of harmony and order in human activities and laws,[20] comes from a kind of fullness that asks to be liberated and flourish. And among those caught up in this generative impulse are those who do not merely generate biologically but who generate on the spiritual plane.[21]

Therefore, Eros impels us to progress in an upward movement.[22] The erotic experience, the desire for the body of a beautiful person, initiates this ascent, and it is through this kind of experience that one is able to begin the climb. Plato describes an ascending sequence in love, culminating in the learning of Beauty itself, which passes through the initial interest in bodily beauty, proceeds with the love of the beauty of social institutions and practices, the beauty of the sciences and the knowledge they deliver to us, and ends with the understanding of Beauty itself. The more we climb the "ladder" of beauty, driven by Eros, the more and more we are stimulated to grasp Beauty in itself transcendent of the object or body we desire. What makes a body beautiful? What attracts us to it? What makes us say that this or that young man, this or that girl, is handsome and beautiful? Those who love, for

18 Plato, *Phaedrus*, 250 e.

19 Plato, *Symposium*, 206e: Τῆς γεννήσεως καὶ τοῦ τόκου ἐν τῷ καλῷ.

20 Reale, *Platone. Alla ricerca della Sapienza antica*, 217.

21 Thomas M. Alexander, *The Human Eros: Eco-Ontology and the Aesthetics of Existence* (Fordham University Press, 2013), 183.

22 Drew A. Hyland, *Plato and the Question of Beauty* (Indiana University Press, 2008), 80, 83 ff.

Plato, begin by sensory perception of Beauty, and the further they proceed down this scale the more they become able to appreciate higher forms of beauty and to appreciate the Beauty in itself more than specific objects.[23] Not everyone is willing, or able, to climb this ladder. Some people will never go beyond a desire for a beautiful body. And yet, for those who are willing to proceed on this path, the erotic desire for beauty leads to moral transformation: it leads them to knowledge of the Justice and the Truth, and to virtue.

Both the theoretical and the sensory-perceptual planes matter, in Plato, and are joined together: the erotic experience of Beauty can lead to the knowledge and practice of Justice. *Kalokagathìa*, in Plato's perspective, lies in this fundamental unity between ethics and aesthetics, certainly, but it also lies in the fact that beauty (the only idea that the eye can grasp) is the place where we can experience Justice because it reveals it. Beauty reveals Justice, because it is the place in which its characteristics (harmony, proportion, order) are visible, and become the object of love and desire: concepts become perceptions, and knowledge and sensory affection overlap. In this vein, properly, beauty is not the expression of goodness but its path: it is a path along which we learn not only to know but also to desire what is right.

Aristotle

The relevance of both the theoretical and the sensory-perceptual perspective must be considered when we analyse Aristotle's perspective, which has mostly been understood with exclusive reference to the conceptual and theoretical plane. Of course, the rationalist and theoretical understanding of aesthetics is of utmost importance in his works, but the question of perception and affect (the ways agentic capacities and choices are shaped by perceptions) is relevant as well.[24]

To discuss this, let's consider the concept of *kalòn*, and the analysis that Aristotle devotes to it. Aristotle makes reference to the *kalòn* in very different contexts, and he attributes it to living beings, to knowledge, to the organisation and government of the state, to art, to God, to virtuous actions, and so on.[25] That is why, as has been rightly noted, even the oldest translations of Aristotelian thought give different meanings to this term, such as 'bonum', that which is desirable and virtuous; 'pulchrum', that which is pleasing to the sight or hearing, or proportionate and resplendent; or "honestum", that which is noble, deserving of appreciation for itself.[26]

23 Plato, *Symposium*, 209–11.
24 Giulia Bonasio, "Kalokagathia and the Unity of the Virtues in the Eudemian Ethics," *Apeiron* 53, no. 1 (2020): 27–57.
25 Aristotle, *Poetics*, 1450b36; *Politics*, 1326a33; *Topics*, 116b21.
26 Terence H. Irwin, "The Sense and Reference of *Kalòn* in Aristotle," *Classical Philology* 105, no. 4 (2010): 382–83. See also Aryeh Kosman, "Beauty and the Good: Situating the Kalon,"

In some cases, Aristotle attributes the term *kalòn* to the colour of some birds, in others to the moral worth of some actions, or more generally what is worthy of appreciation and admiration, what is noble, pleasing, and right.[27] When Aristotle labels some action or person as *kalòn*, it is because he sees in them something appropriate and proportionate (such as an animal whose body is proportionate to its needs for hunting or flight) and because he sees in it those features of order (*taxis*), measure (*symmetry*), and definiteness (*horismenon*) that determine its full conformity to its nature and purposes. After all, we do something very similar. We often attribute the adjective beautiful to a movie, a choice someone has made, the morality of a person, the body of a person, or a specific good. These expressions mirror physical, aesthetic, moral, and technical characteristics but stem from the idea that something or someone is well-made, adequate, or suitable, and is deserving of our and others' appreciation. The aesthetic analysis of kalòn is here, undoubtedly, to be understood from a theoretical and conceptual perspective.

In this vein, is not surprising the strength with which the issue of beauty is linked to that of justice, in Aristotle's thought. When we read the Nicomachean Ethics, we are struck by the fact that Aristotle considers justice to be the most perfect of all virtues, as *beautiful* as the morning and evening star, which is not only the first to appear but also the brightest.[28] This is not surprising even if, while it is easy to recognise justice as more important than other virtues, more complex, and more useful, it is less usual to affirm that it could also be superior to others in beauty. After all, many centuries later, Kant will say something similar, when – in a beautiful sentence often quoted even by those who do not know much else about this author – he affirms that the starry heavens above us and the moral law fill the mind with ever new and increasing admiration and awe.

However, the question of perception and affect, and the role of *aesthesis* in the material ordering of social space, is parallel to this theoretical perspective. It is well-known that Aristotle considers every virtue worthy of admiration (therefore, beautiful, worthy of praise) because of the desire that drives us to perfect the realisation of virtue in our actions.[29] What is *kalòn*, beautiful, noble, and admirable, not only arouses (theoretical) appreciation but in some way urges the person to virtuous action: "it seems proper to a prudent person

in *Virtues of Thought* (Harvard University Press, 2014), 252–60; Kelly Rogers, "Aristotle's Conception of Tò Καλόν," *Ancient Philosophy* 13, no. 2 (1993): 355.

27 Mark K. Spencer, "Beauty and the Intellectual Virtues in Aristotle," in *Beauty and the Good: Recovering the Classical Tradition from Plato to Duns Scotus*, ed. Alice M. Ramos (Catholic University of America Press, 2020), 96.

28 See Kosman, "Beauty and the Good," 265.

29 Bonasio, "Kalokagathia and the Unity of the Virtues in the Eudemian Ethics," 15 ff. See also Katja M. Vogt, *Desiring the Good: Ancient Proposals and Contemporary Theory* (Oxford University Press, 2017), ch. 7.

to be able to deliberate finely (kalōs) about things that are good and beneficial for himself . . . things that promote living well in general".[30] Of course, there may be multiple factors that motivate us to action. But some factors have a stronger motivational capacity than others: according to Aristotle, virtuous actions provide us with motivation in themselves: we do something right (and Kant, again, would agree) because it is right, we behave courageously because courage has a value in itself, we are wise because wisdom is something we consider positive, and so on, regardless of consequences and outcomes. In Aristotle's words, "An activity is choiceworthy in its own right if nothing further apart from it is sought from it. This seems to be the character of actions in accord with virtue; for doing fine and excellent actions is choiceworthy for itself".[31] An action that we would call beautiful (admirable, worthy, extraordinary, in all the variety of adjectives we would ascribe today to praise something) will be performed *because* it is beautiful, because it is in itself worthy of honour, and it has got a value that does not depend on the result to which it leads. It is a beautiful thing to help someone who is in distress, regardless of the outcome (will we save his or her life? Will we get hurt? Will we expose ourselves to a risk?), and therefore it is something we choose to do precisely because we recognise in it some characters of brightness that motivate us to action.[32]

Therefore, it is erroneous to reduce the relationship between beauty and justice to the merely epistemological plane, when in fact both of these dimensions invite action, self-perfection, and planning, rather than contemplation. Virtue is beautiful, in Aristotle, and virtuous actions are motivated by the recognition of this beauty: contemporary difficulties in understanding beauty as a category internal to ethical discourses are probably related to both the tendency to consider beauty as something formal, relating to the conceptual appreciation of what appears, rather than the subjectivity of tastes (after all, it is possible to think that morality is entirely subjective, too). On the contrary, we can better grasp the Aristotelian analysis of *kalòn* if we recognise that it doesn't only belong to theoretical aesthetic sphere but also to that of bodily perceptions and affect.[33] The notion of *kalokagathìa* must be understood, from Aristotle's perspective, similarly: it concerns both the aesthetic (theoretical) appreciation of what is ethically worthy of honour, the shining

30 Aristotle, *Nicomachean Ethics, VI 5, 1040, 25–27,* English trans. Terence Irwing (Indianapolis, Cambridge: Hackett, 1999).

31 Aristotle, *Nicomachean Ethics, X, 6, 1176, 6–9,* English trans. Terence Irwing (Indianapolis, Cambridge: Hackett, 1999).

32 Brian Donohue, "Beauty and Motivation in Aristotle," *Quaestiones Disputatae* 6, no. 2 (2016): 26–43; Spencer, "Beauty and the Intellectual Virtues in Aristotle," 98–99.

33 John Milliken, "Aristotle's Aesthetic Ethics," *The Southern Journal of Philosophy* 44, no. 2 (2006): 319–39: "The noble is fundamentally an aesthetic concept. By this I mean it is a matter of perception and not one of calculation".

of virtue's perfection, and the role of virtues in shaping sensory perception, affecting the beholder, and motivating people's action.

At the end of the *Eudemian Ethics*, one of the three great works that Aristotle devotes to the question of virtue and goodness, he deals with this particular virtue, and describes it, without giving a definition, as a kind of consequence of the others, something that arises from them.[34] It is evident, Aristotle says, that one who has developed all the other virtues also possesses *kalokagathìa*. The same happens with health: we cannot say that someone is in good health unless we assume that all organs, all the parts of which a person is composed, are also in good health. It is from the health of the single parts that the health of the whole body depends. From this perspective, a person *kalòs kai agathòs* is both virtuous and noble, worthy of admiration and praise, and arouses our admiration not because of further purposes, but precisely because her virtue shines, in all its brightness. Whatever is *kalòn* is beautiful and desirable for its own sake: more precisely, virtuous people are both good, pleasant, and objects of admiration because they are good. They possess all the virtues, and their excellence is a unity among all the virtues, those of both the *phrònimos* and the *sophòs*: indeed, they possess the one because they possess the other, and therefore they are people worthy of the greatest admiration.

A good way to understand this virtue as it was understood by Aristotle requires looking at sports[35] and considering the relevance of this activity, within Greek culture, for the moral education of the young people. Even today we think that through sport people can learn certain values (such as loyalty, teamwork, commitment, and dedication), and even today we think that some physical activities should be included in educational pathways. But sports practice can be simply understood as a form of training, which is related to the idea of fitness rather than the idea of virtue or justice. Similarly, while sports at certain levels still arouse our admiration (a skilful play by Messi, an outstanding vault by Simone Biles, a dive by Quan Hongchan), we do not include sports within the so-called 'fine arts', such as dancing, painting, theatre. Neither of these dimensions, however, was separate in Greek culture, and they certainly were not separate for Aristotle: beauty and virtue shine, more than elsewhere, in athletes. The *kalokagathìa* is what we see in athletes, and it is what – as already mentioned – is represented by Myron and Polyclitus in their sculptures. It is the beauty of the athlete, which is both a

34 Aristotle, *Eudemian Ethics*, VIII. 3, 1248 b.

35 Michael Pakaluk, "The Obviousness of the Kalon in Aristotle's Ethics," in *Beauty and the Good: Recovering the Classical Tradition from Plato to Duns Scotus*, ed. Alice M. Ramos (Catholic University of America Press, 2020), 84; Heather Reid, "Athletic Beauty in Classical Greece: A Philosophical View," *Journal of the Philosophy of Sport* 39, no. 2 (2012): 281–97; Heather Reid, "Athletic Virtue and Aesthetic Values in Aristotle's Ethics," *Journal of the Philosophy of Sport* 47, no. 1 (2020): 63–74.

moral virtue and a splendid source of admiration.[36] The *kalokagathìa* is for Aristotle a moral ideal and an educational goal: it is something that is not given a priori, or innate, but must be cultivated and developed.

When we consider today's athletes, we sometimes praise talent, an innate endowment that enables them to excel, and which, through training, serves to make them flourish. Both elements were, certainly, also present in Greek imagination; however the emphasis fell more on the ability to develop one's virtues than on innate talents. Aristotle explicitly says that we become good people and develop the virtue of justice through practice:[37] it is by making the right choices that the virtue of justice takes root in us, just as it is through practice and continuous exercise that we develop the ability to shoot with a bow. Of course, innate talents matter, but athletic and moral virtues depend on the development and exercise of this natural potential until excellent performance is achieved, and it is such excellence that is reflected in the beauty of the pentathlete, and affect the beholder. Nature, says Aristotle, gives us only the capacity for virtue, but this capacity must be developed through continuous practice, both in the ethical and athletic fields.

What is interesting, from our perspective, is that this educational potentiality of *kalokagathìa* can be fully understood if we consider how some phenomena and perceptions (athletes' performances, warriors' deeds, inspiring speeches of rhetoricians, etc.) shape social life: what is *kalòn* shapes the power relations that condition a subject's capacity, makes manifest what is privileged and what must remain in the background, and therefore conditions how sensate subjects live within their social space. It is true that Aristotle, when describing the desire aroused by the *kalòn*, refers to what appears (*to phainòmenon*), whereas the true kalòn appeals to the intellect and rational wish.[38] However, for Aristotle such *phainòmenon* involves desire and pleasure: sense perception concerns both the moral and physical *kalòn*, and does grasp what is shining, fitting, and pleasant. To sense concerns pleasure and desire, and to sense the *kalòn* "is to flourish in one's senses and to delight in the object and in one's living insofar as one senses that object".[39]

Aristotelian *kalokagathìa*, in other words, sheds light on the fact that human beings, on the one hand, understand the commonalities that the notions of harmony, order, and proportion display when they are referred to both aesthetics and ethics. Justice is beautiful, in this sense, because it

36 Reid, "Athletic Virtue and Aesthetic Values in Aristotle's Ethics," 70.

37 See Sarah Broadie, *Ethics with Aristotle* (Oxford University Press, 1993), 104, 109; see also Marta Jimenez, *Aristotle on Shame and Learning to Be Good* (Oxford University Press, 2021).

38 Aristotle, *Metaphysics*, XII. 7, 1072a 28. Spencer, "Beauty and the Intellectual Virtues in Aristotle," 97.

39 Aristotle, *Nicomachean Ethics*, X.4.1174b15–1175a22; *Politics*, VIII.5.1340a15–17. See Spencer, "Beauty and the Intellectual Virtues in Aristotle," 100.

displays the capacity – wonderful and amazing – to recognise an ideal of measure, proportion, and merit, and to realise it regardless of the interest or goals of those who act. On the other hand, *kalokagathìa* stresses the perspective of human beholders as sensory beings, and as embodied subjects: it is the perception of virtue and beauty that affect and motivates our action, and urges people to act. Therefore, on the one hand, Aristotle writes that

> What is just is noble (*kalòn*), justice is proportion to merit, and the perfect man merits these things; or what is fitting is noble, and to the perfect man these things, wealth, high birth, and power, are fitting. So that to the perfect man things profitable are also noble.[40]

On the other hand, in Aristotelian thought, people begin by performing moral actions and develop, through their performances, a proper understanding of the good and beautiful: *kalokagathìa* is not reducible to the theoretical plan. It moves people (and young people, especially) because they are sensate subjects, and virtues affect them and urge them to act: we find the virtue attractive, even apart from any benefits that might flow from it.

Beauty and justice before God

It is well-known that the rationalist approach to aesthetics and beauty, which is present in both Plato and Aristotle, was also taken up by Christian thought in later centuries; however, even medieval aesthetics, and thus the relationship between ethics and aesthetics, cannot be reduced to the merely epistemological plane and a rationalistic approach. The problem of human perception and sensation, the relevance of our sensory engagement with the world, has also been of utmost importance for medieval thinkers.[41]

Of course, medieval thought absorbed much of the rationalism of Greek philosophers. For instance, the idea that beauty has to do with proportion, measure, and order, which is typical of this approach, had extraordinary success throughout the Christian Middle Ages. We know that Plato argues that there is a beauty of geometric forms that is even superior to the beauty of bodies, because in those forms and mathematical ratios, order and harmony are expressed in a particularly evident way.[42] Similarly, Christian thought absorbed the idea that the world is fundamentally ordered and rational, yet

40 Aristotle, *Eudemian Ethics, VIII, 1249a9-10*, English trans. J. A. Smith and W. D. Ross, (Oxford: Clarendon Press, 1915).

41 See, for an overview, José F. Silva and E. J. Brill, eds., *Rationality in Perception in Medieval Philosophy* (Brill, 2023).

42 Plato, *Timaeus*, XX, 53e.

reassessing it from the perspective of a personal God:[43] the world is ordered because it was made that way by the divine reason, which is present in all things and allows us – because our reason is the image of God's – to understand reality. It is the idea of the cosmos, the rational order of the whole, which, for the classical culture, contrasted with primal chaos and, for Christian thought, is the result of God's creation. God creates and then takes pleasure from what he creates: he looks at the stars, the waters, and the animals and appreciates their beauty and goodness. In the first book of the Old Testament, the name for the beautiful is the Hebrew "tov": a term, that God uses when observing his creative work,[44] affirming at the same time the goodness and beauty of creation in the eyes of the Creator.[45]

Within such a rationalist account, the idea of order and harmony is the privileged ground on which beauty meets with justice. Just as beauty flourishes in the proportion between forms, between the parts of the body, in the harmony we perceive when we observe something beautiful, so too is it with justice. This analogy dates back to the pre-Socratics, in whose thought justice was an aspect of that necessary, objective, and rational order that characterises all reality: justice rules reality (it is Justice that keeps the being tightly locked, holding it fast),[46] and the order of reality derives from the *Lògos*, the universal Reason, to which human actions and human societies as a whole must look if they are to be equally ordered. This was also the case in the Eleatic school, where, too, the conception of reality tends to lose much of its naturalistic connotation: for Pythagoras reality is still harmony and order, although this harmony is essentially mathematical, so that justice tends to take on the appearance of a metaphysical and logical necessity.

This idea triumphs in Christian rationalism (i.e., not in all Christianism as a whole), and in Aquinas' thought:[47] the law is an *ordinatio rationis*, an order of reason, in which there is also an imperative element (a command), secondary to the rational one. The order of reality is shaped by the eternal law (*lex aeterna*), and is the expression of God's ordering reason; this order is partially manifested to the rational creature (i.e., endowed with reason that is the image of divine reason) in the natural law (*lex naturalis*), which is that

43 K. L. Nolen, "Personal God," in *Encyclopedia of Psychology and Religion*, eds. D. A. Leeming (Cham: Springer, 2020).

44 Cf. Gen 1:4ff: "And God Saw that this was Good/Beautiful."

45 B. Forte, *La porta della Bellezza. Per un'estetica teologica* (Brescia: Morcelliana, 2000).

46 Parmenides, Diels-Kranz, 28 B 8, vv. 13–14; see David Gallop, trans., *Parmenides of Elea. Fragments. A Text and Translation with an Introduction* (University of Toronto Press, 1984).

47 As we shall see in a later chapter, the same Thomist perspective on aesthetics, and on the relationship between aesthetics and ethics, cannot be reduced to the epistemological plane and a rationalist approach. See ch. 5, on this issue. On Aquinas' thought on beauty see Francis J. Caponi, "Beauty, Justice, and Damnation in Thomas Aquinas," *Pro ecclesia* 19, no. 4 (2010): 389–404.

part of the order of reality that reason can know, or it is partially revealed in the divine law (*lex divina*), and it is the order to which human law must conform. The law that human beings produce in their historical experience is also an order of reason, and it is oriented – *must* be oriented – to constituting human good insofar as it conforms to the natural law, namely, the horizon of this good.[48]

As I have said, however, a purely rationalist approach to Christian aesthetics is reductive; above all, it does not allow for an understanding of the relationship between ethics and aesthetics (and between justice and beauty). If we are to understand this aspect of Christian thought, again, we must recognise Aesthetic experience is never neutral: it is the subjective and sensory engagement with an object or vision, thereby raising moral problems such as that of temptations. Of course, beauty is the order of creation: God is the Cause of the beauty of things and their splendour, insofar as he transmits to them a ray of his light; and this transmission is to be understood as participation, as the reason why we can say that something is beautiful. As a consequence, Christ displays the fullness of beauty. He shines with beauty, not so much (or not only) because of the proportion of his body, but because in Christ "dwells the whole fullness of the deity bodily" (Col. 2:9). Therefore, besides physical beauty, Christ has the beauty of the perfection of moral virtues: he was "full of grace and truth" (Jn 1:14). To see Jesus is to see the fullness of beauty and to know the will of the Father.

At the same time, the harmony manifested in the world serves not only to order reality and avoid chaos but also to orient it toward God. God fills every created thing with beauty: everything is beautiful insofar as it has been created and shows the love of God who willed its existence and its being created. All things, then, speak of God (their Cause) and tend toward Him (as the final Cause) in a dynamism that is not too different from what we have seen in Greek thought. As there Eros drives human beings through their desire for beauty, so here all reality is drawn toward God, the source of all beauty and all love. In other words, the aesthetic appeals to our senses, and not merely to our epistemic capacities, being a force of attraction or repulsion. What is at stake, for Christian thought, is not only a judgement of goodness or rightness concerning aesthetic objects but rather the way they are experienced, and the consequences they produce on the relationship between God and human beings.

48 See Jonathan A. Jacobs, ed., *Reason, Religion, and Natural Law: From Plato to Spinoza* (Oxford University Press, 2012); on Aquinas' thought, see in particular the chapter by Anthony J. Lisska, "Right Reason in Natural Law Moral Theory," in *Reason, Religion, and Natural Law: From Plato to Spinoza*, ed. Jonathan A. Jacobs (Oxford University Press, 2012), 155.

Beauty has the power to attract us, and is the source of human desire; it is at the bottom of human motivation and action. We act because we desire something that we recognise as good for us, and the more intensely we do so the more perfectly we recognise this goodness. If we take Thomas Aquinas, we find this same idea: beauty plays an important role in the system of virtues, particularly in what motivates us and explains how we implement them.[49] In the *Summa theologiae* St. Thomas discusses the *bonum honestum*, and writes that the beauty of the body consists in having well-proportioned limbs, with a certain brightness of due colour. Likewise, spiritual beauty consists of a person's behaviour and acts being well-proportioned according to the light of reason. This – he continues – is the constitutive of honesty, which is identified with virtue, which moderates all human things according to reason. So honesty is identified with spiritual beauty.[50] St. Thomas, in short, does not simply say that *bonum honestum* is identified with beauty but writes that it is at the same time the implementation of virtue. Just as spiritual beauty is manifested in purity and proportion and is achieved when there is agreement between what a person says and does, this is also the case with virtue: to act virtuously means to act in such a way as to manifest, in my actions, reason, and this in turn is a matter of purity and proportion. Honesty, says Aquinas, is the same thing as spiritual beauty (*honestum est idem spirituali decori*).[51] At the same time, there is a beauty that turns away from God, a beauty that seduces and ensnares us in the things of this world and in worldly passions: seductions and temptations draw us toward the world instead of toward God. The idea of the mortification of the flesh, and the denial of a physical beauty that seduces and distracts from God and spiritual things, also belongs to the Christian world: the veil of nuns, sadly similar to other veils that cover the female body in so many cultures, serves to reiterate that they are brides of Christ, and are therefore removed from the gaze of other men. Covering hair, covering bodies, and covering physical forms has also always meant concealing and devaluing physical beauty, assuming it distances us from God and is a source of sin.

However, if we look at Christian art, an opposite scenario emerges. As a matter of fact, temptations come much more from ugliness, deformity, and monstrosity than from beauty. As Castelli explains in a beautiful and important book, demonic temptations often take the form of what is distorted – that is, what has lost the beauty that God imprinted on all creation – and is

49 As Caponi correclty writes, within the order of creation beauty is a task: "Creation is dynamic, receiving its act of being from God and ordered to him as its final end. The initial integrity of the "sixth day" is not self-contained, but ordered to the final cosmic integrity. So, too, any assessment of the beauty of a manmade object must take account of the final end dictated by its form." Caponi, "Beauty, Justice, and Damnation in Thomas Aquinas," 393.

50 Thomas Aquinas, *Summa Theologiae*, II.II, q. 145, a 2.

51 Thomas Aquinas, *Summa Theologiae*, II-II, q. 145, a. 2, resp.

therefore hideous, monstrous, and deformed.[52] Demons with two or three faces, monsters with faces instead of genitals or buttocks, horrible beings whose bodies look like the outcome of a random accumulation of pieces of other creatures. All these serve to represent evil, which is not only ugly but is ugly because it has lost, or destroyed, the proportion and harmony of goodness.[53]

When the world turns away from God it becomes strife, vanity, deceit, and pain: we might think of Bosch's *Hay Wain*, where the two lovers on the haystack are surrounded by charlatans and violent, strange, and deformed beings, starting with the fish-man dragging the chariot itself. The world is prey to chaos and vice, and the two lovers are left with no choice but to be seduced by the monstrous demon playing behind them or to listen to the praying angel on the other side.[54]

Similarly, St. Anthony's temptations are a well-known, and effective, example of this mentality. The saint must retreat from the world to flee its temptations and vices, but he will still be confronted with the temptation of the monstrous, that is, of what turns away from God: winged fish, head-houses, birds-thorns, bodies enclosed within barks in which they feast, men- crocodiles and butterfly-scorpions (so, at least, in the paintings of Bosch, Cranach, or Civetta). Medieval Italian painting is perhaps less imaginative than Flemish painting, but it goes in the same direction. There are fewer hybrids, fewer monsters, and fewer absurdities because the demonic is mostly depicted anthropomorphically, but we are always faced with a degraded and horrific version of nature. From the dome of the baptistery in Florence to the temptations of St. Anthony depicted in Santa Croce, to Botticelli's Infernal Abyss, to Signorelli's frescoes, the demons depict creation in its most degraded form, which is hideous and monstrous because it is degraded.[55]

All this fantastical repertoire visually expresses not only the idea that evil is filthy, horrible, deformed, and disproportionate: it highlights that evil denies the order of creation because it turns people away from it, and destroys the beauty that God has imprinted in creation by its appeal to senses and bodily perceptions. The beholder, whoever is attracted by the fantastic and the monstrous, is lost:[56] the *curiositas* is the means by which evil seduces, the

52 E. Castelli, Il demoniaco nell'arte, in *Introduzione di Corrado Bologna*, ed. Enrico Castelli Gattinara (Torino: Bollati Boringhieri, 2007), 6–7.

53 Dale Jacquette, "Representations of Evil," in *The History of Evil in Antiquity*, eds. Tom Angier, Chad Meister, and Charles Taliaferro (Routledge, 2018), 289–301.

54 On Bosch as creator of "monsters" see Walter S. Gibson, *Hieronymus Bosch* (Thames & Hudson, 1973), 12. See also Nils Buttner, *Hieronymus Bosch: Visions and Nightmares* (Reaktion Books, 2016).

55 Laura Pasquini, *Diavoli e inferni nel Medioevo: origine e sviluppo delle immagini dal VI al XV secolo* (Il Poligrafo, 2017).

56 Castelli, *Il demoniaco nell'arte*, 20.

way it deceives and turns away from goodness and virtue. The problem is not epistemological, but related to *aesthesis*, still: what matters is the way our sensory experiences of beauty or ugliness influence our lives, and draw us away from (or closer to) God.

Such a focus on sensory experience is evident, for example, in Bosch's St. Jerome, that is preserved in the Ghent Museum and depicts the monk lying prone toward the ground, his eyes well shielded from what is not to be seen and focused only on the crucifix. St. Jerome prays and closes his eyes because nothing else is needed for him to escape the temptations of the demonic, and to follow Christ: it is not the monk's task to fight against the monsters, who moreover often hide in recesses and holes in the ground, but to detach himself: salvation comes from the rejection of any sensory relationship with the demonic, and from faith. We can observe the same thing in an engraving by Martin Schongauer (in the Civic Museums of Pavia and the Metropolitan Museum of Art, New York), on the same theme. St. Anthony is lifted by demons, half-human beings, deformed men and women, and half-animals or monsters, who batter and thrash him; they tear out his hair and rip his robe and carry him high into the sky (deluding him, perhaps, that they are not so evil if they rise up to the heavens). But the saint looks fixedly upward; he does not care about the monsters and their tortures/torments, because – Castelli still reminds us – nothingness is what befalls him, "and nothingness, nothing can".[57]

Hell, in short, is an (existential and aesthetic) experience of pain and sadness, of ugliness and sickness. We may observe the image that Il Civetta gives of it, in the rooms of the Doge's Palace in Venice: hell is here depicted as a city in flames, destroyed by a terrible fire and the fury of its inhabitants, invaded by monsters, hybrids of humans and fishes, roosters, birds, and scourged by locusts, mice, spiders, snails. But it is also a place where tables and canteens are set, with reptiles and worms and toads as food. Hell and the demonic are at the same time hideous and meaningless: the loss of measure is the loss of the lògos, of reason, but is also the experience of pain and sadness. The nexus between ugliness and sin belongs to the universe of affect as much as to that of concepts. The Dulle Griet, in 1564, allows Bruegel to portray the senseless, in depicting the absurdity of those recruiting troops for hell. Everything is absurd, devoid of reason: mountains-mouths devouring people, monsters hatching from eggs, people-fish, a man carrying on his shoulders a boat with a sphere in which there are prisoners, and so on. Meanwhile, everything descends into nonsense, violence reigns, and evil seems to have the upper hand. The art of the Middle Ages emphasised the bodily effects rather than the cognitive cause of our yielding to temptation. The horrific union of a human part and an animal part symbolised the fact that evil alters and

57 Castelli, *Il demoniaco nell'arte*, 33 (translation mine).

distorts our natural proportion and measure, both corporal and spiritual. A deformed, beastly figure represents the effects of our turning away from the true beauty that only God can give.[58]

Similarly, references to beauty lie at both the cognitive and sensate level, in Christian theology and mysticism. Angela of Foligno (1248–1309) relates that she saw "a beauty so great that I can say nothing about it, except that I saw the supreme Beauty, which contains in itself all goodness." But already the Book of Wisdom describes God as the source of beauty in the world, and condemns pagans who worship the sun, moon, and stars as gods because of their beauty, reminding them that the true God, creator of all beauty, far surpasses them.[59] Wisdom books repeatedly state that the words of wisdom are beautiful,[60] and the psalmist describes God as "clothed in praise and beauty".[61] In Paul, too, there are many references to beauty from the same perspective: the divine glory and beauty, which sin has prevented us from fully seeing and enjoying, become visible again in the face of Christ, who, by his death and resurrection, has freed us from sin.[62] In other words: the possibility to experience and enjoy the beauty (of God, and creation) go hand in hand with closeness to Christ and the justification that faith offers. It is no accident that when the Gospel of John states that Jesus is "the Good Shepherd," the Greek adjective used to qualify the shepherd is precisely "kalòs". Again, this adjective indicates both external beauty, which attracts and catches the eye, and internal harmony, which makes someone morally good. In short, in the Gospel, too, reference is made to an overall state, in which health, beauty, grace, goodness, and righteousness coincide, and are manifested in fullness. With the difference, of course, that in this case, everything refers to God, who is the source and reason for all beauty and all goodness.

The Kalokagathìa today

Today, what remains of all this? In 1998, Elaine Scarry devoted a famous series of lectures to the relationship between beauty and justice.[63] She proposed an actualization of the discourse we have seen characterising much of classical and medieval thought, arguing that the ideal of kalokagathìa is not so far from our cultural horizon. More precisely, according to

58 It must be stated that sin can reduce human form and the harmonies of soul and body, humanity and cosmos, but not *to nothing*. The human beauty becomes negligible, but even hell exhibits a kind of analogical beauty, displaying corrupted traces of God's creation. See Caponi, "Beauty, Justice, and Damnation in Thomas Aquinas," 396 ff.

59 13, 3–5.

60 Prov 1:9; 4:9

61 Ps. 921; 103:1; 95:6.

62 2 Cor 3:18, 4:6; Rom 3:23; 2; Thess 1:9.

63 Elaine Scarry, *On Beauty and Being Just* (Princeton University Press, 1999).

Scarry, although the classical perspective is far from us, the idea of a fundamental unity between beauty and justice remains still valid in contemporary culture.

First, the Platonic idea that love for beauty leads to love for what we believe in is also valid for us, and this in turn leads to love for the pursuit of truth; and truth is a necessary condition for justice.[64] The desire that beauty arouses in us is not resolved in aesthetic pleasure, in contemplation; this desire is a force that propels our whole life, and drives us to love truth, and therefore also to seek justice. This, Scarry writes, is also true for us. When we see something beautiful, we do not simply stand open-mouthed, in contemplation; the beautiful object prompts us to look for a term of comparison, something to anchor this incomprehensible and elusive perception of beauty, and "the mind keeps tripping backward until it at last reaches something that has no precedent, which may very well be the immortal".[65] It is no accident that we want to preserve beauty when we run into it: the beauty of a landscape, an object (which we keep in a museum or protect as a monument), or a face (with makeup, creams, beauty treatments). The beautiful object always refers back to Beauty itself and kindles the desire for Truth.

Scarry's text goes further and re-proposes in a modern fashion another topic that we have seen to be central to the "classical" *kalokagathìa*. Because we love beauty, argues Scarry, we are led to love what we perceive in it: symmetry and proportion: and so, we similarly love justice, as order of relationships and proportionality in distribution. Since beauty is an opportunity to perceive and love proportion and order, symmetry, and distribution among the parts (of a body, a landscape, a picture), we learn to love and seek these elements in social life as well: we want to live in orderly societies, we seek to distribute proportionately and fairly the goods we have, and so on. Between beauty and justice as fairness (in both cases, in English, the adjective can be the same), there is thus absolute contiguity.[66]

We know from Aristotle that justice can be spoken of both in a retributive sense (as fairness and proportion in exchange) and in a distributive sense (as equality and proportion in distribution). And beauty, Scarry continues, operates in both of these dimensions. Not only does it make us love proportion and harmony (in all levels of our existence, and thus both in what we perceive with our senses and in our relationships with other people), but it urges us to build this harmony: it asks us to achieve it where it is absent, it encourages the widening of our gaze toward the search for distributed beauty in our world, and it creates the conditions for attending to distributive justice. Beauty makes us paint, photograph, write poetry, beget children, and draft

64 Scarry, *On Beauty and Being Just*, 19, 38.
65 Scarry, *On Beauty and Being Just*, 22.
66 Scarry, *On Beauty and Being Just*, 63

laws, because we cannot easily look away from beauty, and we are driven to reproduce and perpetuate it.[67]

Above all, in this impulse to reproduce, we discover the presence of other people: beauty, writes Simone Weil in *Waiting for God*, requires us "to give up our imaginary position as the centre".[68] Contemplating beauty – of a painting, a symphony, a dance, a mountain – changes the weight that at the perceptual level we tend to give to ourselves and our claims: we are not the centre of the world, because Truth and Beauty are elsewhere. At the same time, this decentralization also takes place on the level of social relations, and of law: we stop thinking that what we have is really owed to us, or even that is the result of our autonomous efforts. We stop considering ourselves the creators and sovereigns of our existences, and instead, we recognise next to us countless people with claims, needs, and rights similar to ours. On the one hand, then, beauty keeps the goods of equality and balance constantly visible, through its call to proportion and harmony. On the other, it makes us . . . get off our high horse, it invites us to share and distribute what we have and what has been given to us. If we are not the centre of the world, nor the creators of the goods we enjoy, we can only increase the distribution of it and the possibilities of a common enjoyment.

Scarry's idea is that contemporary culture must rediscover the social and moral value of beauty. There are many reasons that have led contemporary societies to give beauty a marginal prominence, reducing it to something negligible. Beauty may fill magazines, museum halls, and movie theatres, or it may be relevant when we look at ourselves in the mirror or take a picture to post on a social network, but it is socially and politically irrelevant. On the one hand, we are convinced that statements about what (or who) is beautiful are entirely subjective, contestable, and plural, so much so that we should be wary of them: beauty is a matter of taste and opinion, so it cannot have anything to do with what is common and shared, with what is political. On the other, Scarry continues, the political irrelevance of beauty depends on the idea that it distracts from social injustices and makes us indifferent to them. Then, if it is the beauty of a body, of a human being, it even risks being dangerous, because it could conceal a predatory attitude: our gaze, we seem to think, is oriented toward the desire to possess, to make our own, to objectify, so it is politically inappropriate (if not prosecuted under criminal law).[69]

In a similar sense, Arthur Danto points out how the artists of the twentieth century themselves, and especially those who identified themselves with some

67 Scarry, *On Beauty and Being Just*, 75 ff.

68 S. Weil, "Love of the Order of the World," in *Waiting for God*, ed. S. Weil, trans. Emma Craufurd, introd. Leslie A. Fiedler (Harper & Row, 1951), 159.

69 Scarry, *On Beauty and Being Just*, 39.

avant-garde, purposely avoided beauty in their creations.[70] Many artists purposely avoided creating something beautiful and translating the idea of beauty into forms, considering this possibility as in itself naive and irresponsible. Theirs was an art made of activism,[71] indignation, and denunciation, and because beauty is perceived as consoling and pacifying, they rejected it. Precisely because of their commitment to justice, or to a specific issue on which they decided to engage as artists, and in whose service, they directed their art, they refused to associate art with beauty. Modern artists, Danto argues, have sought neither to console nor pacify, but to provoke and accuse.

Scarry's proposal goes in the opposite direction, for it calls for rediscovering the classical perspective, which we have seen permeates Christian thought as well. We should, according to Scarry, rediscover the politically positive value of beauty, namely the fact that it "assists us in the work of addressing injustice".[72] Beauty sharpens our gaze, trains us to look at things with care and attention, and exerts a distributive pressure: when something strikes us for its beauty, we are immediately driven to look for other things of equal beauty, to look around, to turn our gaze to find other beauties to contemplate and protect. Both beauty and justice, in other words, can be both contemplated (where they are exhibited in a body, a landscape, a virtuous action) and realised (where they are not present but arise from the desire to produce new beauty and new justice). Both beauty and justice must be defended and secured where they are present, against all forces that seek to destroy or ruin them; but they must also be built where they are not, obeying a kind of compulsion that requires us to create just arrangements and relationships where they do not yet exist.[73]

Beauty and justice, in short, belong to the human good, so much so that when they are not visible, we miss them, we perceive their absence as a deprivation; in both cases, they impel us to take action to make them real. Many approaches persuasively emphasise a connection between beauty and social justice, both highlighting that beauty is a kind of "aesthetic necessity" for human beings, then a crucial part of the educational process,[74] and focusing

70 Arthur Danto, *Embodied Meanings: Critical Essays and Aesthetic Meditations* (Farrar Strauss Giroux, 1994); Arthur Danto, *The Abuse of Beauty: Aesthetics and the Concept of Art* (Open Court Publishing, 2003).

71 Kathleen M. Higgins, "Whatever Happened to Beauty? A Response to Danto," *The Journal of Aesthetics and Art Criticism* 54, no. 3 (1996): 281–84.

72 Scarry, *On Beauty and Being Just*, 42.

73 Rawls writes of a 'desire for justice' that derives from the desire to express a potentiality, and to realise it, on the part of free and equal subjects endowed with the freedom of choice. Such subjects, in other words, realise their freedom by giving effect to this desire for justice, which drives them to choose principles of justice, to express them in their lives as members of a community, and to act in a way that conforms to them. Cfr. John Rawls, *A Theory of Justice* (Harvard University Press, 1971), 83–87.

74 John Armstrong, *The Secret Power of Beauty* (London: Penguin Books, 2005).

on how an aesthetic tension is internal to legal experience, so much so that it influences our very view of justice and our propensity to realise it.[75] Others argue that beauty is a pivotal factor for the expansion of our moral sense and society's ethical universe in general.[76]

Above all, it seems to me that a perspective like Scarry's correctly grasps that both justice and beauty are processes rather than objects: both are perspectives to be realised, and their content is certainly variable, and yet it is necessary to strive to realise them. Indeed, it is necessary to encourage a way of living in the world in which commitment to both is central.[77] As we will see in the next chapter, both justice and beauty can be described as a tension or, more precisely, as an *ordo factivus*: something to be realised, not simply known or contemplated. But this, once again, is only possible if the cognitive and rational approach to aesthetics and law, to beauty and justice, is complemented by an awareness of the role played in both cases by subjective perceptions and sensations, and the way law and aesthetics structure our perceptions.

75 Scarry, *On Beauty and Being Just*, 46.

76 Jose Luis Bermudez and Sebastian Gardner, eds., *Art and Morality* (London, New York: Routledge, 2003).

77 Desmond Manderson, *Songs without Music: Aesthetic Dimensions of Law and Justice*, vol. 7 (University of California Press, 2000), 45.

Chapter 3

The beauty of law

Introduction

Sometimes, legal texts are considered very beautiful, aesthetically speaking. These are often constitutional texts, although not exclusively. In Italy, for example, the beauty of the Constitution is often extolled, and in Germany or France the beauty of the civil code is just as frequently praised.[1] Whether these statements are true or not, it seems to me that they cannot be taken for granted. The fact that a legal text can be judged in many ways, and from many perspectives, including not strictly legal ones, is indeed a well-known fact. Anyone can state with some confidence that a single norm, or a legal text of any level, is just or unjust, politically important or inappropriate, economically useful or socially beneficial, morally appreciable or despicable, and so on. Whether they can be beautiful or ugly is less obvious. And even if a long tradition of scholarship has interpreted law as an aesthetic object, the question of the meaning of such judgements is not entirely clear. In particular, even assuming that law can be studied as an aesthetically relevant fact, and with the epistemic tools of aesthetics, three questions must be answered. First, it is unclear whether an aesthetic evaluation of law is possible (Is it beautiful? Is it ugly?). Second, it is unclear in what sense this evaluation should be made (What do we mean when we say that law is beautiful?). Third, it is unclear what the purpose of this evaluation is (Why do we care whether it is beautiful or ugly?).

Let me try to clarify these questions by moving them to a non-legal plane. It may happen, of course, that a philosophical text is also very beautiful: Plato's dialogues, for instance, are certainly texts of immense philosophical importance, but they are also texts endowed with extraordinary literary value: they are works of art, true literary masterpieces. We can say the same of St. Augustine's Confessions or, citing some more recent examples, certain texts by Nietzsche or Kierkegaard. But it is very difficult to assert an equal

1 Anne-Marie Le Pourhiet, "La beauté du droit," in *L'art et le Droit. Écrits en hommage à Pierre-Laurent Frier*, ed. Maryse Deguergue (Editions de la Sorbonne, 2010), 195–201.

DOI: 10.4324/9781003589426-3

aesthetic value with respect to every philosophical text, however relevant it may be. Of course, we can say that Hegel's thought is beautiful, or that Being and Time is a beautiful text, but we mostly mean that we are dealing with arguments that are stimulating, interesting, exciting, fundamental from a historical point of view, or something else again. Rarely do we mean that they have a particular aesthetic relevance and that on this level they deserve to be appreciated and valued.

Similarly, a legal text can be also beautiful from a literary point of view. We certainly can, for example, consider the Mosaic law, the law that God through Moses gave to the people of Israel, to be very beautiful on a literary level. More generally, we are not surprised that some parts of the Pentateuch are both aesthetically appreciable – that they are literature, properly speaking – and provided with an important normative and religious value. More recently, the writings and judgements of Cardozo and Brandeis[2] – two well-known Supreme Court Justices who, from a liberal orientation, served during the Roosevelt presidency – can also be considered to be works that are appreciable on an aesthetic level, because of the language they use, the words and styles, the arguments they elaborate, and the way they organise the timing of linguistic communication.[3]

But what does it mean that a legal text can be appreciable, from a literary point of view, however different personal tastes and sensibilities are? To what extent is an aesthetic judgement relevant to law and to the goals we intend to achieve through law? When we evaluate a building from an aesthetic point of view and say that in addition to being functional, and safe, it is also beautiful, we are implicitly affirming that the aesthetic factor is a level on which it makes sense to place the analysis of architectural works. That is to say, we expect a building to be suitable for its intended use, and to be safe for those who live or work in it, but that it also makes sense to evaluate the beauty of that building, although we know that personal tastes vary and we do not claim to make an objective judgement. We can certainly live in a house that is comfortable and spacious but ugly; and yet, if it were also beautiful (to us), it would be better. Similarly, we can eat a well-cooked and tasty dish that looks unappetising (e.g. a deflated soufflé): but of course, "we eat first with our eyes", and if we could also enjoy that food from an aesthetic point of view, it would be better. It is not evident whether we can say the same thing about the law.

I am convinced that this is not simply a matter of words. Of course, it is possible that when we speak of beautiful legal text, a beautiful sentence, or a beautiful Constitution, we are simply using the word 'beautiful' to refer to

2 Benjamin N. Cardozo, "Law and Literature," in *Selected Writings of Benjamin Nathan Cardozo*, ed. Margaret E. Hall (Fallon, 1947), 339–56; Judith S. Kaye, "Cardozo: A Law Classic," *Harvard Law Review* 112 (1999): 1027, 1030–31; Richard H. Weisberg, "Law, Literature and Cardozo's Judicial Poetics," *Cardozo Law Review* 1 (1979): 283.

3 Weisberg, "Law, Literature and Cardozo's Judicial Poetics," 309 ff.

the subtlety of the argumentation used in a judgement, the rigour of legal reasoning, the clarity and comprehensibility of a normative text, or the political and social value of a constitution.[4] However, I think that even if we appreciate these features, when we evaluate a legal text as 'beautiful', we are using an aesthetic category consciously, and still quite accurately. More precisely, we want to show our appreciation for that text, either because we think it manifests a certain idea of beauty that we appreciate (the harmony of the text, the geometric precision of the arguments, the rigor and purity of the linguistic uses, etc.), or because that text has aroused in us peculiar reactions, feelings, and emotions.

Years ago, one of the most important Italian jurists of the twentieth century, Francesco Carnelutti, entitled one of his writings precisely "The Art of Law" (in the preface he specifies that he wrote it while reading Miguel de Unamuno on a boat trip to Latin America). Carnelutti reminds us, right from the title, that if from Celsus onwards law has been defined as *Ars boni et aequi*, for centuries we have concentrated on the last two terms, the Right and the Fair, and have forgotten the reference to art, to the law as art. For Carnelutti, reducing law to a science is, in fact, a diminution, a short-sighted choice that does not grasp the mystery of law and its nature. The mature legal scholar, he writes, no longer has the naive faith in the scientific approach, because he knows that the reality of law is more complex, and accessible only with an – even – poetic approach:

> The young man had faith in science; the old man has lost it. The young man believed he knew; the old man knows that he does not know. And he reaches the awareness of not knowing, then science is converted into poetry. The young man was content with the scientific concept of law; the old man feels that in this concept he loses his impetus and drama and, therefore, his truth. The young man sought the sharp contours of definition; the old man prefers the nuances of a comparison. The young man did not believe except in what is seen; the old man no longer believes except in what he cannot see.[5]

Law, in short, is art, and not only in a metaphorical sense. Law, like music or poetry, works by selecting its elements (be they notes, colours, words, or interests and rights) and organises them by ordering them and giving them harmony and meaning. The result of this artistic work of selection may, of course, be beautiful or ugly: aesthetics is not, in short, a dimension extraneous to the world of law. On the contrary, it is a perspective from which to

4 Jacqueline Morand-Deviller, "Ordre du droit, ordre du beau," in *L'art et le Droit. Écrits en hommage à Pierre-Laurent Frier*, ed. Maryse Deguergue (Editions de la Sorbonne, 2010), 249, 252.

5 Francesco Carnelutti, *Arte del diritto*, ed. Daniele Cananzi (Giappichelli, 2017), 18 (my translation).

observe legal phenomena, legitimately and sensibly. After all, law is made of words, and all the problems, potentialities, and issues that language produces are typical of the legal experience. The structure and construction of the text, the use and value of rhetoric, the presence of ambiguities, the interpretation and search for the meaning of words are all aspects proper to every literary work, and law is one of them.

Some (possible) approaches to the beauty of law

When we explore the relevance of aesthetics to law, different approaches are possible.[6] A first approach analyses the aesthetic representations of law and how law, lawyers, and legal issues are depicted by literature or other works of art (textual, visual, or even performative arts). Within this approach, works of art are used to better understand legal issues, the human nature, or problems of justice.[7] Second, legal texts can be analysed *as* aesthetic objects, with a specific focus on forms and by using methodologies typical of the arts and humanities. Within this approach, for instance, judgements and legislation are interpreted as literary texts, highlighting rhetorical or stylistics devices used by the law.[8] A third approach focuses on how aesthetics is *used* by lawyers or legislators, to support their political objectives, legitimise their choices, or enhance political consensus. Well-known are studies on courtroom architectures, emblems and iconographic tools mobilised by law, as well as procedures and rituals.[9] Finally, a fourth approach takes aesthetics

6 I'm reducing possible approaches to those that I consider more relevant for this analysis: however, other are possible, ore some of the mentioned approaches could be further specified. For these additional distinctions, see Kamil Zeidler and Agnieszka Plata, "Law and Literature: A New View from Six Perspectives," in *Aesthetics of Law: From Methodology to Manifestations*, eds. K. Zeidler and J. Kamień (Springer, 2024). For a good overview, see Greta Olson, *From Law and Literature to Legality and Affect* (Oxford University Press, 2022).

7 Among the many, a rightly famous book is Martha Nussbaum, *Poetic Justice: The Literary Imagination and Public Life* (Boston: Beacon Press, 1997); with a specific focus on movies and visual representations of legal issues, see Austin Sarat, Lawrence Douglas, and Martha Merrill Umphrey, "On Film and Law: Broadening the Focus," in *Law on the Screen*, eds. Austin Sarat et al. (Stanford University Press, 2005); the focus on visual art can be found in Oren Ben-Dor, *Law and Art: Ethics, Aesthetics, Justice* (Routledge, 2011).

8 Examples of this approach are the works of James Boyd White, *Heracles' Bow: Essays on the Rhetoric and Poetics of Law* (University of Wisconsin Press, 1985); James Boyd White, *Justice as Translation* (University of Chicago Press, 1990), 235–67; and Ronald Dworkin, *Law's Empire* (Belknap Press, 1986), especially 45–86.

9 See the works of Costas Douzinas, *Justice Miscarried: Ethics, Aesthetics, and the Law* (Harvester Wheatsheaf, 1994); Peter Goodrich, *Oedipus Lex: Psychoanalysis, History, Law* (Berkeley: University of California Press, 1995); Costas Douzinas and Lynda Nead, eds., *Law and the Image: The Authority of Art and the Aesthetics of Law* (University of Chicago Press, 1999); Desmond Manderson, ed., *Law and the Visual: Representations, Technologies and Critique* (University of Toronto Press, 2018).

as a dimension of human experience which is internal to law. From this perspective, legal practices of language, dress, and argumentation are taken as aesthetic objects: therefore, we cannot understand the ideas and practices of legislators or judges without considering the way they see the world, on the one hand; and we cannot understand the way the law shapes our world without considering how these legal objects are used to affect our perception and senses.[10] In line with this approach, the task is to go beyond linguistic logic and rationality, in search of meanings and effects that are non-linguistic but no less real and intense than others.[11]

As Manderson rightly suggests, most of the approaches dealing with legal aesthetics take law and aesthetics as separate and distinct domains. Similarly to what we can do when we talk about law and economics, law and science, law and politics, these approaches – with the exception of the last one – consider law and literature "as two separate disciplines with certain aspects in common and certain things to teach each other . . . fit subject for comparison but not of interaction":[12] aesthetics is a separate discipline useful to shed light on law and its challenges, rather than an intrinsic aspect of it.

This separateness is particularly evident in the studies on law in literature, that is, studies on how law, procedures, legal issues, and the people who produce and apply law, are represented in literature. It is possible, for instance, to discuss literary works in which legal procedures, such as a trial or a stage of a trial, are described: from legal thrillers, for example, to *The Merchant of Venice* and the debate between Shylock and Portia; from Racine's *Les plaideurs,* which not only makes theatre out of the trial but turns the trial into a theatre, to the Rabelais's *Gargantua*, in which Pantagruel attends the trial of Judge Bridlegoose, who decides the cases before him by a throw of the dice; from *The Brothers Karamazov*, to Kafka's *The Trial* or Melville's *Billy Budd*, the list of titles and authors is truly impressive, testifying to the literary fascination of the law and the characters that animate it.

Besides this approach, we can also consider texts in which one of the characters, not necessarily the main one but someone who plays a central role, is a lawyer (predominantly male). We can certainly think of the figure of Azzeccagarbugli ("Quibble-weaver") in Manzoni, whose fearfulness constitutes one of the novel's developmental factors; but extraordinary figures are the lawyer Derville in Balzac's *Colonel Chabert*, or Bartleby the scribe

10 Patricia Clough and Jean Halley, eds., *The Affective Turn: Theorising the Social* (Duke University Press, 2007); Ben Anderson, *Encountering Affect: Capacities, Apparatuses, Conditions* (Routledge, 2014); Olson, *From Law and Literature to Legality and Affect*, 96 ff.

11 See, for a peculiar implementation of this approach, Desmond Manderson, *Songs without Music: Aesthetic Dimensions of Law and Justice*, vol. 7 (University of California Press, 2000), 190 ff.

12 Manderson, *Songs without Music*, 31.

in Melville, or Atticus Finch in *To Kill a Mockingbird* (who could also fall into the previous category), in a very 'male' list that certainly reflects the centuries-old exclusion of women from the legal horizon. To find a female figure, we have to go back to more recent times, perhaps widening the field to movies and TV productions, with Erin Brockovich and Lidia Poët among the many possible.[13]

Finally, a third group of works legitimately falls within this category, being perhaps the best-known group among legal scholars: it is a set of works that deal, more or less explicitly and directly, with the theme of justice, in one of its many possible dimensions. From Oresteia to Antigone, from Cervantes to Milton, from Shakespeare to Dickens, and from Dante to Hugo, it is indeed difficult to find a text or author that is irrelevant to the analysis of the topic of justice. Not surprisingly, such works have always attracted the interest of legal scholars: some of these texts have indeed been recognised as capable of raising questions and analyses with a similar acuity to that of philosophical and legal works.[14]

However, and even if I share the opinion of Manderson, I argue that within this approach law and literature are not *merely* juxtaposed: the very fact that visual or literary works could be used in analysing and understanding legal issues means that these two domains touch each other more than it may seem. More explicitly, the law and literature approach is meaningful to the extent we recognise that literature or visual arts contributed to the development of Western thought, also for what concerns the topics of justice, as well as the relationship between the individual and the state, and the limits of power, at least as much as authors and works more traditionally recognised as 'classics' of philosophical and juridical thought. These works are not mere examples, but they are part of a history of mutual influences, such that the points of contact are not merely contingent but reveal an intrinsic relationship.

This is the reason why literature may be considered in itself a privileged channel for understanding legal and political phenomena; that is, besides more usual analyses (philosophical, political, and legal), literature can open up spaces of understanding and levels of interpretation that would otherwise be inaccessible, or almost inaccessible.[15] This seems to be the reason for

13 Analyses of law in movies and tv series are offered by Steve Greenfield, Guy Osborn, and Peter Robson, *Film and the Law: The Cinema of Justice* (Hart Publishing, 2010); Austin Sarat et al., eds., *Law on the Screen* (Stanford University Press, 2005).

14 Among the many, a very good discussion of legal issues within literature, and literature as a form of law, is provided by Maria Aristodemou, *Law and Literature: Journeys from Her to Eternity* (Oxford University Press, 2000).

15 This is also due to the creative potential that literature opens up, opposing to a merely passive and receptive thought; concerning this aspect see Richard Weisberg, *Poethics: And Other Strategies of Law and Literature* (Columbia University Press, 1992), 222 ff.

the opening of 'law and literature' courses in law faculties; and this is, after all, the idea that emerges in a justly famous book, *Poetic Justice*, written by one of the most read contemporary philosophers, Martha Nussbaum.[16] In her reflections, Nussbaum emphasises how literature allows us to force a boundary that we experience when we attempt to understand reality on an exclusively rational basis. In this vein, literature is not only a digression but becomes a crucial tool for public discussion and decision-making,[17] both because it shows how our lives are filled with the questions and problems of justice, and it develops empathy, an ability to grasp the consequences on human life of problems that are otherwise too theoretical and abstract, the ability to care about the good of other people whose lives are distant from us. These are all indispensable qualities in public debate and legal work. Flexibility in judgement, foresight, the ability to recognise the humanity and dignity of others, the absence of preconceptions, and care for the most diverse people are qualities that, in Nussbaum's opinion, literature can develop in legal professionals, and we value more than ever.[18]

Many scholars also combined law and literature from a hermeneutic perspective. Their underlying idea[19] is that it is possible to study law and literature as parallel and to some extent analogous fields for the analysis of the relationship between the reader, the interpretative community, and the texts (legal or literary, precisely) that are the basic structure of a cultural horizon. Whether we are searching for the original 'meaning' of a text (a constitution, for example, or a literary text) or have to unravel certain ambiguities, we are faced with questions that arise for the understanding of legal texts as much as for the analysis of literary texts. Therefore, studies on the interpretation of literary texts and semiotics have also been used by legal scholars to analyse the decision-making mechanisms used by specific courts, or to formulate interpretative solutions.

The results of this parallelism between law and literature in terms of interpretation have been highly variable. Certainly, the different theories of interpretation have played their part, thereby influencing these analyses: more

16 Martha C. Nussbaum, "Poetic Justice: The Literary Imagination and Public Life," *Political Theory* 26, no. 4 (1998): 557–83; Martha C. Nussbaum, *Poetic Justice: The Literary Imagination and Public Life. The Alexander Rosenthal Lectures* (Beacon Press, 1997).

17 Nussbaum argues that reading can guide judges toward adopting specific mental and emotional attitudes. In this context, emotions do not hinder rational decision-making but instead shape and inform it. See Nussbaum, *Poetic Justice*, 2 ff.; see also Martha C. Nussbaum, *Love's Knowledge: Essays on Philosophy and Literature* (Oxford: Oxford University Press, 1990), 148.

18 For a critical analysis of these approaches, see James Seaton, "Law and Literature: Works, Criticism, and Theory," *Yale Journal of Law & the Humanities* 11, no. 2 (1999): 479–508.

19 This concept is grounded in the ideas of several classical theorists of interpretation (from Gadamer to Betti to Saussure) and some more recent authors: Derrida, first and foremost, but also Goodrich or Fish.

than in determining specific judicial decisions or specific interpretations, these theories contributed to shaping a cultural climate in which the relationship between author and interpreter has been analysed and discussed. Thus, the deconstructionism of Derrida,[20] the intertextuality of Kristeva[21] and Eco,[22] Marxist criticism and New Criticism, the intentionalism of Hirsch,[23] the anti-intentionalism of Barthes[24] and Gadamer,[25] and many other perspectives have been able to give life to a cultural debate which has involved legal scholars and conditioned interpretative practices.

However, legal interpretation still seems to be largely conditioned by the search for the legislator's intention, the original meaning of the text: still, to a very large extent, courts and interpreters tend to read legal texts in search of objective meaning, an intention, and to consider the text in question as a communication content elaborated by an author (Parliament) and intended for a community of interpreters and addressees.[26] In short, they tend to do what most contemporary theories of interpretation criticise or denounce as false, wrong, and illusory.[27] In the opposite sense, it is precisely the nature of legal acts that makes interpretation consistent with wide margins of creativity, much more so than in the literary sphere: after all, a legislative text is not the product of a single author, of someone who (like the author of a novel) actually wanted to communicate something specific, someone whose subjective intention is, at least in theory, determinable. The legislature is a collective body, and legislative texts are not bound by the intentions of those – whoever they were and may have been – who drafted and approved that text. This is, among others, the reason why Posner, writes with a little irony and a lot of wisdom that the theory of interpretation is "the great, false hope of law

20 Jacques Derrida, *Deconstruction in a Nutshell: A Conversation with Jacques Derrida, with a New Introduction* (Fordham University Press, 2020).
21 Julia Kristeva, "Word, Dialogue, and Novel," in *Desire in Language: A Semiotic Approach to Literature and Art*, ed. Leon S. Roudiez (Columbia University Press, 1980), 64–91.
22 Umberto Eco, *The Role of the Reader. Explorations in the Semiotics of Texts* (Indiana University Press, 1979).
23 Eric D. Hirsch, "The Aims of Interpretation," *Journal of Aesthetics and Art Criticism* 35, no. 3 (1977).
24 Roland Barthes, "The Death of the Author," in *Image – Music – Text*, ed. Roland Barthes (Fontana Press, 1977), 142–48; also in *Art and Interpretation: An Anthology of Readings in Aesthetics and the Philosophy of Art*, ed. Eric Dayton (Broadview, 1988).
25 Hans G. Gadamer, *Truth and Method*, trans. Joel Weinsheimer and Donald G. Marshall (Continuum, 1975).
26 Consider the recent US Supreme Court decision, *Dobbs v Jackson Women's Health Organization*, no. 19-1392, 597 U.S. 215. An interpretation of originalism, from the perspective of legal aesthetics, is provided by Manderson, *Songs without Music*, 163.
27 Jeremy Waldron, "Legislators' Intentions and Unintentional Legislation," in *Law and Interpretation: Essays in Legal Philosophy*, ed. A. Marmor (Clarendon Press, 1995), 329–56.

and literature":[28] it is a suggestive field but with very uncertain results, on a practical level.

More convincing are other approaches, such as those of Costas Douzinas[29] or Peter Goodrich,[30] where aesthetics is recognised as an effective analytic perspective for legal texts, and artworks are understood as appropriate points of view to explore legal issues. These approaches consider the ways in which legal texts – including judgements, constitutions, and statutes – operate as aesthetic objects, thereby illuminating the rhetorical and stylistic devices that support legal texts' authority and coherence. Pioneering works of James Boyd White, Guyora Binder, and Richard Weisberg[31] highlighted that law is not merely a technical system of rules but a cultural practice deeply rooted in language, and legal texts and literary works share modes of expression and interpretation. White's concept of "constitutive rhetoric," for instance, posits that legal texts shape communal identities through their performative and persuasive qualities.[32] Legal judgements, like works of literature, deploy narrative strategies to structure facts, create coherence, and legitimise outcomes. Law settles conflicts and contrasts between interests, needs, and values: the building of a community depends on how these conflicts are decided. Law is an end-oriented technique, which uses words and language to build relationships and strengthen communities: as a consequence, legal rhetoric is not (only) the art of persuasion but a strategy by which, with words and signs, legislators build communities and transform them.[33]

On the one hand, these approaches capture the aesthetic dimensions of legal texts, by highlighting metaphors, analogies, and other figures of speech, and the ways evocative language is used to ground abstract principles in relatable terms or facilitating the evolution of legal norms.[34] The narratological structure of legal texts becomes a central issue, and the narrative choices made by judges are understood as ways to discuss their implicit aesthetic and ethical judgements. On the other hand, these studies analyse how style and language are used to facilitate the reception of legal texts and affirm their

28 Richard A. Posner, "Law and Literature: A Relation Reargued," *Virginia Law Review* 72, no. 8 (1986): 1360.

29 Douzinas, *Justice Miscarried.*

30 Goodrich, *Oedipus Lex.*

31 Richard H. Weisberg, "Comparative Law in Comparative Literature: The Figure of the 'Examining Magistrate' in Dostoevsky and Camus," *Rutgers Law Review* 29 (1975–1976): 237–58; Guyora Binder and Robert Weisberg, *Literary Criticism of Law* (Princeton University Press, 2000).

32 James Boyd White, *Heracles' Bow: Essays on the Rhetoric and Poetics of the Law* (University of Wisconsin Press, 1986).

33 Boyd White, *Heracles' Bow*, 28, 116 ff.; Boyd White, *Justice as Translation*, 235 ff.

34 James Boyd White, *The Legal Imagination* (University of Chicago Press, 1985), 56 ff.; Robert M. Cover, "Foreword: Nomos and Narrative," *Harvard Law Review* 97, no. 1 (1983): 4–68.

authority: for instance, by contributing to affirm law's traits of objectivity and rationality, or signalling the urgency of specific political outcomes.[35] For instance, dissenting opinions in Courts' decisions often adopt a more impassioned tone, aiming to sway future legal developments or public opinion.[36]

Besides these studies, other authors have analysed how the aesthetics of law, the symbols and emblems of power, the architectures and liturgies of law, have been used to stage power itself and its values. For instance, scholars like Austin Sarat and Thomas R. Kearns explored the performative dimensions of law, highlighting how its rituals and ceremonies embody aesthetic as well as legal significance. Beginning with Huizinga's pioneering studies, scholars discussed how aesthetics is used by legislators, to support their political objectives, legitimise their choices, and enhance political consensus. Studies on courtroom architectures, emblems and iconographic tools mobilised by law, as well as procedures and rituals, contributed to a better understanding of legal practices and values.[37] In this vein, Peter Goodrich described the semiotics of courtroom behaviour, highlighting how its visual architecture inculcates alienation and disempowerment: the size and space of the courtroom, as well as the placement of seats or the isolation of the dock, and the antiquity of modes of dress and address, everything contributes to the exaltation of power and its super-ordination over the position of the individual.[38] The space of the courtroom, as in the architecture of the great cathedrals of the Middle Ages, stages the sacredness and grandeur of power and law to justify obedience.[39]

While these approaches tend to view law and aesthetics as separate disciplines, focusing on reciprocal influences and the advantages of using similar methodologies for the study of both, the last group focuses on how aesthetics emerges within the legal sphere and the specific form of legal aesthetics that is given as a result. The focus of these theories is not merely the possibility of parallel analyses that can be conducted from an aesthetic perspective in relation to law, or the intersection between law and aesthetics. Rather, these analyses explore the internal dynamics of law, considering aesthetics as an

35 John M. Conley, William M. O'Barr, and Robin Conley Riner, *Just Words: Law, Language, and Power* (University of Chicago Press, 2019).

36 Robert F. Blomquist, "Dissent, Posner-Style: Judge Richard A. Posner's First Decade of Dissenting Opinions, 1981–1991-Toward an Aesthetics of Judicial Dissenting Style," *Missouri Law Review* 69 (2004): 73.

37 The role played by visual depictions, such as portraiture, architectural symbols, statuary, or costumes is analysed extensively in Peter Goodrich and Valérie Hayaert, eds., *Genealogies of Legal Vision* (Routledge, 2015).

38 Peter Goodrich, *Languages of Law, From Logics of Memory to Nomadic Masks* (Northwestern University Press, 1980), 53; Peter Goodrich, "Modalities of Annunciationo. An introduction to Courtroom Speech," in *Law and Semiotics*, ed. Roberta Kevelson (Springer Science & Business Media, 2012), 143–45.

39 Manderson, *Songs without Music*, 42.

internal dimension of legal experience. The transition of legal studies from aesthetics to what is called *aesthesis* highlights the awareness that sensory, emotional, and affective dimensions are internal to law:[40] it is not only the political use of images and emblems that brings an aesthetic dimension within the legal field, because legal experience (acting subjects, objects, languages, relations) is per se experienced by sensate bodies and belongs to aesthesis.[41] In this vein, legal *aesthesis* focuses on the way law conditions our sensory perception, and the way senses and perceptions affect our understanding of law and shape law's power: as Wall and Matthews rightly write, sovereignty itself has an inner aesthetic dimension, and is "within the aesthetic (affective and imaginative) registers that the lawful and material relations associated with sovereignty are first visualised, represented, felt, and given sense".[42]

Approaches focused on legal aesthesis do not take law and aesthetics as separate fields; rather, it is argued that the aesthetic dimension is not only relevant but also necessary to understand law and legal phenomena: without aesthetics, the legal also blurs.[43] The words of the law are never a mere means to transmit informative content, and by which human behaviours are ordered, forbidden, or regulated: they are comparable to the parts of a painting, something that asks to be understood, but first of all also observed, seen.[44] Similarly, Gary Bagnall, in his book *The Law as Art*, assumes that law should be explained as a kind of artistically valuable action type: law, according to Bagnall, is a performance of artistic value, whose elements are verbal and non-verbal human actions, and whose structure is typical of dramatic action.

Law has an *iconic* dimension because it aims not only to communicate a content of thought or will but to stage the foundation of power, to represent sovereignty in a visible and perceptible manner.[45] This is why, as totalitarian regimes have always well understood, the discipline of social relations cannot do without a liturgical dimension, rituals, parades, visible manifestations of sovereignty, scenic arrangements, and representations. Law is a

40 see Terry Eagleton, *The Ideology of the Aesthetic* (Blackwell, 1990), 13: "Aesthetic is the whole of our sensate life together – the business of affections and aversions, of how the world strikes the body on its sensory surfaces, of that which takes root in the gaze and the guts and all that arises from our most banal, biological insertion into the world".

41 Jacques Rancière, *Aisthesis: Scenes from the Aesthetic Regime of Art*, trans. Zakir Paul (Verso, 2013).

42 Illan Wall and Daniel Matthews, "Sovereignty and the Persistence of the Aesthetic," *The Modern Law Review* 87, no. 6 (2024): 1396.

43 Paolo Heritier, *Estetica giuridica. A partire da Legendre. Il fondamento finzionale del diritto positivo*, vol. II (Giappichelli, 2012), 45.

44 Heritier, *Estetica giuridica*, 26.

45 See Zenon Bankowski and Geoff Maugham, *Images of Law* (London: Routledge, 1976); Zenon Bańkowski, "Images of Images of Law," *Social & Legal Studies* 11, no. 3 (2002): 445–53.

phenomenon of communication addressed to the human being as a whole, and thus not only to the sphere of rationality. Rules are at the same time instruments oriented to the sphere of passions, feelings, fears, and ideal aspirations, which are necessary for the effective communication of law. As Douzinas rightly writes, images "speak directly to the senses and affect the psyche, they address the labile elements of the self and avoid the calming intervention of logos".[46] The icon does not 'resemble' reality; it represents it. It does not aim to persuade through verisimilitude, but orients the mind of the beholder: the person who looks at the icon is driven by the observation of the limited formal similarity towards the desire to perceive what is absolute, invisible, and ineffable.[47]

In the same way, law depicts an absence: it stages sovereignty, or a certain model of community and coexistence, not only by describing it in a rational and definite way, but by directing reality towards what is desired, and which at the same time is not present.[48] Legal texts – as already discussed – are understood as emblems, representations of something that is not present. As Goodrich explains, we should consider law as a plastic art, made up of architecture, statuary, clothing, heraldry, painting, and emblems that provide people with a representation of justice that they can see and remember. The judge's robe, the ritual use of oaths and seals, everything is aimed at reinforcing the appearance of a just authority. The same architecture makes most courts temple-like, and even the most visible institution in the private sector of law, the lawyer's office, is aesthetically packaged to link the power of law to the authority of tradition, culture, and knowledge.[49]

To say that law is a *mise-en-scene* is a statement that we should not view in a negative light. Many elements allow us to bring the trial closer to the theatre, starting with certain architectural solutions that recall typical theatrical forms (as well as responding to functional requirements): the audience stalls, decorated wings, certain grandiloquent sets typical of courtrooms, etc.[50] Moreover, the element that is often emphasised is the separation of the judicial space: like the stage for actors, the judicial action takes place in a

46 Costas Douzinas, "The Legality of the Image," *Modern Law Review* 63, no. 6 (2000), 817.

47 Douzinas, *The Legality of the Image*, 820.

48 Wall and Matthews, "Sovereignty and the Persistence of the Aesthetic," 1402; Desmond Manderson, "Here and Now: From Aestheticizing Politics to Politicising Art," in *Sensing the Nation's Law: Historical Inquiries into the Aesthetics of Democratic Legitimacy*, eds. Mark Antaki et al. (Springer, 2018); Peter Goodrich, *Legal Emblems and the Arts of Law: Obiter Depicta as the Vision of Governance* (Cambridge University Press, 2013).

49 Peter Goodrich, "Specula Laws: Image, Aesthetic and Common Law," *Law and Critique* 2, no. 2 (1991): 233 ff.

50 See among the countless texts devoted to architecture and judicial iconography Robert Jacob, *Images de la justice. Essai sur l'iconographie judiciaire du Moyen Âge à l'Âge classique* (Le Léopard d'Or, 1994). For a description of the affinities between theatre and trial, see also Jacques Vergès, *La justice est un jeu* (Albin Michel, 1992), 41–48.

separate space, closed towards the outside and identifiable with certainty; it is a *tèmenos*,[51] a separate sacred space, a space within which the action, from mere discussion, becomes judgement.

But it is also from other places and cultures that one can draw, apparently, a confirmation of the theatrical character of the process, and the legitimacy of an aesthetic approach to the understanding of law: one of the most beautiful examples, in this sense, is that of the procedure adopted by the Inuit, in which the theatrical and aesthetic element comes to the fore with great force. Among the various possible strategies for resolving a conflict and settling a dispute – all with a strong competitive and ritual character – perhaps the most characteristic is the song contest: in this procedure, the parties challenge each other to a duel in which the weapons are exclusively musical, namely songs. Victory is awarded to the party that manages to be applauded most warmly by the community, on account of the beauty of the song performed. Nothing of direct relevance to the substantive issue is considered for judgement. One can try to make people laugh, to move, to involve them with rhythm, one can slander and one can make false accusations, harass one's opponent, and all to the rhythm of the music. However, two basic rules must be respected: the first is not to be offended by the accusations one receives (after all, it is only a staging), and the second is never to refer to reasons of personal resentment, complaining instead of attacking.[52] The spectators, at the same time, participate in the chants, and can applaud and cheer the parties against each other, in a procedure that, in stage and theatre form, performs a very important jurisdictional function.[53]

Pierre Legendre effectively captured this dimension when he described the *Corpus Juris Civilis* as an extraordinary example of the mythical and iconic dimension of legal texts, especially when they are endowed with founding ambitions. The *Corpus* is precisely born with the idea of collecting the

51 The term is used by almost all authors: see, however, Joan Huizinga, *Homo Ludens. A Study of the Play-Element in Culture* (Routledge, 2002), 77. See on this the essential analysis by Mircea Eliade, *Traité d'histoire des religions* (Payot, 1975), 313.

52 Inuit procedure was first studied by Edward Adamson Hoebel, *The Law of Primitive Man: A Study in Comparative Legal Dynamics* (Harvard University Press, 1954); for an example of a song duel see pp. 139–49, in which two men challenge each other over a woman: K. wants to get back the woman he divorced, and clashes with E., the woman's new companion; the two therefore challenge each other to a song duel, a duel in which accusations and insults are not spared. K., for example, accuses E. of being a 'deformed man with black skin', a thief of women, and a 'miserable scoundrel who loves human flesh'; E., conversely, replies that K. treated the woman like a servant, always leaving her alone and never showing affection towards her. On the Inuit procedure, see also Max Gluckman, *Politics, Law and Ritual in Tribal Society* (Blackwell, 1965), 304 ff. Studies on similar procedures in the Melanesian system have been carried out by Bronislaw Malinowski, *Crime and Custom in Savage Society* (Routledge and Kegan Paul, 1966), 71 ff.

53 Huizinga, *Homo Ludens*, 78.

pre-existing legal tradition and giving it the organic structure and harmony of a body; it has, however, the ambition of founding a social and political structure. The normative text thus becomes a scenic object, a mechanism for staging fragments of centuries-old legal wisdom, giving them a place, a role, selecting and organising them. The Code is a powerful fresco that unifies and – precisely because of this ability to organise the multiple harmoniously, like a painting – becomes canon and foundation, by taking the place of what is invisible (sovereign power) and representing it visually.[54]

Law as a text, and the importance of *style*

Within this complex and various set of studies, an interesting question concerns the beauty of the legal text. It is an important aspect for several reasons: first, because it is often overlooked by more general analyses, in which the focus is on the relationship between law and aesthetics, or between the different methodologies used by these disciplines. Second, because this question puts at the center the problem of beauty, that is, of a positive aesthetic evaluation of law: in other words, the issue here is not whether law and aesthetics have points of contact, or whether they are somehow intertwined dimensions, but whether it is possible to give an aesthetic evaluation of law, as beautiful or ugly. Not only do I think such an aesthetic evaluation of law is possible, but I think it is relevant, and allows us to highlight the need to take into account both perspectives of legal aesthetics and the question of *aesthesis*.

One caveat must be stressed: the notion of beauty – similarly to the notion of justice – is extremely elusive and variable. Both in the sense that it can be considered an exclusively subjective notion dependent on individual preferences – that is, impossible to define objectively – and in the sense that even the objective definitions that may be proposed differ from each other. In other words, we do not have a unified definition of either beauty or justice. Yet, the question of the beauty of law is not epistemologically incorrect, if we understand it in a very narrow way: we can ask whether the subjective, and widespread, perception of the beauty of law has relevance, regardless of definitions. That is, the fact that law meets the tastes and aesthetic sensibilities of the recipients of norms, does matter, even though these tastes may vary over time, or may be different from each other. In other words, the fact that a legal text is considered beautiful by the recipients of the norms (or by most of them, at least) is a relevant aspect of the law's ability to shape social relations and individual behaviors.

54 Pierre Legendre, *Nomenclator. Sur la question dogmatique en Occident, II* (Fayard, 2006), 353 ff.; Heritier, *Estetica giuridica*, 80 ff.

If aesthetic dimensions are internal to law and justice, since "the discourse of law is fundamentally governed by rhetoric, metaphor, form, images, and symbols",[55] the question of the beauty of law (even limited in the aforementioned way) becomes relevant: if law is portrayed as a form of literature, "the debates among major jurisprudential traditions can be viewed as aesthetic contrasts among competing narrative methods and visions",[56] and the aesthetic quality of texts becomes relevant as much as that of literary works. From this point of view, therefore, it is legitimate to ask whether the language of law, the prose of judgements and laws, is aesthetically appreciable or not.[57] Gustav Radbruch, one of the greatest jurists of the twentieth century, wrote a very short text on precisely this aspect,[58] arguing that if in modern times the law is kept separate from poetry and mythology, it has nevertheless gained, through this separation, its specific aesthetic value. The language of law is cold, renouncing any emotional tone. It is harsh, far from all justification; it is brief and lapidary because it expresses the force of the state; it could even be – writes Radbruch – for this reason alone an excellent stylistic example for many novelists. But at the same time, the language of the 'struggle for law' (today, we might say, of activism) is ardent and full of rhetoric, reflecting the fervour of individual passions and the urgency of needs. Both of these styles are part of the legal experience, and both show how aesthetics is an appropriate paradigm for understanding and evaluating law.[59]

It is a fact that legal text, because of their language and structure, can be considered beautiful by many, even without going so far as to claim, as Paul Valéry did, that the Civil Code (the Napoleonic one, in his case) was a masterpiece of literature. And without necessarily having to do as Stendhal did, who, in a letter sent from Civitavecchia, confided to Balzac that while he was writing *The Charterhouse of Parma* he felt the need, every morning, to read at least two or three pages of the Code, to be 'natural' and not deceive the reader. With a little chauvinism, but also a great deal of reasonableness, it has been recalled that the drafters of the French Civil Code were entrusted with the mission of writing a text that had the value of a universal pact and that this objective has been achieved thanks to a style that was not only limpid,

55 Manderson, *Songs without Music*, ix.

56 Robin West, "Jurisprudence as Narrative: An Aesthetic Analysis of Modern Legal Theory," *New York University Law Review* 60, no. 2 (1985): 145–211.

57 Anne Teissier-Ensminger, *La beauté du droit* (Descartes & Cie, 1999); Stéphane Bernatchez, "Oh! le beau droit. La pertinence du jugement esthétique pour le jugement juridique," *Les Cahiers de droit* 58, no. 1–2 (2017): 91.

58 Gustav Radbruch, "Aesthetik des Rechts," in *Rechtsphilosophie* (Muller Verlag, 1999), 103–6.

59 Radbruch, "Aesthetik des Rechts," 104.

but evocative, endowed with a force similar to that found in other, and justly famous, Universal Declarations of Rights.[60]

It must be acknowledged, however, that this way of thinking and looking at law is not so common. Stendhal may be right, and the Civil Code could be a literary masterpiece, but the common opinion is that contemporary legal texts are really far from beauty, and the language of legal texts is boring, complex, obscure, and technical: in short, anything but beautiful.[61] Of course, some phrases or expressions may arouse admiration and aesthetic appreciation, especially in texts of constitutional level, and especially – we must confess – in texts that are not very recent, but the linguistic and aesthetic quality of the most recent normative texts is very questionable.[62] My goal is to show, through some examples, that the (aesthetic) quality of legislation is a crucial aspect of the relationship between rulers and ruled, and in general for the construction of social relations. Above all, I intend to show that the 'quality' of legal language is to be understood both on the level of aesthetics and from the perspective of *aesthesis*: on the one hand, whether a law is appreciated aesthetically depends on the presence of certain features that we rationally find appreciable, and in some way represent the canon of a well-written law. On the other hand, law's aesthetic value depends on the way that text affects people as sensate subjects and embodied readers.

Let's consider a few examples. The first part of Article 1 of the French Constitution states that "La France est une République indivisible, laïque, démocratique et sociale. Elle assure l'égalité devant la loi de tous les citoyens sans distinction d'origine, de race ou de religion".[63] It is perfect: clear, precise, evocative, fascinating. But even better is Article 1 of the Déclaration des Droits de l'homme et du Citoyen, stating that "Les hommes naissent et demeurent libres et égaux en droits. Les distinctions sociales ne peuvent être fondées que sur l'utilité commune".[64] Similarly, it is impossible not to be fascinated by the beauty of the preamble to the US constitution. The text is

60 Gabriel de Broglie, "La langue du Code Civil," https://www.academie-francaise.fr/sites/academie-francaise.fr/files/broglie-code_civil.pdf.

61 For a comprehensive analysis of legal language and its characteristics, see Peter Tiersma, *Legal Language* (University of Chicago Press, 1999).

62 Gemma Pastore, "L'arte della lingua sta nell'essere inteso: la comunicazione legislativa," *Sociologia del Diritto* 3 (2011): 152–61.

63 (France is an indivisible, laïc, democratic and social Republic. It ensures the equality of all citizens before the law, without distinction of origin, race or religion): https://www.conseil-constitutionnel.fr/le-bloc-de-constitutionnalite/texte-integral-de-la-constitution-du-4-octobre-1958-en-vigueur.

64 (All people are born and remain free and equal in rights. Social distinctions can only be based on the common good): https://www.elysee.fr/la-presidence/la-declaration-des-droits-de-l-homme-et-du-citoyen#:~:text=%2D%20Les%20hommes%20naissent%20et%20demeurent,et%20imprescriptibles%20de%20l'homme.

so well-known that it is almost part of the Western literary heritage, and it is indeed beautiful:

> We the People of the United States, in order to form a more perfect Union, establish Justice, insure domestic Tranquility, provide for the common defence, promote the general Welfare, and secure the Blessings of Liberty to ourselves and our Posterity, do ordain and establish this Constitution for the United States of America.

In three lines, ideals, aspirations, political objectives are united, with an almost poetic rhythm and cadence. And yet, such expressive force is rare, even in normative texts of the same level or importance. Again, let me conclude with Article 1 of the Italian Constitution, stating that "Italy is a Democratic Republic founded on labour". Here, we are struck by the expressive force of this rule, which in a few words founds the Italian Republic and democracy by linking them to work, sweeping away any aristocratic and classist reading of democracy itself, and making the commitment to building society the place of citizenship.[65] All this, in less than ten words, with a clarity, simplicity, and efficacy worthy of the most famous literary incipits. This is not surprising: in 1948, the Italian Constituent Assembly chose to entrust several writers and literati with checking the linguistic quality of the final text of the Constitution.[66] Commenting on this choice, a member of the Assembly observed:

> The use of the subjunctive, the elegance of the subjunctive, was renounced and the indicative was preferred. There are no periods exceeding twenty words, except in the transitional and final provisions. We normally stay at 19 words. In other words, the Italian citizen is able to read and understand the Italian Constitution, even if he is of average or inferior culture.[67]

On the other hand, just as not all novels have memorable beginnings (it is hard to forget *Anna Karenina*'s first line, "Happy families are all alike; every unhappy family is unhappy in its own way",[68] or that of *Pride and Prejudice*, "It is a truth universally acknowledged, that a single man in possession of a good fortune, must be in want of a wife",[69] but the list is long and very subjective), not all normative texts, however fundamental they may be, have an

65 Michele Ainis e Vittorio Sgarbi, *La Costituzione e la bellezza* (La Nave di Teseo, 2016).
66 Roberto Zaccaria, ed., *La buona scrittura delle leggi* (Camera dei deputati, 2012), 14.
67 Speech by MEP Sannicandro, in the verbatim report of the Parliament session of 11 February 2015 and following days, page 633.
68 Leo Tolstoy, *Anna Karenina* (Penguin Classics, 2025), 3.
69 Jane Austen, *Pride and Prejudice* (Oxford University Press, 1974), 1.

equally fine Article 1. The European Convention on Human Rights, though fundamental, has a more ordinary Article 1, which somewhat bureaucratically states that "The High Contracting Parties shall secure to everyone within their jurisdiction the rights and freedoms defined in Section I of this Convention". Somewhat better, from an aesthetic perspective, is the Charter of Fundamental Rights of the European Union, which states in Article 1 that "Human dignity is inviolable. It must be respected and protected". But certainly poor from an aesthetic point of view is Article 1 of the Treaty on the Functioning of the European Union: "By this Treaty, the High Contracting Parties establish among themselves a European Union, hereinafter called 'the Union', on which the Member States confer competences to attain objectives they have in common". The mediocrity doesn't concern the content: it stems precisely from the misuse of language for expressive purposes. Equally poor is Article 2 of the same Treaty, which affirms the fundamental rights of Union citizens. And yet, even if the content is appreciable, the language that is used to express it is formal and bureaucratic, turning a statement of value into an unattractive list:

> The Union is founded on the values of respect for human dignity, freedom, democracy, equality, the rule of law and respect for human rights, including the rights of persons belonging to minorities. These values are common to the Member States in a society in which pluralism, non-discrimination, tolerance, justice, solidarity and equality between women and men prevail.[70]

To find better beginnings we have to go far back and look at the main declarations of rights; the Universal Declaration of Human Rights, in 1948, adopted by the General Assembly of the United Nations, offers us a beautiful Article 1: "All human beings are born free and equal in dignity and rights. They are endowed with reason and conscience and must act towards one another in a spirit of brotherhood". The image of birth, the idea of natural freedom and original equality of all human beings, the affirmation of a value (dignity) that does not depend on what we do or do not do – on our merits and faults – but on the simple and original fact of being human, all this and much more is affirmed in a language that is clear, limpid, concise, and at the same time evocative and rich in images. Beautiful, indeed.

In other words, the language of normative texts is not always beautiful, we know that. But it *can* be, and to a degree that is in no way inferior to masterpieces of literature, which we are accustomed to considering excellent

70 https://eur-lex.europa.eu/legal-content/EN/TXT/HTML/?uri=CELEX:02016M/TXT-20200301.

examples of beauty and expressive capacity.[71] Such an aesthetic value depends on two factors: on the one hand, as said, it is related to the quality of the legislative drafting, that is, to the process of transposing government policy into the text of the law. Thus, when we appreciate the aesthetic quality of a legal text, we are valuing the work of legislative drafters concerning the quality of regulatory provisions. In this vein, if legislation was merely a tool of the government, then a good law would simply be that able to produce the regulatory results expected by the policy.[72] However, a well-drafted law is more than this: cost efficiency, clarity, precision, and unambiguity are the principles that when applied, at least in most cases, allow the creation of good laws. Of course, the use of plain language, defined as "clear and effective for its audience," is certainly important.[73] Plain language is the medium that promotes barrier-free communication between the legislative drafter and the recipients of the law text, and is not reduced to a choice of terminology. Words, syntax, and even punctuation are important, but the structure, layout, and overall look of all legal text are also elements that the plain language movement takes into account.[74] From this perspective, legal texts deserve an aesthetic appreciation concerning their language, form, effectiveness, communicative efficacy, or synthesis and harmony. All these characteristics are related to a rationalistic understanding of the "beautiful" normative text, such that if they are present, and to the extent that they are present, the text deserves appreciation.

On the contrary, the language of legal texts can be aesthetically poor, and it seems to agree with Hamlet, who points out the *law's delay* (also coming from linguistic contortions and obscurities) among the ills of life.[75] See

71 It must be said that the fact that Article 1 of the Constitution is beautiful, is debatable. And it is so debatable that Calamandrei himself, who also took part in the Constituent Assembly, criticised precisely the wording of these articles, and Article 1 itself. "In our Constitution," he said, "to articles that consecrate real and proper enforceable rights, accompanied by sanctions, articles that regulate and distribute powers and establish bodies to exercise these powers, there are interspersed several vague provisions (on ethical-social relations and economic relations), which are not real legal norms in the precise and practical sense of the word, but are moral precepts, definitions, ambitions, programmes, intentions; perhaps electoral manifestos, perhaps sermons: which are all disguised as legal norms, but legal norms they are not'. On the subject of Article 1, he observed: 'When I have to explain to my students what it means legally that the Italian Republic has "the work" as its foundation, what will I be able to say?' (quoted in Luciano Vassalli, "Pietro Calamandrei e la Costituzione," 621, https://culturaprofessionale.interno.gov.it/FILES/docs/1260/instrumenta_08_05_vassalli.pdf).

72 Luzius Mader, "Evaluating the Effect: A Contribution to the Quality of Legislation," *Statute Law Review*, no. 22 (2001): 119–31.

73 Peter Butt, *Modern Legal Drafting: A Guide to Using Clearer Language* (Cambridge: Cambridge University Press, 2013).

74 Brian Hunt, "Plain Language in Legislative Drafting: Is It Really the Answer?," *Statute Law Review*, no. 23 (2002): 24.

75 Shakespeare, *Hamlet*, III, 1.

for instance the former paragraph 1 of Article 19 of Regulation 820/97 EC, which read:

> A compulsory beef-labelling system shall be introduced which shall be obligatory in all Member States from 1 January 2001 onwards. However, this compulsory system shall not exclude the possibility for a Member State to decide to apply the system merely on an optional basis to beef sold in that same Member State.

It is not only a text lacking in literary quality: it is obscure, ambiguous, barely readable, and confusing.

Obscurity, polysemy, and vagueness are due to various factors, including a lack of conceptual clarity, the desire not to take a clear position concerning opposing interests, or even the mere attempt to refer more precise decisions to other instances and other subjects (jurisprudence, for example). Moreover, as Amato rightly notes,[76] reality itself has become complex, much more complex than in the past, and it is not always possible to regulate in a few lines, in the manner of the nineteenth-century legislators, the interests and rights that intertwine in our pluralist and globalised societies. Finally, the language of the law is – like the language of medicine – a technical language that is also intended for non-technical interlocutors, and it presents certain structural obscurities if we consider this objective of communication: some terms may be obscure to anyone unfamiliar with legal jargon, and it is necessary, if the goal of clarity is to be pursued, to consider not only the vocabulary, but the broader context of the communication, and the text as a union of form and content.[77] A sentence written like a novel, with the emphasis and lexical choices we appreciate in a literary text, would not necessarily be a good sentence: it might even be a bad one. We have to look at the context in which the normative texts fit, and which they modify, to assess their beauty or ugliness.

However, the beauty of law does not boil down to this, because the law – whether law-in-books or law-in-action – is not just a formal structure; it can never be, and the mediocre quality of legal texts is not just an aesthetic problem: it is a problem of justice.[78] Therefore, the quality of legislation is the degree to which a regulation complies not only with the requirements of legality and lawfulness, enforcement, effectiveness, efficiency, and so on

76 Giuliano Amato, "Ricordi in tema di chiarezza della legislazione," in *La buona scrittura delle leggi*, ed. Roberto Zaccaria (Camera dei deputati, 2012), 25.

77 Gabriella Alfieri, "Non c'è grammatica: la scrittura legislativa e la sua funzione testuale," in *La buona scrittura delle leggi*, ed. Roberto Zaccaria (Camera dei deputati, 2012), 107.

78 Wim Voermans, "Concerns About the Quality of EU Legislation: What Kind of Problems, by What Kind of Standards?," *Erasmus Law Review* 2, no. 1 (2008): 59–95.

but also with those of simplicity, readability, and accessibility.[79] Legislation must be as simple and clear as possible to allow the public and those responsible for interpretation and enforcement to understand the law. Poorly written legislation is not only a missed opportunity but entails problems with application and compliance.[80]

It is important to grasp this aspect because there is often a tendency to think that the beauty of law is identified with the clarity and comprehensibility of normative texts or legal acts. Laws are coded in language and are mediated through language. The legal system voices a society's beliefs and values,[81] and the way it communicates this message (the style of legislation) obviously matters. In other words, the beauty of law does not depend solely on its content (in terms of justice), nor on the mere form of the linguistic expressions used by the legislator. It depends on the ability of the normative language to convey a framework of values and make it comprehensible and desirable.

The beauty of law, and the order to be built

Law is beautiful when its language is perceived by people as suitable for building a community: when, besides formal characteristics of its language, it conveys narratives, affect people, and stages a possible/desirable future. This idea is well labelled by White as the law's *constitutive rhetoric*, or the poetics of a community.[82] Law settles conflicts and contrasts between interests, needs, and values: the building of a community depends on how these conflicts are decided. Law is a technique, certainly, but it is an end-oriented technique, which uses words and language to build relationships and strengthen communities. Rhetoric is not (only) the art of persuasion, in short, but a strategy by which, with words and signs, legislators build communities and transform them.[83]

We can compare the beauty of law to a medal with two sides. These aspects are not alternatives, but they must be held together to understand in what sense, and to what extent, an aesthetic judgement about law can make sense. On the one hand, an aesthetic assessment of law can focus on the presence in the text of elements that we consider rationally appreciable and capable of

79 Claudio M. Radaelli and Fabrizio de Francesco, *Regulatory Quality in Europe: Concepts, Measures and Policy Processes* (Manchester: Manchester University Press, 2007).

80 Voermans, "Concerns About the quality of EU legislation," 79.

81 John Gibbons, "Language and the Law," *Annual Review of Applied Linguistics* 19 (1999): 156–73; see also Wim Voermans, "Styles of Legislation and their Effects," *Statute Law Review* 32, no. 1 (2011): 38–53.

82 James Boyd White, "Law as Rhetoric, Rhetoric as Law: The Arts of Cultural and Communal Life," *The University of Chicago Law Review* 52, no. 3 (1985): 688.

83 Boyd White, *Heracles' Bow*, 28.

bringing the text to its best. On the other hand, within a focus on *aesthesis*, the beauty of law refers to the way in which it is able to affect our senses, arouse perceptions, and motivate.

The first approach identifies the beauty of law with the harmony of the system, the balance between the parts of a text or the words that are used, exalting symmetry and proportion, clarity and perfection of a text's composition.[84] In this vein, it is possible to appreciate what makes the law beautiful for the beholder when reading or applying it. In a way, we value legal texts as spectators, like someone who visits a museum and stops in front of a painting or a statue, or someone who stands in front of a building and appreciates its structure and proportions. It is also in this sense that we complain about regulatory confusion, the absence of internal coherence, and regret a golden age of codification in which all law was organically and systematically reducible to a *corpus*. After all, the idea behind the *Corpus Juris Civilis* was that of unifying the legal thought of the time – indeed, its best part, since the sources had been selected at the outset – in an organic work, unifying the pre-existing law by integrating it with the new needs of society. The same idea is also present in modern codifications.[85] It is true, as we have already discussed, that codes are scenic objects, theatrical mechanisms for staging power and knowledge, but at the same time this goal is pursued by giving tangibility to the idea of harmony between the parts. If the purpose of power is to rule over the parts of the social body, the harmony of the legislative text is the means of making this goal visible: and this harmony was the kind of beauty that Balzac praised concerning the 1804 French Civil Code.

Accordingly, the second approach also relates the beauty of law to the concept of order, but focuses on the fact that this order has to be constructed, not being something we can merely contemplate in its perfection. The order of law is, in this second perspective, a goal, a community's achievement, whereas in the first it is a prerequisite. There is nothing to be contemplated, no normative and social order that must be defended and protected against chaos or degradation (this is what we are inclined to do when we contemplate something perfect and complete: we want to prevent it from being ruined, from being destroyed; we want to prevent its degradation). Here, on the contrary, there is a road to be travelled and a building to be erected. The order of law is a process that has an asymptotic trend, that proceeds towards a fullness that is never fully given. St Bonaventure, in the *Breviloquium*, uses this same opposition to describe the order of justice (which, we know, has much in common with beauty): the order of justice is an order that must be

84 Ernest J. Weinrib, *The Idea of Private Law* (Oxford University Press, 1995), 22 ff.

85 Paolo Cappellini, "La forma-codice: metamorfosi e polemiche novecentesche," in *Enciclopedia italiana Il Contributo Italiano alla Storia del Pensiero. Diritto*, eds. Paolo Cappellini et al. (Istituto dell'Enciclopedia Italiana, 2012), 550–58.

built, an *ordo factivus*. It is the order of nature (the God's creation, the *ordo factus*) that must be merely admired and protected because it is already fully accomplished:[86] the order of justice is our task.

The beauty of law, in a similar fashion, does not lie in the way a normative text is written, however clear and coherent it may be. It lies in its capacity to build the order of social relations, to edify, and to fulfil its function by pacifying human coexistence. From this perspective, we can understand why law can be beautiful and why it is good that it is, at least in some parts and at a certain level. The beauty of law is always linked to its function, and is at its service: it is not a matter of elegance, ornament, or pure aesthetic pleasure, but of motivation and sensate experience of an ideal; it is harmony and balance, at the service of peaceful coexistence between free individuals.

This way of understanding the beauty of law was very well analysed, in my opinion, by Karl Llewellyn, who, in a lecture at the University of Chicago in 1941, explained that the words of law can never be understood as an ornament, but always as function-oriented architecture. This does not mean that the beauty of law can be reduced *to* its ability to fulfil its function: a public building is not beautiful just because it is appropriate to its function (this way of thinking is, unfortunately, at the origin of some architectural aberrations that are increasingly frequent today, whereby churches and courtrooms end up looking like garages or shopping centres). On the contrary, Llewellyn argues that in law, form and content go hand in hand, and when they are well balanced, law can be truly beautiful. The beauty of the German Civil Code (this is the example Llewellyn gives) lies in its being an example of intellectual architecture: a clean, rigorous, and chiselled structure able to realise the social project, at every turn, in every line, and in every corner.[87] The beauty of law is analogous to the beauty of a cathedral, in which every ornament, every volute, and every decoration is never an end in itself, but is always (or should be) consistent with the function of that place.[88] And just as a cathedral can be built over years, decades, or centuries, by different workers and different artists, modifying original plans and styles, so the law is built by superimpositions and modifications, like a building that does not respond to any hypothetical original plan,[89] but which nevertheless, at least in some cases, produces a peaceful, just, and free space of coexistence. A space of beauty and justice.

86 Bonaventura da Bagnoregio, *Opera Omnia, V* (Quaracchi, 1981), 239: "Ordo justitiae est non solum factus, sed etiam factivus, ordo vero naturae est ordo factus".

87 Karl Llewellyn, "On the Good, the True, the Beautiful," *The University of Chicago Law Review* 9, no. 2 (1942): 224–65.

88 Maurizio Manzin, "Architetture del ragionamento giuridico Architecture of Legal Reasoning," *Teoria e Critica della Regolazione Sociale* 2, no. 19 (2019): 209.

89 Friedrich von Hayek, *Law Legislation and Liberty. A New Statement of the Liberal Principles of Justice and Political Economy*, vol. 19 (Routledge, 1973–1979), 50.

Plato precisely discusses this aspect when he distinguishes in *The Laws* three methods in legal drafting. The law can be purely coercive, or it can be a mixture of persuasion, rhetoric, and compulsion. But it can also operate in a third mode, by writing a *preamble.* All discourses and vocal exercises have preludes and overtures, says Plato, intended to help the strain which is to be performed: these parts are intended "to create goodwill" so that, because of this goodwill, people "might more intelligently receive his command, that is to say, the law".[90] The legislator who operates by pure compulsion behaves, according to Plato, like the doctor of slaves: he orders, prescribes medicines, passes quickly from one sick person to another, and offers no explanation of what he imposes. Different is the behaviour of the freemen doctor, who not only prescribes cures but also informs, persuades, and discusses with the sick person and his family.[91] Similarly, the legislator should motivate to obedience, not merely compel. He should convince, persuade, resorting to any means to hatred of iniquity, and love of right or even acquiescence in right.[92] Not differently, Rousseau writes in *The Social Contract* that 'Si vous voulez qu'on obéisse aux lois, faites qu'on les aime'.[93]

The ability of a community of people to cooperate and coordinate is not taken for granted, nor can the legislator achieve it by mere imposition. On the contrary, it is important to put in place 'incentives' that create the conditions for jointly identifying the problems to be solved and the acceptable solutions.[94] A rule can be *clothed*, so to speak, in a form that reinforces the scope of the rule itself, because it makes it more comprehensible, enhances its consistency with the needs of the subjects, and makes it evident through those words its rightfulness.[95] Alternatively, that same rule may be transmitted by a deluge of obscure words and formulae, through an incomprehensible bureaucratic jargon, a language full of gaps, repetitions, or contradictions: and then, even if the effects are not entirely lost, the possibility of understanding its value and sense is much smaller.

The beauty of a principle or a rule (their rhythm, sound, and ability to strike the senses of those who read or listen) is not a frill, but the place where cooperation between legislators and citizens can best be realised. Beauty makes values perceptible by affecting us as sensate bodies, and arouses feelings of

90 Plato, *The Laws*, 722 d.
91 Plato, *The Laws*, 720 c.
92 Plato, *The Laws*, 862 d.
93 Jean-Jacques Rousseau, *Discours sur l'économie politique, in Œuvres complètes*, vol. 5 (Raymond Gagnebin, Bibliothèque de la Pléiade-Gallimard, 1959–1995), t. III, 250.
94 Jacques Lenoble et Marc Maesschalck, *L'action des normes. Éléments pour une théorie de la gouvernance* (Éditions Revue de droit de l'Université de Sherbrooke, 2009), 353.
95 Elaine Scarry, *On Beauty and Being Just* (Princeton University Press, 1999), 71; See also Kent Roach, "The Uses and Audiences of Preambles in Legislation," *MCGILL Law Journal* 47, no. 1 (2001): 129, 138–40; Liav Orgad, "The Preamble in Constitutional Interpretation," *International Journal of Constitutional Law* 8, no. 4 (2010): 714–38.

approval that underpin social cooperation: in other words, beauty can provide the motivational basis for achieving the social cohesion that coercion alone cannot guarantee. In a similar vein, Legendre understands law as the transmission of the fundamental social myth: and taking from Augustin the idea that the liturgical order is a structure of love, Legendre rightly argues that subjects must fall in love with the institution.[96]

The construction of the edifice of law is not the work of a solitary artist nor an omnipotent and deaf legislator. Rather, it is a communication between legislators and individuals. And for this communication to take place, beauty is necessary, or at least opportune. One can 'love' the law, to quote Rousseau, when one finds it beautiful; and one finds it beautiful certainly not on a merely aesthetic level, as if it were a poem, but because one perceives its appropriateness concerning the needs of people's life. A law is not beautiful as an object of pure contemplation, but it can be beautiful because of its ability to motivate people: subjects must be emotionally convinced that law's answer to the issues in the life of individuals and society are adequate (just, equitable, efficient). When the purposes of a rule are correctly understood, when these purposes are deemed appropriate and just by people, and when all this is expressed linguistically in a precise and clear way, we can experience the harmony between life and law. And this is something we can truly consider as beautiful.

All 'fundamental' texts can be thought of as large-scale staging, as mechanisms whose normative effect is closely linked to the ability to give order from something that is represented, staged, even when it remains absent. They are images that make visible and perceptible what is absent, be it imperial sovereignty or an equally mythical 'social contract'. When we speak of the "constituent (or founding) fathers and mothers" we evoke mythical figures, who are certainly absent, but fundamental as well: we are not so much interested in knowing much about the individual persons, in flesh and blood, who drafted a specific Constitution or Treatise (this may be interesting for a small number of scholars, certainly), nor are we interested in the real contribution of each to the work of that legislative body, their statements, and the results of their interventions. As subjects and citizens, we are interested in evoking their figure because the representation of the Constituents as people endowed with legal wisdom and political prudence enables us to experience a sense of belonging, love for the architecture of the legal system, and gives life to a common ideal.

Conclusions

The preceding analysis shows, on the one hand, that an aesthetic analysis of law is possible and necessary, because law and aesthetics are intertwined

96 Pierre Legendre, *L'Empire de la Vérité: Introduction aux espaces dogmatiques industriels* (Fayard, 1983), 132.

dimensions and in many ways internal to each other; on the other hand, it demonstrates that an aesthetic judgement of law (in terms of beauty or ugliness) is also possible. In both cases, however, it is necessary to hold together an aesthetic understanding of law, and to consider from the epistemological point of view the possibilities and limits of aesthetic analysis of law, and a consideration of law from the point of view of sensate subjects. The rational understanding of forms and contents of law must go along with the consideration of how law affect people's bodily sense perception: how and what their body sees, hears, and feels.

Both aspects matter, and should be kept in mind, when we analyse law from an aesthetic point of view and when we ask to what extent a judgement of law in terms of beauty is possible. Thus, if we say that law (a constitutional norm, a decision, or whatever) is beautiful, we must refer to both an epistemological plane (regarding form, harmony, language, etc.) and the way in which this law is perceived by subjects, the feelings it arouses, and its ability to stage the poetic of a community. Of course, this judgement is largely subjective. What is important is not to objectively define what elements the law must have in order to affect and motivate sentient beings: this depends on varying cultural and social circumstances. What matters is that law can be deemed beautiful depending on how it affects subjects and sentient bodies, and that this judgement is socially and politically relevant.

As Kafka teaches, a purely rational access to the law is not sufficient. If in the story "Before the Law" he tells us about the impossibility of accessing the meaning of the Law, *An Imperial Message* points to a different, meta-rational way of access. Somehow, it is an access that refers to *aesthesis*, and allow us to grasp something, even not by reading, analysing, understanding, knowing rationally. Kafka writes that the Emperor on his deathbed dispatched a message. He sent it "to you", Kafka writes, and therefore to each of us, to one of the miserable subjects, a 'tiny shadow' compared to the splendour of the imperial sun, entrusting it to a herald, in whose ear it was whispered. The message makes sense, it has been correctly understood by the herald (the Emperor has had it repeated to him), but the journey is surprisingly long and tiring. The crowds are large, the rooms through which to pass are endless, so are the staircases, the courtyards, and then more palaces and rooms; and even if the herald managed to get out of the palace, there would remain the immense imperial city to traverse, the heart of the world with its debris. Does anguish prevail even here? No, because surprisingly you "sit at your window and dream of that message when evening comes".

The image, the dream, is the place where the message can be heard. There is not only the unbearable fatigue of understanding, in the unsuccessful attempt to enter the gate of the Law, or to traverse the imperial city to obtain or give information and content. There is the dream, there is another way, and it is a way that fully justifies the focus on *aesthesis* concerning law.

Chapter 4

The right to beauty

Beauty: a legal issue

The cultural, social, philosophical, and anthropological importance of aesthetics is evidenced by its legal relevance in contemporary legal systems. It is quite common, in fact, that either art or artistic and natural heritage is mentioned in fundamental charters: legal systems protect beauty and grant it relevance by sometimes protecting cultural heritage, the freedom of artistic and cultural production, as well as the landscape and the beauty of nature. This system of rules, I argue, is focused on people's right to access and enjoy beauty. As we shall see, in doing so, legislatures make a choice that is both understandable and risky: it is an understandable choice, because they implement an aesthetic pedagogy with a political and social value. But it is also a risky choice, because in doing so legislatures are forced to seek objectivity where it cannot be, generating contradictions and problems that are not easy to overcome.

In most cases, rules and policies concern art and artistic heritage. The Spanish Constitution, for instance, at Article 20.1. states

> The following rights are recognized and protected: . . . b) the right to literary, artistic, scientific and technical production and creation; c) the right to academic freedom; . . . 2. The exercise of these rights may not be restricted by any form of prior censorship.

Similar provisions may be found in other national Constitutions: the Croatian Constitution, Article 69, states that "The freedom of scientific, cultural and artistic creativity shall be guaranteed. The state shall encourage and support the development of science, culture and the arts. The state shall protect scientific, cultural and artistic assets as national spiritual values". In Greece, Article 16 (1) of the Constitution of the Hellenic Republic states that "Art and science, research and teaching shall be free and their development and promotion shall be an obligation of the State. Academic freedom and freedom of teaching shall not exempt anyone from his duty of allegiance to the Constitution". Again, the Grundgesetz of the Federal Republic of Germany

DOI: 10.4324/9781003589426-4

contains Article 5 (3), where it is granted that "Arts and sciences, research and teaching shall be free". Finally, and more extensively, the Italian Constitution also covers the relevance of the beauty of nature, stating that both "The Republic promotes the development of culture and scientific and technical research. It safeguards natural landscape and the historical and artistic heritage of the Nation", and (Article 33) "The Republic guarantees the freedom of the arts and sciences, which may be freely taught".

All these examples show how much importance is accorded to the aesthetic dimension by Western legal systems: the protection of art and artistic heritage is an integral part of the system of fundamental rights, at times, or is recognised as a fundamental task for state policies. Beauty is not mentioned, but it is at the core of this system. First, it stems from the text itself, the thoughts, the spirit, and the words that are used, thereby making Constitutions themselves aesthetically relevant or even appreciable (in the sense that has already been discussed in the previous chapter). Second, beauty is an *issue* of contemporary legal systems, and according to some scholars it should even be understood as an "absolute right",[1] constitutionally protected: both as the right *to* beauty, that is, the right of individuals to the possibility of enjoying beauty, and as the right *of* beauty, as the totality of the measures protecting and guaranteeing artistic and cultural heritage, as well as natural landscape and natural beauty.

Most of the mentioned constitutional rules (of course, some more explicitly than others) should be understood in this second sense. Western legal systems regard the aesthetic dimension as a fundamental part of the human experience, so much so that they must protect at least that peculiar possibility of access to beauty that is provided by art and the artistic and natural heritage. At least this portion of the many possible aesthetic experiences available for human beings is afforded protection by law: it preserves artistic heritage for the benefit of future generations, in order to pass on what has been produced over the centuries, as well as the beauty of the territory and natural landscapes.

As Bobbio appropriately highlighted, liberal democracies should take on the objective of promoting culture, at the same time turning down the temptation of promoting a state cultural policy:[2] art and science shall be free, and no cultural policy can – top-down – orient them towards politically relevant goals or objectives. No enslavement of research or artistic activity to politics and its objectives is acceptable. But if art and science are free, they are

1 Clammer argues for a "visual justice," as the right to access aesthetically pleasing objects, environments and situations. See J. Clammer, "Visual Justice: The Right to Beauty?," in *Cultural Rights and Justice* (Singapore: Palgrave Macmillan, 2019). See also M. Ainis and V. Sgarbi, *La Costituzione e la bellezza, La Nave di Teseo* (Milano: La Nave di Teseo, 2016).

2 Norberto Bobbio, *Politica e cultura* (Einaudi, 1955), 205.

not neglected or left to their own devices, as if they were politically irrelevant things. They are promoted, protected, guaranteed, and at the same time their freedom is guaranteed: any policy of culture is oriented bottom up and stems from the demands and needs of those who produce culture, science, and art. With Bobbio's words, cultural policy is rejected not because it reduces art to an instrumental value, but because it denies the value of freedom.[3]

It is not clear whether, and to what extent, these constitutional rules concerning art and landscape, with their implicit reference to beauty, are such as to justify not only obligations, but even a real right to beauty, as some seem to believe,[4] or whether in the end it is not just a mixture of rhetoric and good intentions, in varying proportions. It is certainly important that constitutions and other national or international regulations aim at protecting artistic and natural heritage: however, it is not evident what this means, and in what way it is good to do so. Similarly, it is not always easy to understand how to protect the landscape and the beauty of nature, nor where the boundary is between landscape protection and environmental protection. Again, it is important to emphasise that beauty certainly deserves to be protected when it manifests itself in and through art: however, if what we want to protect is beauty, first and foremost, and not just art, we should recognise and protect beauty also when it reveals itself in other, less usual places.

The right to beauty, and the protection of artistic and natural heritage

Legal systems, or many of them, protect the country's natural, artistic, and cultural heritage. Laws, in other words, seek to preserve the beauty people have made, written, produced, and the beauty that surrounds them: such a protection is both justified by private interests (the moral right of the artist), as well as public or collective interests (the protection of a heritage).[5] But why? And what, or in what way, does the law seek to protect?

A good starting point might be the recognition of the fact that such an attempt to protect art and beauty is much older than our modern constitutions. While the attention of contemporary legislators to art and beauty is certainly admirable, the idea that culture, art, and everything beautiful that human beings produce should be protected, well, this itself is an ancient idea. Certainly, so old that we may find rules and policies aimed at protecting artistic and natural heritage in Roman law (to limit our analysis to the Western tradition).

3 Bobbio, *Politica e cultura*, 92 ff.

4 Rubén Martínez Dalmau, "Arte, derecho y derecho al arte," *Revista derecho del estado* 32 (2014): 35–56.

5 Giampaolo Frezza, "Art and Law: Authentication and Assessment within the Italian Legal System," *Italian Law Journal* 8, no. 1 (2022): 135.

The care reserved to culture and the necessary protection of artistic and cultural production began to be present as early as the Republican era when contacts with Greece spread in Rome – among the Roman elite, at least – the sensitivity to beauty and culture that still flourished there. In the second of the *Actiones in Verrem*, for example,[6] Cicero praises the beauty of the Domus of Caius Aelius, adorned with statues of Praxiteles and Myron and other artworks; however, he also praises the activity of those officials (the *aediles*) who, instead of plundering the provinces of such beauties, or stealing them from their allies, borrowed these works from the nobles who had them at home to adorn the forum and the basilicas. In his oration against Verres, Cicero highlights the idea that art and beauty must be protected, not plundered for political or private ends. The aediles that Cicero praises, in fact, return statues and art treasures to their several owners: they did not carry them off from the cities, pretending, as aediles, to be borrowing them for a four-day festival, and then transport them to their own town-mansions and country-houses.[7]

The first set of rules aiming to protect artistic heritage dates back to the Imperial age. In a context in which political power tended to use culture and art as instruments of propaganda, the valorisation of artistic heritage and the necessity of protecting it began to gain relevance.[8] To get an idea of the change in perspective, consider the imprint left by Augustus on the city of Rome in terms of urban planning and architecture. Suetonius, very effectively, writes that Augustus rightly gloried in having found a city of bricks and having left a city of marbles: *"iure sit gloriatus marmoreum se relinquere, quam latericium accepisset"*.[9] In this context, the protection of art was implemented through civil actions, which could be brought by anyone – the *actio iniuriam*, for example – in the event of damage to a good that was considered as publicly significant. In this same perspective, limitations were introduced on the ownership of goods of public interest, a sort of anticipation of the constraints that are imposed today to protect artistic and natural heritage: to give some examples, we can mention the ban on keeping houses in a non-decent condition;[10] the prohibition for citizens to demolish their buildings in order to sell their marble and statues;[11] the prohibition of alienating libraries and works by separating them from the buildings in

6 Cicero, *Actio in Verrem*, II 4, 3–6.
7 Cicero, *Actio in Verrem*, II 4, 6.
8 Francesca Rossi, "Cura urbis, monumenta e patrimonio culturale nell'esperienza di Roma antica," in *A New Role for Roman Taxonomies in the Future of Goods?*, eds. Marco Falcon and Mattia Milani (Jovene, 2022), 31–58.
9 Suetonius, *De Vitis Caesarum. Divus Augustus*, II, 97.
10 D. 1.18.7.
11 D. 18.1.52.

which they were housed, unless they were destined for public use.[12] And in this same direction, some primordial town-planning rules should also be mentioned, some of which were precisely enforced to protect the public interest in the enjoyment of the landscape and its beauty.[13]

This attention, already in ancient Rome, for the protection of artistic and natural heritage (there are Justinian regulations on the protection of façades in coastal cities, of what today we would call the skyline, with relative prohibitions on the construction industry)[14] is rooted in the desire to protect a *traditio*, in the proper sense of the term. It is a matter of protecting something that comes from the past (from the *patres* and previous generations, but also as part of the landscape that past generations appreciated for its beauty) and that must be handed down to future generations: a *traditio*. Beauty must be protected because it must be 'handed down' (*tradita*) to those who come after us.

It is interesting to note that reasons for the protection of artistic and cultural heritage were expressed, among the first,[15] by one of the greatest artists of the Renaissance, Raphael, in a letter addressed to Pope Leo X.[16] It is an extraordinary text, because already two centuries before the foundation of the first European museums, Raphael clearly states the reasons why artistic heritage deserves to be protected, precisely from the perspective of *traditio*. The text was written in 1519, shortly before Raphael's death. Left in the archives for a long time, it was initially attributed to Baldassare Castiglione, a friend of Raphael, who actually helped him write it, and published it in 1733. Not surprisingly, the value of this text began to be understood at the end of the eighteenth century, when the Italian artistic heritage was being plundered by French troops. The public debate, even in France, became heated, and Raphael's letter had a new and unexpected fortune: Quatremère de Quincy wrote a pamphlet in 1799 to contest the legitimacy of these confiscations and used Raphael's letter to support his thesis.[17]

12 D. 30.41.4 ff.

13 Zeno, in a constitution reported in C.8.10.12, on the regulation of the reconstruction of buildings that have been destroyed by fire, mentions the principle of the *prospectus maris* i.e. the prohibition of building, impairing the view of the sea by others. See Barbara Cortese, "Patrimonio culturale, diritto e storia," in *Patrimonio culturale: profili giuridici e tecniche di tutela*, eds. Ettore Battelli et al., vol. 2 (Roma TrE-Press, 2017), 14.

14 Léon Homo, *Roma imperiale e l'urbanesimo nell'antichità* (Mursia, 2022), 475 ff.

15 As far as I know, this is one of the earliest documents concerning the need for public protection of cultural heritage.

16 Francesco P. Di Teodoro and Timothy Stroud, "Raphael and the Letter to Leo X: Drawing Like the Ancient Romans," *Le Visiteur* 25, no. 1 (2020): 193–98.

17 Dorothy Mackay Quynn, "The Art Confiscations of the Napoleonic Wars," *The American Historical Review* 50, no. 3 (1945): 437–60. JSTOR, accessed March 9, 2024, https://doi.org/10.2307/1843116.

In this letter, Raphael writes to Leo X (a Medici pope, and great intellectual) to suggest how to manage and govern the monuments, which the pope himself had asked him to map and catalogue. Raphael emphasises his love for ancient art but writes that the study of that heritage gives him pain: that heritage, he writes, is like a torn corpse. And the fault lies not only with the Goths and the Vandals, but with those who were supposed to protect these monuments and did not, or even helped to destroy them. Raphael has in mind the Roman aristocrats and popes, who ruined temples and statues and monuments to build their villas and palaces out of ancient materials.

Raphael, who had seen the old St Peter's Basilica demolished to make way for the new one (which we admire today) reflects on this destructive attitude towards the past. For the first time, he proposes the idea that to build the present, one should not erase the past but rather unite and pacify the present and past. He therefore invites the pope to cherish the past and to care for the beauty that comes from the past, because this beauty can "excite to virtue" the spirits of those who live today. The defence of ancient ruins is not about commemorating the past, but about building the future:[18] "Holy Father" – writes Raphael –

> let it not be the lowest of Your Holiness's priorities to ensure that – out of respect to those divine spirits, the remembrance of whom encourages and incites to virtue the intellects among us today – what little remains of this ancient mother of the glory and renown of Italy is not to be completely destroyed and ruined by the wicked and the ignorant. Unfortunately, even here these people have perpetrated evil deeds against those souls who, with their blood, brought so much glory to the word, to this state and to us. Rather, by preserving the example of the ancients, may Your Holiness seek to equal and better them, as indeed you have done through your magnificent buildings, by supporting and favoring the virtues, reawakening genius, rewarding virtuous endeavors, and by sowing that most holy seed of peace among Christian princes.

The contemporary system of international protection of the artistic and natural heritage still moves in this same perspective. The first element of this ensemble is probably the 1954 Hague Convention for the Protection of Cultural Property in the Event of Armed Conflict, which introduced a dual

18 Source: Bayerische Staatsbibliothek, Munich, cod. it. 37b, in Francesco P. Di Teodoro, *Raffaello, Baldassar Castiglione e la 'Lettera a Leone X'* (Nuova Alfa Editoriale, 1994), 115–27; translated as "The Letter to Leo X by Raphael and Baldassare Castiglione, c. 1519," in *Palladio's Rome: A Translation of Andrea Palladio's Two Guidebooks to Rome*, eds. Vaughan Hart and Peter Hicks (New Haven: Yale University Press, 2006), 180.

regime of protection for cultural property and specific obligations for states.[19] This Convention, which builds on some references already present in the Hague Conventions of 1899 and 1907 on the protection of cultural property in the event of war, provides a first important definition of 'cultural property'. Indeed, when law protects culture or art, it always refers to 'goods', to material or immaterial (but still perceptible) manifestations of these dimensions of human experience. And so too is beauty, which is protected insofar as it is made perceptible, and thus made the object of a possible *traditio*, a transfer between one generation and the next. Cultural assets, according to the Convention, are movable or immovable properties, archaeological sites, and complexes of buildings that, taken as a whole, offer historical or artistic interest, as well as works of art, manuscripts, scientific collections and museums, great libraries, and so on in a very long list that is certainly incomplete (Article 1).

Such an idea of *traditio* plays a crucial role in community-building, and not surprisingly is considered so crucial both nationally and internationally that the destruction of certain artefacts must be considered a crime. The destruction of artistic, natural, or historic heritage is a crime because it means depriving future generations of something to which they are not only entitled but which is fundamental to their prosperity and flourishing. Many examples could be given, but one seems particularly significant to me and goes back to the war in the Balkans. Between October and December 1991, hundreds of grenades were thrown at buildings in the old town of Dubrovnik: the ancient city was destroyed, and what at the time was already recognised as a UNESCO World Heritage Site was lost. The International Criminal Tribunal for the former Yugoslavia, set up to judge war crimes, crimes against humanity, and genocide committed in the former Yugoslavia since January 1990, in a 2004 judgement[20] convicted Commander Miograd Jokic of war crimes, specifically sentencing him for the destruction of a cultural asset on the *World Heritage List*. Intentionally destroying an ancient and marvellous historical centre means destroying a part of humanity's heritage, depriving future generations of a chance to access and enjoy its beauty: and this is, no more and no less, a war crime.[21]

19 UNESCO, "Convention for the Protection of Cultural Property in the Event of Armed Conflict," https://www.unesco.org/en/legal-affairs/convention-protection-cultural-property-event-armed-conflict-regulations-execution-convention#item-1.

20 International Criminal Tribunal for the former Yugoslavia (ICTY), *Prosecutor v Miodgrad Jokic*, Case no. IT-01–42/1-S, Trial Chamber I, Sentencing Judgment.

21 Francesco P. Cunsolo, "L'UNESCO: struttura, competenze e funzionamento," in *Tutela e valorizzazione del patrimonio culturale mondiale nel diritto internazionale*, ed. Elisa Baroncini (Bononia University Press, 2021), 14; see also Patty Gerstenblith, "The Destruction of Cultural Heritage: A Crime Against Property or a Crime Against People?," *John Marshall Review of Intellectual Property Law* 15, no. 336 (2016); Marc Balcells, "Left Behind?

Two aspects of the legal relevance of artistic and natural heritage must be stressed. First, I argue that legal protection of artistic and natural heritage is certainly aimed at building and preserving the collective memory of a community, but it also aims at protecting the individual's opportunity to access beauty. A vast literature has been concerned with studying the relationship between collective memory and artistic heritage from different perspectives,[22] highlighting that heritage is a means of transmission of ideas, values, and knowledge,[23] at the same time focusing on the complexities in the definition of memory.[24] However, if destruction and/or transformation of heritage can even be ways to re-define a community culture, therefore necessary for politically and socially positive change,[25] these actions always constitute a loss of opportunity to access beauty.[26] That is why, in my opinion, these two aspects deserve to be kept separate, on a conceptual level.

Second, the notion of 'world heritage', introduced into international law by the Convention Concerning the Protection of the World Cultural and Natural Heritage (Paris, 1972), further expands the idea of *traditio*. Certain goods, certain manifestations of beauty, are a *common* heritage: not in the sense that they cannot be traced back to the culture and forms of expression of a certain group or a specific community, but because they constitute a

Cultural Destruction, the Role of the International Criminal Tribunal for the Former Yugoslavia in Deterring it and Cultural Heritage Prevention Policies in the Aftermath of the Balkan Wars," *European Journal on Criminal Policy and Research* 21 (2015): 1–13.

22 For a very good survey, see Veysel Apaydin, "Introduction: Why Cultural Memory and Heritage?" in *Critical Perspectives on Cultural Memory and Heritage: Construction, Transformation and Destruction*, ed. Veysel Apaydin (UCL Press, 2020), 1–10; see also Katharine Hodgkin, *Contested Pasts: The Politics of Memory* (Routledge, 2003); Astrid Erll et al., eds., *Cultural Memory Studies: An International and Interdisciplinary Handbook* (Walter de Gruyter, 2008).

23 Gregory Ashworth, "1848 and All That," *International Journal of Heritage Studies* 13, no. 6 (2007): 511–13.

24 Pierre Nora, *Les lieux de mémoire* (Gallimard, 1984); Pierre Nora, "La loi de la mémoire," *Le débat* 1 (1994): 178–82; Paul Ricoeur, "Memory and Forgetting," in *Questioning Ethics: Contemporary Debates in Philosophy*, eds. Richard Kearney and Mark Dooley (Routledge, 1999), 5–14; Beverley Butler, "Heritage and the Present Past," in *Handbook of Material Culture*, eds. Christopher Tilley, Susanne Kuechler-Fogden, and Webb Keane (Sage, 2006), 463–79; Tim Benton, *Understanding Heritage and Memory* (Manchester University Press, 2010).

25 Rodney Harrison, *Heritage: Critical Approaches* (Routledge, 2012); Caitlin DeSilvey, *Curated Decay: Heritage Beyond Saving* (University of Minnesota Press, 2017); Cornelius Holtorf, "Embracing Change: How Cultural Resilience is Increased through Cultural Heritage," *World Archaeology* 50, no. 4 (2018): 639–50.

26 With a focus on natural beauty, see Nora Mitchell et al., *Study on the Application of Criterion VII: Considering Superlative Natural Phenomena and Exceptional Natural Beauty within the World Heritage Convention* (IUCN, 2013); for a literature review, see Meng Zhang et al., "Natural Beauty and Esthetic Value of Natural World Heritage Sites: a Literature Review and Implications for Karst Geoheritage Sites," *Geoheritage* 14, no. 84 (2022).

possibility of access to beauty that, as such, must be offered to every human being.[27] If there is a right to beauty, that is, a right to access and enjoy beauty, in all its forms, it must certainly be a universal right.[28]

For this reason, the notion of common heritage crystallises some ideas of beauty and culture that transcend the boundaries of states, precisely because of their universal value (the *exceptional universal value* is the fundamental requirement to enjoy the protection regime provided by the Convention). Not only that: the fact that the Convention introduced a further distinction, by including both cultural and natural heritage in the protection, confirms that the value at stake is not only art and other significant things humankind has produced, but beauty itself, and the possibility for every human being to have access to it. Natural heritage owes nothing to human activity, it has nothing to do with what past generations can teach us, but it is a fundamental possibility to access beauty, which must be preserved between generations.[29] Certainly, human activity and its legacies dominate the landscape of the international protection system: from the 1982 Mexico City Declaration on Cultural Policies to the 2001 Universal Declaration on Cultural Diversity, to the Convention for the Protection of the Intangible Cultural Heritage, at the heart of this system is certainly the capacity of human beings to produce beauty, culture, and value: one may consider the notion of 'cultural landscapes', that is, those areas where human activity and nature combine: among the many examples are the Amalfi Coast and Cinque Terre in Italy, the Loire Valley between Sully-sur-Loire and Chalonnes, or the Champagne Hillsides, houses and cellars in France, the Upper Middle Rhine Valley in Germany, the Cornwall and West Devon Mining Landscape in the UK, etc..[30] However, as mentioned, the beauty that is protected by the Convention is not only understood as the fruit of human ingenuity and work. There is a beauty to which the human being has not contributed in any way but has only ever contemplated: again, to mention only a few examples, one may think of the Dolomites, the Great Barrier Reef in Australia, the Iguazu National Park in

27 Ralph O. Slatyer, "The Origin and Evolution of the World Heritage Convention," *AMBIO: A Journal of the Human Environment* 12 (1983): 138–40.

28 Yvonne Donders, "Cultural Heritage and Human Rights," in *Oxford Handbook on International Cultural Heritage Law*, eds. Francesco Francioni and Ana Filipa Vrdoljak (Oxford University Press, 2020); Luigi Lombardi Vallauri, ed., *Il meritevole di tutela* (Milano: Giuffré, 1990).

29 Allen Carlson and Sheila Lintott, eds., *Nature, Aesthetics, and Environmentalism: From Beauty to Duty* (Columbia University Press, 2008); Ronald Hepburn, "Contemporary Aesthetics and the Neglect of Natural Beauty," *British Analytical Philosophy* (1966): 285–310.

30 On the complexities underlying the concept of cultural landscape, and its evolution, see Michael Jones, "The Concept of Cultural Landscape: Discourse and Narratives," in *Landscape Interfaces: Cultural Heritage in Changing Landscapes*, eds. Hannes Palang and Gary Fry, vol. 1 (Springer Science & Business Media, 2003).

Argentina, and all the other places included in the UNESCO list as natural heritage.

The same perspective is adopted in the Council of Europe Framework Convention on the Value of Cultural Heritage for Society (the so-called Faro Convention), which entered into force in 2011.[31] The Convention recognises that "rights relating to cultural heritage are inherent in the right to participate in cultural life, as defined in the Universal Declaration of Human Rights" and that "the conservation of cultural heritage and its sustainable use have human development and quality of life as their goal".[32] The idea of *traditio* is confirmed once again, and it is stated that "cultural heritage is a group of resources inherited from the past which people identify, independently of ownership, as a reflection and expression of their constantly evolving values, beliefs, knowledge and traditions" in order to "sustain and transmit to future generations".[33]

A similar approach has been adopted by many national legal systems. I cannot make a comparative analysis of the different regulatory solutions: I lack the expertise to do so, and it is not my objective in these pages. However, a couple of examples can give an idea of legal assumptions that underlie national policies for the protection of art and beauty. It is true, of course, that the analysis of different systems of public intervention in cultural heritage protection highlights a great variety of models. Some countries (e.g. Italy) use specific administrative procedures and provide for intervention by institutions with legally defined functions. Other countries adopt the devolution strategy (Austria, Germany, Spain, for example), and others refer to free trade mechanisms (Netherlands, United Kingdom, Sweden, Norway).[34] In terms of objectives, cultural policies focus on different sectors, ranging from more traditional ones, such as historic heritage, performing arts, libraries, and archives, to sectors such as intangible heritage and cultural/creative industries. It is the very notion of cultural heritage that is constantly evolving, concerning different artefacts, movable and immovable goods, tangible

31 For a legal analysis of the Faro Convention, and arguing for an ethical approach to heritage, in terms of participation to a range of social activities and cultural diversity, see John Schofield, "Forget About Heritage: Place, Ethics and the Faro Convention," in *The Ethics of Cultural Heritage*, eds. Tracy Ireland and John Schofield (Springer, 2015).

32 Art 1, a–c, CETS 199 – Value of Cultural Heritage for Society, 27.X.2005.

33 Art 2, a, b, CETS 199 – Value of Cultural Heritage for Society, 27.X.2005.

34 Nobuko Kawashima, "Comparing Cultural Policy: Towards the Development of Comparative Study," *International Journal of Cultural Policy* 1, no. 2 (1995): 289–307; Rick van der Ploeg, "In Art We Trust," *De Economist* 4 (2002): 333–62; Frederick Van der Ploeg, "The Making of Cultural Policy: A European Perspective," in *Handbook of the Economics of Art and Culture*, eds. Victor A. Ginsburgh and David Throsby (Elsevier, 2006), 1183–221; Joaquim Rius-Ulldemolins, Alejandro Pizzi, and Juan Arturo Rubio Arostegui, "European Models of Cultural Policy: Towards European Convergence in Public Spending and Cultural Participation?," *Journal of European Integration* 41, no. 8 (2019): 1045–67.

and intangible products, and historic and industrial areas: such a variability demonstrates that the notion itself is culturally conditioned and shaped by specific national needs and cultural values.[35] Similarly, the subjects involved and charged with tasks of protection, funding, and definition vary from country to country: the specific overlap between public and private institutions that are responsible for the implementation of cultural heritage policies reflect different national traditions, as well as "differing philosophies and objectives regarding the whole area of culture and the arts".[36] Consequently, some countries (such as France, Italy, and Ireland) have a centralised organisation, where a ministry or an administrative bureau bears responsibility for the implementation of cultural policies, while others adopt a decentralised model, where lower levels of government, such as regions or municipalities are involved. Some countries distribute competencies among different ministries and institutions, and others combine public and private (profit and non-profit) interventions, to different degrees, and entrust central authorities with control and coordination tasks.[37] Finally, differences are also relative to the specific measures adopted, which can take the form of both direct public expenditure (distribution of funds, awards, and grants to public and private institutions), indirect support (through the tax system and incentives), and systems where funds are allocated at arm's length, through the intervention of different institutions and bodies that act to filter government influence.

Despite all these differences, it seems to me that on one aspect these different legislations converge. Beauty and art are protected (in various ways, and for different purposes), but it is never made clear what they are. The Italian case, in this perspective, is interesting. On the one hand, Italy developed one of the oldest regulations and most articulate legislation on cultural and artistic heritage; on the other hand, the Italian legal system is built on a void: art and beauty are protected, without a definition of art and beauty being provided.

Indeed, the Italian regulation on the protection of the artistic, cultural, and natural heritage has had a long evolution. From the Nasi law of 1902,[38] the protection of beauty has never disappeared from the legal system. The Italian Constitution of 1948, in Article 9, confirmed that "the Republic promotes the development of culture" and protects "the landscape and the historical

35 Arjo Klamer, Anna Mignosa, and Lyudmila Petrova, "Cultural Heritage Policies: A Comparative Perspective," in *Handbook on the Economics of Cultural Heritage*, eds. Ilde Rizzo and Anna Mignosa (Edward Elgar Publishing, 2013), 37–86.

36 Milton C. Cummings and Richard S. Katz, eds., *The Patron State: Governments and the Arts in Europe, North America, and Japan* (Oxford University Press, 1987).

37 Klamer, Mignosa, and Petrova, "Cultural Heritage Policies," 43.

38 Cortese, "Patrimonio culturale, diritto e storia, 17.

and artistic heritage of the Nation".[39] The objective of this regulation is also clear: as ruled by the Constitutional Court,[40] the valorisation of the artistic and cultural heritage, and of the goods that are "material evidence" of this tradition, goes hand in hand with the need to "take care of the cultural education of citizens", enrich their sensitivity as persons, and promote "the progress of their spiritual as well as material development". The idea of *traditio*, in other words, is the foundation of this regulatory system.

Subsequent interventions had more practical purposes: they are normative acts that hold firm to the idea of a protection functional to human development but which focus on the definition and categorisation of assets of historical and artistic interest and the organisation of an efficient protection system. Among these, the most important is certainly the Code for the Protection of Cultural and Natural Heritage.[41] With the Code, the category of 'cultural heritage' is broadened to include both artistic, historical, archaeological, ethno-anthropological, archival, bibliographic assets, and "other things having a civilisational value", as well as landscape assets, that is, buildings and areas "constituting an expression of the historical, cultural, natural, morphological and aesthetic values of the territory".[42] It is precisely this civil function of beauty and artistic and landscape assets that justifies any restrictions on the enjoyment or circulation of these assets.

The fact that the interest deserving protection is an asset endowed with a social function underlines the inadequacy of public interventions aimed solely at preservation.[43] It is not enough to protect beauty and prevent it from being ruined, to hand it down intact to future generations. Protection doesn't mean inaccessibility. On the contrary, there is no true protection of beauty (and art, or landscape) without that beauty being offered to the enjoyment of mankind. For this reason, very wisely, the Code regulates a series of activities aimed not only at identifying the assets constituting the cultural heritage but above all at "guaranteeing their protection and conservation for public enjoyment".[44] The memory of identity (which is embodied and testified by monuments, works of art, and landscapes) is oriented to the future: since it educates and promotes human development, it can never be protected retrospectively. Either an asset manifests its capacity to say something to human beings, or it has little (civic) value.

39 Maria A. Cabiddu, "Diritto alla bellezza," *Rivista Associazione Italiana Costituzionalisti*, no. 4 (2020): 367–85.

40 Corte Costituzionale, sent. no. 118/1990.

41 Legislative Decree no. 42 of 22 January 2004, s.c. Urbani Code, from the name of its promoter: http://www.bncrm.beniculturali.it/getFile.php?id=466.

42 Article 2 of the Urbani Code.

43 Cabiddu, "Diritto alla bellezza," 377. Frezza, "Art and Law," 133.

44 Art. 3(1) of the Urbani Code.

In a very similar perspective, the German system of cultural heritage protection is based on the idea that this heritage is the mirror of the country's history and identity and is fundamental for self-understanding as a nation. Art and culture deserve protection because they mirror the social identity of a community, helping to consolidate this identity among future generations.[45] With this in mind, German legislation protects both cultural goods in Germany against being exported abroad and cultural goods from other countries that have been illegally brought into Germany from these countries and that must be returned. The German Protection of Cultural Property Act 2016,[46] together with regional regulations on specific issues (such as the protection of cultural property against natural disasters), constitutes the main reference for this system.

The provisions of the National Cultural Property Protection Act aim to protect German cultural property from damage, destruction, and expatriation, as well as to ensure that illegally removed cultural property is protected and returned. This law, adopted in 2016, summarises the most important regulations on the protection of cultural property at the federal level. At the same time, the individual states are responsible for the preservation of monuments, and the relevant laws protect cultural property from destruction, damage, or other alterations that prevent witnessing the past which – as mentioned – is at the heart of this regulatory system.

Beauty: in search of a legal definition

Our legislations protect beauty, therefore, both in the sense that they guarantee everyone the right to enjoyment of artistic heritage and in the sense that they protect beauty from ruin and destruction. But the question concerning a possible definition of beauty, which has vexed anyone interested in aesthetics for centuries, becomes a non-trivial one for jurists.[47] Can we protect something if we do not know what it is? What do we pass down to future generations if we lack criteria to identify with certainty the object of such a *traditio*?

Mindful of the saying *omnis definitio in iure periculosa est*, legislators have never given definitions of beauty, that is, of that value which they, in so many ways, intend to protect. Past experiences in other domains teach us

45 For a contextual analysis of the peculiar management of German memory, see Silke Arnold-de Simine, *Memory Traces: 1989 and the Question of German Cultural Identity*, vol. 5. (Peter Lang, 2005). See also Sina Hartwigsen and Jasmin Oschkinat, "The Convention for the Safeguarding of the Intangible Cultural Heritage and Its Relevance for Germany," *German Yearbook of International Law (GYIL)* 57 (2014): 667.

46 Kulturgutschutzgesetz, "KGSG," https://www.gesetze-im-internet.de/englisch_kgsg/englisch_kgsg.html#p0022.

47 Janet Blake, "On Defining the Cultural Heritage," *International & Comparative Law Quarterly* 49, no. 1 (2000): 61–85.

that when the law tries to come up with definitions, it usually creates more problems than it succeeds in solving: think of the cases of Scientology or, even more so, Pastafarianism, and the decision of the European Court of Human Rights not to recognise the Church of the Prodigious Flying Noodle as a religion. This decision is not motivated by public policy, nor is it based on the need to protect other values or interests, but it is rooted in a definitional problem: Pastafarianism is not a religion because it lacks "seriousness and cohesion", characteristics necessary to attract the protection of Article 9 ECHR.[48] It is the Court, in short, that determines what is a religion and what is not, and although the decision was very reasonable – in that case – the theoretical problems raised by such a definition are not small. What is seriousness? When is a religion serious? And in what sense is it or should it be cohesive? A heretical sect is cohesive internally, but its very existence manifests disunity within the larger, orthodox group. We all have a vague idea of what a religion is, but if we try to come up with an all-encompassing definition (lumping together Christianity and Hinduism, Scientology and Voodoo) we fail miserably. Definitions are therefore dangerous, and legislators should keep their distance from them.[49]

However, even if art is difficult to define, perhaps even impossible,[50] it may fall on jurists to provide some definition. Likewise, it is the law that establishes what human life or death is, and doctors are left with the much easier task of ascertaining the recurrence of those characteristics that the law considers relevant to the definition of human life and its end. Legal system contains definitions of death introduced by law, by democratically elected and legitimised parliaments (whether the criterion adopted is brain death, or cardiac death, or whatever, is irrelevant).[51] Yet, in the case of art, the tension between definitional needs and the possibility of finding shared definitions seems even more arduous. There is no legislative definition of what art is: probably, this is because – admittedly – that of art is a less urgent definition. We must know with certainty when a person should be considered clinically dead, or when that biological life in front of us can be still considered

48 *Hermina Geertruida de Wilde v the Netherlands* App. no. 9476/19, ECtHR, 9 November 2021.

49 Fabrizio Macagno, "Definitions in Law," *Bulletin suisse de linguistique appliquée* 2 (2010): 199–217; Michael D. Bayles, "Definitions in Law," in *Definitions and Definability: Philosophical Perspectives*, eds. James H. Fetzer, David Shatz, and George N. Schlesinger (Netherlands: Springer, 1991), 253–67.

50 On this impossible challenge see Dominic Lopes, *Beyond art* (Oxford University Press, 2014).

51 The most common criterion in Western legal systems is irreversible cessation of cardiorespiratory function or irreversible cessation of all brain function. See Brendan Parent and Angela Turi, "Death's Troubled Relationship With the Law," *AMA Journal of Ethics* 22, no. 12 (2020): E1055–61, https://doi.org/10.1001/amajethics.2020.1055.

a human life; we can, however, more calmly accept the uncertainty as to the quality of an art object.[52]

It is useful to consider both the poles of the alternative between a rationalist and cognitive approach to aesthetics, and an approach focused on the perception of sensate bodies (*aesthesis*), which has already discussed in previous chapters. If, for example, we focus on the protection of natural beauty and landscape, the object of protection involves both specific features of the landscape itself, such as elements and form, or specific physical properties or characteristics (scale, complexity), *and* the perspective of the beholder of that beauty, that is, the perceptual interaction between natural beauty and the subject. In the assessment of landscape, and thus in the assessment of the level of protection, the properties of the landscape cannot be separated from the consideration of the interaction with the beholder.[53]

On the one hand, the analysis of the beauty (and thus the value) of the landscape can be centred on an aesthetic or ecological approach (in which what counts is the natural value of the landscape and the absence of human modification): in both cases, what is relevant is the presence in the landscape of certain characteristics that can be detected almost objectively, on the basis of an expert assessment.[54] From this perspective, expert professionals should be able to objectively analyse landscape beauty and translate its qualities into formulas that can be used in legislation.[55] However, on the other hand, the consideration of landscape can focus on subjective perceptions and human-landscape interaction. This emphasis on experience and how a particular landscape affects the beholder as sensate bodies sheds light on the fact that aesthetic quality also lie in what the landscape means for people; in this sense, the aesthetic value of the landscape is understood within the framework of an emotional experience, rather than a rational understanding of certain characteristics.[56] In other words, while expert-based approaches translate biophysical features of the landscape into indicators of quality, which are in line with some standardised models of aesthetic judgement,

52 As Philippa Foot writes "When thinking about art we do not, it seems to me, have the same worry about relativism as we do when thinking about morals". Concerning morality – says Foot – "we maintain a fiction of inescapability", while in art we do not. Philippa Foot, "Morality and Art," in *Philosophy As It Is*, eds. Ted Honderich and Myles Burnyeat (Penguin Books, 1979), 7–28.

53 Terry C. Daniel, "Whither Scenic Beauty? Visual Landscape Quality Assessment in the 21st Century," *Landscape and Urban Planning* 54, no. 1–4 (2001): 267–81.

54 For a review of methods and results of this approach, see Daniel, "Whither Scenic Beauty?," 267–81; see also Beate Jessel, "Elements, Characteristics and Character–Information Functions of Landscapes in Terms of Indicators," *Ecological Indicators* 6, no. 1 (2006): 153–67.

55 Ian C. Laurie, "Aesthetic Factors in Visual Evaluation," in *Landscape Assessment: Values, Perceptions and Resources*, eds. Ervin H. Zube et al. (Halstead Press, 1975), 102–17.

56 Ervin H. Zube et al., "Measuring the Landscape: Perceptual Responses and Physical Dimensions," *Landscape Research* 1, no. 6 (1974): 4–6.

perception-based approaches understand landscape as affecting psychological/emotional responses through sensory-perceptual processes.[57]

Between these two poles of evaluation, and taking into account that an assessment of aesthetic quality of a landscape or artefact must be accompanied by a valuation of aesthetic quality – the balance between aesthetic worth and other values, such as economic development or respect for private property – viable solutions must be found. After all, law abounds with definitions, which are essential insofar as they serve to establish the boundaries of legal protection. To proclaim the right to health without defining health, for example, is to protect an empty box: the right to health becomes concrete, actionable, and real only when we define it as an individual and collective right, specify that it implies the right to access health services and infrastructures and implies the right to refuse treatments, as well as when we widen the concept of health, including physical, mental and social well-being.

In the same vein, the whole system of protection of artistic and natural heritage cannot stand without some definitions, at least in more limited or specific areas.[58] Therefore, even if the law does not protect beauty in itself nor does it define art, the law protects beauty in the places where it manifests itself: works of art, culture, and landscape. Thus, we might say, there is no legal definition of beauty because what matters is the protection of those specific *loci* of beauty that a specific community considers significant, as places of access to beauty worthy of being handed down to posterity.[59] The problem, however, is by no means solved but only shifted. And this displacement is not always an effective solution.

Landscape and culture, as far as possible, find some fairly accurate definitions in the legal system; or at least, some attempts at definition are at times provided. The Italian Code for Cultural heritage and landscape (Urbani code), for example, defines 'cultural' assets as those that have a certain artistic or historical interest, and have a *value of civilisation*.[60] Such things are generally considered to be very diverse, such as museum collections, and painting galleries, but also testimonies of past civilisations, photographs, films, parks, and gardens, and much more. The list is long and often generic, and wisely refers to verification of the 'existence' of artistic, historical, archaeological,

57 Daniel, "Whither Scenic Beauty?," 268.

58 Blake, "On Defining the Cultural Heritage," 65.

59 In a similar manner, Soucek argues that focusing on individual arts and single mediums of expression instead of looking for a single definition of art is more likely to succeed, especially from a legal point of view: Brian Soucek, "The Constitutional Irrelevance of Art," *North Carolina Law Review* 99, no. 685 (2021): 724 ff.

60 Urbani Code, Art. 10–11, speaks of movable and immovable property that "has an artistic, historical, archaeological, ethno-anthropological, archival and bibliographical interest" (Art. 2) and the other things identified by law or based on the law as assets having civilisation value. It indicates as landscape 'the territory expressive of identity, the character of which derives from the action of natural and human factors and their interrelationships' (Art. 134).

or ethno-anthropological interest.[61] If we consider the landscape, the reference to beauty is also evident. In the same text, when reference is made to natural heritage, it includes "immovable things having conspicuous features of natural beauty", or gardens and parks "distinguished by their uncommon beauty", or "scenic beauties" and "viewpoints . . . from which the spectacle of those beauties can be enjoyed".[62]

Once again, beauty is placed at the centre of legal definitions and still presupposed as the foundation of the protection that the law guarantees to certain goods; and even if the reference to beauty introduces into the norm no small degree of vagueness and discretion (how is *uncommon beauty* determined?), the appreciable attempt of the legislator is to offer a list, a catalogue, that bit of precision that is inevitably needed when one wants to construct instruments of protection. In this case, the subjectivity of aesthetic judgement is tempered by recourse to 'experts', to special regional commissions,[63] but some areas are protected by law, precisely on account of their specific aesthetic value.[64]

The German Protection of Cultural Property Act is not less vague. Cultural properties are defined as "any movable object or aggregates of things of artistic, historical or archaeological value or from other areas of cultural heritage, in particular of paleontological, ethnographic, numismatic or scientific value".[65]

If no definition of beauty is given (and no definition is feasible), neither is possible a legal definition of art (or even desirable). As we have seen, the law protects artistic assets, because it recognises their aesthetic and social value: it recognises a 'value' that deserves to be protected and safeguarded for the benefit of all. The question is how to assess this value. The evaluation of experts and commissions can be a valid strategy, or at least a reasonable way to balance the subjectivity of aesthetic judgement with the need for objectification of the artistic and aesthetic value of an asset, but it will always be a partial and provisional assessment.

61 Regulated in Articles 12–16 of the Code.

62 Art. 136 "a) immovable things that have conspicuous features of natural beauty, geological singularity or historical memory, including monumental trees; b) villas, gardens and parks, not protected by the provisions of Part Two of this Code, that are distinguished by their uncommon beauty c) complexes of immovable things that compose a characteristic appearance having aesthetic and traditional value, including historical centres and nuclei; d) panoramic beauties and also those viewpoints or belvederes, accessible to the public, from which the spectacle of those beauties can be enjoyed".

63 Art. 137 et seq.

64 These are areas that are subject to general restrictions due to their landscape interest under the sc. Galasso Law: valuable areas, coastal stretches of seas and lakes, rivers and shores, glaciers, and glacial cirques, national or regional parks and reserves, territories covered by forests and woods, volcanoes, and areas of archaeological interest. In these cases, however, the protection regime is conditioned by a positive assessment to determine whether these areas should continue to be subject to protection.

65 Kulturgutschutzgesetz, "KGSG," sect. 2 (10).

In the American context, and with specific reference to the issue of copyright protection, the VARA (Visual Artists Rights Act) of 1990, which provides its protection to paintings, drawings, prints, sculptures, and still photographic images, give some definitions that are similarly vague, and more precise criteria come from the Courts and specific cases. For instance, while the VARA states that the author of a work of art has the right to "prevent any destruction of a work of recognized stature", the New York federal district court set forth a test to assess the "recognized stature" of a work, trying to give content to such a formal definition. The test requires a plaintiff to show that "(1) the visual art in question has stature, i.e. is viewed as meritorious, and (2) that this stature is recognized by art experts, other members of the artistic community, or by some cross-section of society".[66] As one can easily understand, no definition is provided: rather, the "stature" is linked to the notoriety and the recognition by members of the artistic community.

Additionally, a not insignificant difference must be considered: the protection of cultural heritage set forth by the mentioned legal systems does not have beauty as its object, in the strict sense. If in the case of landscape, beauty is expressly mentioned and placed at the centre of protection,[67] this is not the case with cultural heritage. We protect a landscape for its exceptional beauty, as it would be a natural picture, as well as places accessible to the public from which the spectacle of such beauty can be enjoyed. Surprisingly, law does never (for what I know) protect a sculpture, or a collection of seventeenth-century paintings, for their beauty. Protect is awarded for the (specific) 'cultural' value they convey, for the importance that such works have in shaping and moulding culture, identity, and the common feeling of contemporary society and future generations. The beauty of such works is not even mentioned, but only their 'interest' (artistic, historical, archaeological, ethno-anthropological, archival, and bibliographical).

The category of interest is a social one, and goes beyond the aesthetic domain. A cultural good can be of ethno-anthropological, or historical, interest, without necessarily being of great aesthetic value. Thus, if no one doubts the beauty of the statue of *The Dying Galatian*,[68] or of Artemisia Gentileschi's *Judith*, the aesthetic value of the Pyrgi laminae is relative, and in any case irrelevant compared to the importance of a bilingual text (Etruscan and Phoenician) for the understanding of the Etruscan language, or the relations between Etruscans and Carthaginians.

66 Derek Fincham, "How Law Defines Art," *John Marshall Review of Intellectual Property Law* 14, no. 314 (2015).

67 The UNESCO criterion for being included on the World Heritage List is to be "areas of exceptional natural beauty and aesthetic importance".

68 Byron commemorates the statue in his *Childe Harold*, Canto IV (1818), stanzas 140–41.

To avoid definitional fallacies and the inevitable failures of expert judgement concerning cultural and natural heritage, the approach of Western legal systems takes a *retrospective* point of view: we protect those assets and goods whose relevance has been consolidated, and which we consider to be of interest not only from an artistic point of view but also from a historical or anthropological point of view. This is a 'museum-like' approach: time is the necessary means for this interest to emerge. Only the test of time can tell us – through the experts – whether these goods are of interest in relation to political and military history, literature, art and culture, and the identity of public, collective, and religious institutions, or are collections of exceptional artistic and historical interest.[69] This is what George Dickie proposed as an institutional theory of art,[70] considering where the object has been exhibited, and whether the work or the artist already achieved a certain recognition in the artistic community, as both indicators of its artistic value that can be profitably used by courts.[71]

This approach is not surprising. On the contrary, it is consistent with the history of aesthetics and the changing perception of beauty in modernity. Once the hope (or illusion) of giving an objective definition of beauty has been abandoned, aesthetic judgement tends to bind itself more and more to subjective taste and sensibility, even when the distinction between good taste and bad taste is not arbitrary.[72] Western legal and social mainstream is far away from the idea of an objective *canon* of beauty, and from the idea that this canon can be expressed in measurements and proportions, such as the ratio, in a body, between the head and the rest of the human figure. Within such a horizon and in the light of such a sensibility, we entrust 'museums' and other aesthetic institutions with the role of proposing and disseminating a kind of minimum aesthetic commonality, an official standard that distinguishes the beautiful from the ugly, and with the task of educating people's taste through works that we consider exemplary.[73] Museums have been established with many social and political aims,[74] but despite the fact that

69 Art. 10 (3) D, E.

70 George Dickie, "Art and the Aesthetic: An Institutional Analysis," *The British Journal of Aesthetics* 16, no. 2 (1976): 174–76.

71 On the use of this Dickie approach by Courts, see Brian Soucek, "Aesthetic Judgment in Law," *Alabama Law Review* 69, no. 2 (2017): 381–468.

72 See David Hume, "Of the Standard of Taste," in *Of the Standard of Taste and Other Essays*, ed. John Lenz (Bobbs-Merrill, 1965), 6: "Beauty is no quality in things themselves; it exists merely in the mind that contemplates them; and each mind perceives a different beauty". See, for an analysis of Hume's thought, Noel Carroll, "Hume's Standard of Taste," *The Journal of Aesthetics and Art Criticism* 43, no. 2 (1984): 181–94.

73 Tony Bennett, *The Birth of the Museum: History, Theory, Politics* (Routledge, 2013); Remo Bodei, *Le forme del bello* (il Mulino, 1995), 51.

74 Donald Preziosi, "Philosophy and the Ends of the Museum," in *Museum Philosophy for the Twenty-First Century*, ed. Hugh H. Genoways (Altamira Press, 2006), 69–78.

the function of museums has long been the subject of criticism and analysis,[75] they still affirm and disseminate a sort of minimum aesthetic standard, without in principle questioning the relevance of subjective taste in the enjoyment of works of art: museums do not propose an aesthetic theory but *spread certainties* (in short, everyone can have their legitimate aesthetic perspective, but what is conserved in a museum, be it a Caravaggio or a Degas or a Pollock, must *certainly* be considered a work of art).

As is well-known, museums have not always existed: there were private collections or public exhibitions of works for political and propaganda purposes, but it was not until Sixtus IV (who in 1477 donated some bronzes to the city's magistracy for public display, including the she-wolf that is still the symbol of the city of Rome) that an entire building was set up for the public enjoyment of works of art, and then the foundation of the first nucleus of the Capitoline Museums (in 1733) by Clement XII. Museums therefore become in modernity the temples of a secular religion, and of a public pedagogy that the sovereign proposes despite (or against?) the loss of objective criteria for the recognition of beauty and art: everything that enters a museum becomes, by right, a work of art, so much so that it loses any original function or purpose. An altarpiece no longer has any liturgical purpose, just as a Sèvres porcelain service has no practical function; an Egyptian sarcophagus loses its funerary function, and a painting is taken out of the context for which it was created (a refectory, the chapter house of a monastery, a merchant's study) and is admired in series, alongside other works of art, for the use and consumption of a mass audience. That mass is the audience for increasingly large and capacious museums, which become instruments for the construction of national identity. The Louvre, which is perhaps the largest museum in the world and certainly one of the best known, was inaugurated in 1793 expressly to house a collection of the arts to show the superiority of the post-revolutionary republican regime; and it grew in size thanks to Napoleonic plundering, which brought to Paris works such as the *Apollo of the Belvedere* or the *Laocoon*, Veronese's *The Wedding at Cana*, and the bronze horses of St. Mark's, as public demonstration of the glory of imperial France.

The category of interest is thus constructed at the intersection between aesthetics and politics. The law protects a cultural or artistic heritage, something that is preserved and handed down as an instrument of public pedagogy. And if this pedagogy does not have (not explicitly, at least) the objective of political propaganda or the exaltation of the regime, it nevertheless serves to disseminate an aesthetic standard, a sort of certified beauty, which is worthy of protection beyond subjective taste insofar as it has been recognised as cultural heritage. This approach is indeed prudent, but it takes time: time is

75 For an overview, see Wendy Earle, "Cultural Education: Redefining the Role of Museums in the 21st Century," *Sociology Compass* 7, no. 7 (2013): 533–46.

necessary for a work to become part of the public aesthetic canon, especially when the recognition of experts is at stake.

The necessary and impossible distance

Time, as noted, provides the useful perspective of distance which allows us, with greater clarity, to judge the public interest, and value, of a work. When Manet proposed the *Déjeuner sur l'herbe* at the Salon in 1863, the work was rejected as scandalous (and only exhibited at the Salon des Refusés, where artists rejected at the official salon could exhibit their work); a similar fate befell Klimt with *Judith* (the first version), in which the young protagonist of the biblical tale is a seductive woman of Viennese society, or with the paintings he was commissioned to paint for the lecture hall of Vienna University.[76] In this case, the works – which were representations of philosophy, jurisprudence, and medicine – were rejected as scandalous and ugly, so much so that one of Klimt's friends and supporters, Franz Wickhoff, gave a lecture entitled "What is Ugly?" precisely in response to the controversy stirred up by the works. It is only standing the test of time that has allowed these works[77] to be considered masterpieces of art and examples of beauty, and to become part of the museum canon: what scandalises contemporaries can be judged as 'interesting', or be perceived as beautiful, by later generations.

However, while time is an important factor, since it facilitates judgement and allows the consolidation of a widespread opinion on a work, it is not a sufficient element: the provenance from the past of an asset is not enough to make it culturally significant, especially when what is to be assessed is its artistic (aesthetic) interest. In other words, there is a margin of appreciation that goes beyond the mere ascertainment of historical significance, so much so that cultural goods are distinguished into goods of artistic, historical, archaeological, ethno-anthropological, archival, and bibliographic interest. Therefore, the question is what makes a good worthy of protection in terms of its 'artistic interest', and how this interest is distinguished from the merely historical, archaeological, and so on. A Roman fibula, of modest workmanship, may have considerable archaeological interest, but no artistic value. In the same way, Raphael's *Fornarina* has immense artistic value but may have no ethno-anthropological value (or at any rate be of modest value, from this point of view, and no more so than the painting of an obscure artisan). The concept of interest, in short, can also be used the other way round, in

76 An interesting analysis of Klimt's *Jurisprudence* is provided by Manderson, who highlights the depiction of the relationship between a sovereign power beyond juridical control, and a bare life beneath it: Desmond Manderson, "Klimt's Jurisprudence – Sovereign Violence and the Rule of Law," *Oxford Journal of Legal Studies* 35, no. 3 (2015): 515–42.

77 Not those of Klimt, which were unfortunately lost in a fire that Nazi troops set in Immendorf Castle, where they were kept.

a non-museum function: we can recognise an interest in the protection of an artistic good, even if it is of recent manufacture, not yet canonised by a museum institution.

As we already mentioned, the assessment of this 'interest' is entrusted by contemporary legal systems to expert professionals: it is neither the legislator nor judges who assess the merits and ascertain the interest of a work of art. They both, as we have seen, merely establish the circumstances in which such an assessment is necessary, and the legal consequences, but they entrust the substantive evaluation to others. It is not for lawyers to say what goods and artefacts have some artistic or cultural importance, but for those who are experts in the field. Judge Holmes' famous warning sounds like a *silete iudices in munere alieno*:

> It would be a dangerous undertaking for persons trained only to the law to constitute themselves final judges of the worth of pictorial illustrations, outside of the narrowest and most obvious limits. At the one extreme, some works of genius would be sure to miss appreciation. Their very novelty would make them repulsive until the public had learned the new language in which their author spoke. It may be more than doubted, for instance, whether the etchings of Goya or the paintings of Manet would have been sure of protection when seen for the first time.[78]

Unfortunately, even expert assessment is not always conclusive. It may happen that such an evaluation has not yet taken place or that there is no widespread consensus on a certain artefact or artist. Moreover, from a legal point of view a further complication may arise: the expert evaluation has a declaratory nature and is not constitutive, at least within some legal systems. This means – for instance, according to the Italian Supreme Court – an asset either is of artistic interest or is not: the expert evaluation merely declares this value, but does not constitute it. Experts do not confer artistic value on an asset, they merely recognise and declare it.

A recent case can be cited as an example. In 2010, a man was stopped at Ponte Chiasso customs with a painting by Carlo Carrà, which he was trying to take out of Italy. He was sentenced in the first instance to a fine of EUR 40,000 for the attempted transfer abroad of "things of artistic, historical, archaeological, ethno-anthropological, bibliographic, documentary or archival interest".[79] The conviction was then confirmed on appeal. On appeal, however, the defendant pointed out that no assessment or subsequent

78 *Bleistein v Donaldson Lithographing Co.*, 188 U.S. 239, 249–51 (1903).

79 As provided for in Article 174 of Legislative Decree 42/2004 (article now repealed and replaced by Art. 518-undecies of Law no. 22 of 9 March 2022.

declaration of cultural interest had ever been made on this painting. In other words, he argued that since there was no formal recognition that the work had artistic and cultural interest, there was no limit to export, and therefore no offence. Against this interpretation, the Court of Cassation held that the protection outlined in the Italian legal system does not only cover "recognised" cultural heritage but also those "goods protected because of their intrinsic value", regardless of whether they have been recognised as such or not.[80] In other words, some assets *objectively* present a cultural or artistic interest: evaluation procedures entrusted to experts may declare and give public evidence of this interest, but they do not create it. The fact that a good has artistic value is a characteristic of the object, not something that depends on its inclusion in a list of protected assets. For this reason, the Court overruled the appeal judgement:[81] the painting could not be taken abroad because of its objective value. As we can see, the Court took an objective approach, understanding artistic value as an objective quality, something that some assets possess even before they are declared as such, and regardless of such a declaration.

On the one hand, the law appears to rely retrospectively on a museum-like approach, enforcing a system of rules that protect a 'heritage', what communities have accumulated and catalogued over the centuries: this heritage becomes canonical and avoids the variations of subjective taste (at least, in the short run) and aesthetic orientations. Some things are unquestionably (one might say: *iuris et de iure*) worthy of aesthetic appreciation, insofar as they are catalogued, institutionalised, and recognised: no one could ever deny artistic value to Twombly's paintings, although it is legitimate that such paintings may or may not be liked. On the other hand, reality cannot be enclosed in stringent catalogues, and it is not always possible to simply rely on established judgements or experts' opinions. While the law needs precise definitions, and clear-cut boundaries (between what has artistic value and what does not), this clarity and precision is not always possible, when one leaves the halls of museums. When Courts have to decide whether an object is of artistic interest or not, assuming that this decision shall be based on the objective characteristics of the object itself, all these contradictions and pitfalls become evident.

That contradictory nature of legal judgement on artistic and aesthetic value is inescapable. The whole history of art is made up of a continuous reshaping of distinctions, between what is beautiful and what is ugly, what is

80 It is the cultural interest – writes the Court – 'which, constituting a predicate of the "thing", attracts it into the orbit of the discipline of protection of cultural heritage': Cass. Sent. no. 10468, of 8 March 2018.

81 It is "necessary and sufficient, for there to be an offence, that the thing has an objective cultural interest (and that, obviously, the author of the conduct is aware of this)" (Cass. Sent. no. 10468, of 08 March 2018).

high and what is low, the beautiful and the sublime, the harmonious and the vague, what elevates us and what lowers us, what is 'permitted' and canonically beautiful and the dissonant, the repudiated, and the excluded. When Giotto painted the *Lamentation* (The Mourning of Christ), in which even the angels are torn by grief and cry out for the death of Christ, he broke down every idea of order, harmony, and the cosmos, typical of previous art: feelings break through the banks and give shape to images. Byzantine art, and early Christian art, had never dared so much, especially in the representations of the celestial spheres and angelic bodies. When Baudelaire published *Une Charogne*, in which he writes that "Les mouches bourdonnaient sur ce ventre putride /D'où sortaient de noirs bataillons/ De larves, qui coulaient comme un épais liquide/ Le long de ces vivants haillons",[82] he dropped the boundary between beauty and the disgusting, between a decent and orderly existence and the chaotic putridity of life. After all, Rimbaud opens *Une saison en l'Enfer* by saying: "Un soir, j'ai assis la Beauté sur mes genoux. Et je l'ai trouvée amère. Et je l'ai injuriée".[83] When, again, Duchamp began the Ready-Made series, first with the bicycle wheel and then with the 'bottle-drainer' (ironically, thrown away by the artist's sister, who evidently had not grasped its artistic value) and the fountain-urinal, he broke down the distinction between object of art and object of use: art moves from the sphere of manual ability (the ability to sculpt, paint, compose) to that of the idea. Again, this is what Warhol did with the Brillo-Boxes, and this is indeed what happens with contemporary industrial design, which democratises beauty and makes it internal to everyday objects and mass consumption.[84] In short, if there is one thing that the history of art shows, it is the ability of art to be conveyed in different forms and ways and objects, to break down boundaries and canons, and to break out of codes and lists.

Law, in this evolution, is overwhelmed by art and its changing manifestations, and the claim to find objective elements to prove the artistic interest of a good is anything but an illusion. In 1910, Marinetti's novel *Mafarka le futuriste* was published in Paris by Sansot. It was an immediate sales success and aroused admiration in the intellectual circles of the time. The Italian edition at the Edizioni Futuriste di Poesia, which followed shortly afterwards, was immediately seized by the Milan police headquarters for outraging public decency, and Marinetti himself was sentenced to two months in prison. To be honest, it was not a book for innocent souls: rapes by soldiers

82 "The flies swarmed on the putrid vulva, then / A black tumbling rout would seethe / Of maggots, thick like a torrent in a glen, / Over those rags that lived and seemed to breathe": Charles Baudelaire, *The Flowers of Evil*, eds. Marthiel Mathews and Jackson Mathews (New Directions Book, 1962), 38.

83 "One night, I sat Beauty on my lap. And I found she was bitter, and I called her names". Arthur Rimbaud, *A Season in Hell*, trans. Paul Schmidt (Bulfinch Press, 1997), 5.

84 Arthur C. Danto, "The Abuse of Beauty," *Daedalus* 131, no. 4 (2002): 35–56.

drugged with hashish, sadomasochism, gigantic penises, emasculated horses, dog fights and mechanical giraffes, uxoricides, and much more, in a flood of images and words employed admittedly to describe a crazy and extravagant existence, but certainly one that is also disruptive and *futurist*. The Court of Milan, called to judge whether the book was pornography or art, held that "this is no longer art, but filth and despicable turpitude that literary decadentism is certainly not worth mitigating".[85] The sentence was later overturned on appeal, thanks in part to the expert judgement of some novelists who, infusing quotations from Italian literature and contemporary aesthetics, argued for the morality of the work, and emphasised its artistic value. The following year, the Court of Cassation overruled the sentence of appeal and condemned the work.[86] A different fate, however, befell Casanova's memoirs, when in 1923 the Court of Appeal of Florence separated the content and the judgement on the morality of the work from the aesthetic one, noting how "the obscene element of the work remains overwhelmed and, so to speak, purified by the element of its literary and historical value that has been affirmed for a century".[87]

One of the most famous cases relating the legal qualification of an object as a work of art – and thus relating to the formulation of a universal aesthetic judgement on a specific object – is probably the 1927 case *Brancusi v. United States*. It is an interesting case, from our point of view, because the legal question (whether certain taxation should be applied to customs) depends precisely on the aesthetic one: is the object in question a work of art or not? A technical (fiscal) question opens up an incredibly complex epistemological and aesthetic question.

The facts are fairly known: in 1927, US Customs classified a work by Constantin Brancusi – the *Bird* – as a mere artefact, rather than a work of art, and therefore levied a series of customs duties under the Tariff Act of 1922.[88] Brancusi sued to have the artistic quality of his work recognised and thus brought into the United States duty-free. In the process, again, the expert-based approach was used, and an evidentiary path was constructed to prove the work's artistic quality. The work itself was deposited, together with a photo of the original (the work was a multiple of the original), a copy

85 Court of Appeal Milan, 25 January 1911 and Court of Cassation, 26 May 1911, in *Supplemento alla 'Rivista Penale'*, 64 (1911): 376.

86 Filippo Tommaso Marinetti, *Il processo e l'assoluzione di" Mafarka il Futurista"*, vol. 2 (Soldiershop Publishing, 2018).

87 Florence Court of Appeal, 29 April 1923, Pres. Bertolli, imp. Nerbini, in *'Monitore dei Tribunali'*, 64 (1923): 439–40; cited in Elisabetta Fusar Poli, "Oltraggi d'autore. Questioni novecentesche d'arte, diritto e cripto-censura," *LawArt Rivista di Diritto, Arte, Storia. Journal of Law, Art and History* 1 (2020): 139–77.

88 Thomas L. Hartshorne, "Modernism on Trial: C. Brancusi v United States (1928)," *Journal of American Studies* 20, no. 1 (1986): 93–104.

of an art magazine with reproductions of some of Brancusi's works, and the artist's deposition. In addition, various experts on modern art were called in as witnesses: among others, Edward Steichen, an artist, collector, and dealer; Jacob Epstein, a sculptor; Forbes Watson, editor-in-chief of *The Arts* magazine; William Henry Fox, director of the Brooklyn Museum of Art; Henry Mc Bride, an art historian.

Many arguments and counter-arguments were used in the hearing: all of these arguments are indicative of the fact that the approach to aesthetic judgement here was exclusively conceived in rational and cognitive terms, and concerned the absence or presence of certain features.[89] Among the many, the fact that the work was not "unique" but a replica was contested by assuming that in the process of creating the replica, the artist always introduces something original and different (in this case, Brancusi moved from the original marble to the bronze replica), and therefore the work could be considered as having value in itself. The fact that the object bore no resemblance to what was represented (a bird) was contested by introducing a distinction between external resemblance and inner, subjective, and suggestive resemblance. The competence and the very qualification of the witnesses, the prosecution, and the defence were also called into question (who is to say that Steichen is actually an artist? Is this a qualification that one can attribute to oneself? At the same time, who guarantees that the editor of an art magazine is competent to decide what is art and what is not?), and Brancusi himself was challenged (is he an artist too?). On the other hand, the consensus of experts and institutions was called upon – once again, the museum and reputational approach came to the fore – and it was emphasised that Brancusi was recognised as an artist by the most qualified international museums and cultural institutions. Again, it was pointed out that the object in question had no special characteristics that could distinguish it from a mere artefact, as it could be made by any medium-level craftsman (this is, after all, the comment of the layman who, having arrived at a contemporary art museum, says: I can make this too!); and it was asserted, conversely, that it is the artist who makes the work of art, not the other way around (it is the artist who gives content and artistic value to the work, not the work of art that qualifies as an artist the person who created it).

Finally, it is interesting to note that one of the arguments used by the defense (the US administration), even if used in an anti-relativist perspective, was related to the issue of taste and perception. To devalue the aesthetic quality of Brancusi's sculpture, thereby not qualifying it as art, the defense argued that this qualification should be reserved by law only to that category of fine arts that imitate natural objects as perceived by the artist, and whose mere

89 Nathalie Heinich, "It's a Bird: Brancusi vs USA: When Law Defines Art," *Droit et Société* 34 (1996): 649–72.

sight is capable of arousing emotions, to the exclusion of purely decorative objects. To this objection, Brancusi's lawyers took a decidedly post-modern perspective: they asserted that, in the field of art and aesthetics, every opinion is legitimate because the judgement on beauty is subjective; that beauty – as each person perceives it – is what makes an object a work of art; and finally, that art has no connection with utility or a specific function. In other words, Brancusi's lawyers argued that a court of law, or any other court, has no authority to determine what constitutes a work of art and what does not, not so much because of a lack of competence (as Holmes argued), but because the question does not relate to the legal nature of an object. While a court may well decide – indeed, it must – whether a certain document is a contract, and what kind of contract it is, it cannot decide whether an object is a work of art or not; because this is not its task, and because no one can make this decision on its *authority*, that is, with the pretence of imposing it *erga omnes*. Each person interested in the matter can, with equal authority, decide on the artistic value of an object, and this decision is irretrievably subjective.

The Court agreed with Brancusi. In its ruling, without explicitly adhering to any aesthetic perspective, the Court emphasised that – no matter how much one may be in favour of contemporary art trends – taste and avant-garde artistic currents are *facts* that a court cannot but accept as such. And therefore, since the object does not have a direct and explicitly practical purpose, it must be treated like any other sculpture, in short, like a statue by Phidias. Since everything suggested that it was the original production of an artist, the work had to be *treated as* a work of art, and therefore exempt from import duties on artefacts and objects of use.

As Danto wrote, in times of radical openness, pluralism extends to aesthetics itself: if everything can be art, everything is possible, including aesthetics.[90] We can also put it another way: aesthetic pluralism does not dissolve the relevance of art, just as – for Kant – taste does not eliminate the legitimacy of aesthetic judgement, nor its universal value. It is well-known that according to Kant aesthetic judgement is, by its very nature, a subjective judgement, and raises the question of the subjectivity of taste and the possible universality of aesthetic judgement, that is, the question of the capacity of reason to make judgements on beauty that are not exclusive to the person making them.[91]

Likewise, the fact that courts or legislatures recognise the subjectivity of aesthetic judgement, overcoming the purported objectivity of expert judgement, does not mean they have solved every problem. And this is because while aesthetic judgement may be subjective, legal judgement has a claim to

90 Arthur C. Danto, "Embodied Meanings, Isotypes, and Aesthetical Ideas," *The Journal of Aesthetics and Art Criticism* 65, no. 1 (2007): 121–29.

91 Immanuel Kant, the Critique of Judgement, § 6.

objectivity, or at least stands on authority above subjective judgements.[92] Legal reasoning of courts claims to substantial interpersonal validity, even if reasonable people can disagree about the precise force of reasons: the force of law allows a sentence to impose its content over any contrary opinions. Yet, judges and public officers all over the world are constantly having to decide whether an object can be considered a work of art or a cultural good, for many different reasons: to avoid taxes and customs duties, as in the Brancusi case, or to assess the relevance of the outrage to the common sense of decency concerning an image, or to distinguish fakes from originals, or to activate forms of protection with respect to the export or sale of a certain good.[93]

This difficulty of combining expert judgement and judgement based on perception and taste is also reflected in another, legally relevant aspect. I have said that an assessment of aesthetic quality of a landscape or artefact must be accompanied by a valuation of its aesthetic quality, thereby balancing between aesthetic worth and other values, such as economic development or respect for private property. Even then, an expert-based approach is useful, but may not be sufficient. Street art and graffiti are very obvious examples in this respect. We have no objective criteria to distinguish a defaced wall from a work of art,[94] just as we have no criteria to decide whether Brancusi's bird is a work of art or not. Yet, even in this case, the evolution of taste and social perception of such art forms has led to a phenomenon of progressive decriminalisation of street art, which has not only culturally legitimised both these forms of expression but has sometimes led to legal recognition and exhibitions of graffiti in museums. Street art, after being criminalised for decades, is now used in many cities as a tool for the renewal of the suburbs, with works financed by the municipality and located in various areas of the city on social housing properties.[95]

92 Kent Greenawalt, *Law and Objectivity* (Oxford University Press, 1992; online ed., Oxford Academic, October 31, 2023).

93 John A. Walker, *Art and Outrage: Provocation, Controversy and the Visual Arts* (London: Pluto Press, 1999).

94 Tomasz Rychlicki, "Legal Questions About Illegal Art," *Journal of Intellectual Property Law & Practice* 3, no. 6 (2008): 393–401; Marisa A. Gómez, "The Writing on Our Walls: Finding Solutions through Distinguishing Graffiti Art from Graffiti Vandalism," *University of Michigan Journal of Law Reform* 26 (1992): 633; Lori L. Hanesworth, "Are They Graffiti Artists or Vandals – Should They be Able or Caned: A Look at the Latest Legislative Attempts to Eradicate Graffiti," *De Paul Journal of Art, Technology, and Intellectual Property* 225 (1996): 225.

95 Alexandra Parker and Samkelisiwe Khanyile, "Creative Writing: Urban Renewal, the Creative City and Graffiti in Johannesburg," *Social & Cultural Geography* 25, no. 1 (2024): 158–78; Joaquim Rius-Ulldemolins and Ricardo Klein, "From Top-Down Urban Planning to Culturally Sensitive Planning? Urban Renewal and Artistic Activism in a Neo-Bohemian District in Barcelona," *Journal of Urban Affairs* 44, no. 4–5 (2022): 524–44.

This change in social understanding of street art (mainly) and graffiti (rarely) is a social process: criteria of taste and aesthetic perspectives are constantly changing, and the margins of uncertainty remain wide. And this is why – wisely – many courts decide to overlook aesthetic issues altogether, and focus on the legal aspects of an issue. In 2016, in the same days that an exhibition of street artists' works was organised in Bologna by the municipality (*Street Art. Banksy & Co. – L'arte allo stato urbano*), the street artist Alice Pasquini was condemned by the Court of Bologna for defacement.[96] The sentence did not take into account the decorum of the property defaced or the possible artistic nature of the work of art that was created. The decision on the offence of defacement, stated the Court, cannot be based on "very personal and therefore unquestionable evaluations linked to artistic value, being a parameter linked to taste and variable social or individual feelings and often influenced by fashions". This is because, whatever the artistic relevance of the work, the protection of the property rights is such as to guarantee the owner the freedom to decide whether and how to decorate that property. And so, the Court of Bologna did not enter into the merits of the work: whether it is art or just paint thrown on a wall is not for the judge to say.

This approach is certainly prudent: but it does not resolve the issue, it merely avoids it. Which is sometimes impossible, as we have seen. The law does protect art and landscape also because of their beauty, but it can do so quite smoothly only when it takes a retrospective, museum-like approach. This happens when aesthetic value is institutionalised, or embodied in objects that are socially recognised as works of art, either because they are exhibited in a museum, or because a widespread aesthetic judgement has been formed on them over time. However, this approach is plausible only when a social consensus has already been formed and consolidated on the artistic and cultural interest of certain goods. When this recognition has not (yet) taken place, everything becomes more slippery, and any evaluation, although necessary in the specific case, becomes contradictory: the given examples show, after all, how Courts seek to do what cannot be done, because it must be done. Distinguishing art from mere imbrication, or a piece of furniture, is almost impossible. In this 'almost', there is the scope for intervention by law.

The beauty of bodies

So far, we have dealt with the beauty of artefacts, or nature and landscape, and how the law protects these assets. However, when analysing the possibilities and limits of what some called the right to beauty, and the way in which legal systems protect the aesthetic value of objects and nature, one issue is generally overlooked: the legal relevance of the bodily aesthetic. However,

96 Court, Bologna, judgment 15 February 2017, no. 674.

and in line with a tradition that – since ancient Greece – understands the human body as the first place to experience beauty, law protects beauty even when it concerns the living body. Or, better, it protects the subjective wish of matching a certain ideal of beauty. And just as the evaluation of art or landscape involves balancing it against other values protected by the law, so it is with the pursuit of a bodily aesthetic ideal: it must be balanced against the protection of the right to health.

The legal and social status of cosmetic surgery is at stake. That is, the status of a specific medical practice with aesthetic purposes, different from plastic and reconstructive surgery: while the latter is a surgical practice aimed at treating anatomic-functional alterations of pathological value, the former is mostly aimed at intervening in somatic alterations of a morphological order, or in any case producing alterations and modifications of a morphological type due to an autonomous choice of the subject.[97] More precisely, we can distinguish between operations aimed at reconstructing a somatic condition following injuries and accidents of various kinds (road accidents, injuries at work, surgery, etc.) such as breast reconstruction following the removal of a breast tumour; operations necessary to correct natural but dysfunctional features (for example, operations to correct cleft lip and palate, the so-called harelip); and finally, operations not motivated by any clinical need, and motivated solely by the desire to correct and alter somatic features that have no pathological character.

This last group is where we find the interventions that we commonly label as cosmetic surgery. Aesthetic purposes are indeed detectable in various types of intervention, but the desire to conform one's body to an aesthetic model motivates, even if not exclusively, the practices of the third group.[98] The interventions that we classify as examples of cosmetic surgery may be motivated by the search for greater self-acceptance, by the desire to correct somatic traits that are a source of discomfort or insecurity, but they may also be linked to the mere desire to shape one's body following an ideal of beauty, whatever that may be. What characterises these interventions is not so much the presence, alongside the search for an ideal of beauty, of other motivations that can be traced in some measure directly to the psychophysical well-being of the person, which the actual intervention should guarantee. These are possible motivations, certainly, but not necessary. Rather, what is important is the absence of a clinical reason for the intervention, also because there is no

97 Monique Devereaux, "Cosmetic Surgery," in *Medical Enhancement and Posthumanity*, eds. Bert Gordijn and Ruth Chadwick (Springer, 2009), 159–74; Franklin G. Miller, Howard Brody, and Kevin C. Chung, "Cosmetic Surgery and the Internal Morality of Medicine," *Cambridge Quarterly of Healthcare Ethics* 9, no. 3 (2000): 353–64.

98 Susan Bordo, *Unbearable Weight: Feminism, Western Culture, and the Body* (University of California Press, 1993); Kathryn P. Morgan, "Women and the Knife: Cosmetic Surgery and the Colonization of Women's Bodies," *Hypatia* 6, no. 3 (1991): 25–53.

obligation on the part of the subject undergoing such a surgical procedure to justify his or her request.[99] In this case, the two poles of aesthetics and *aesthesis* seem to coincide. The person acts to embody a model of beauty that he or she not only considers appreciable, but that can contribute to his/her well-being and define his/her identity.

The path that led jurisprudence to recognise the lawfulness of cosmetic surgery was not easy. Western legal systems have initially justified plastic surgery based on the therapeutic purposes of the intervention: plastic and reconstructive surgery (the first two types indicated earlier) were immediately equated with surgical activity in the general sense, and therefore with a practice comprising obvious therapeutic purposes and founded on clinical reasons.[100] On the contrary, cosmetic surgery, that is, surgery not motivated by clinical reasons and morphological alterations or pathologies, appeared unjustifiable from the outset, because "affecting a healthy patient would have done so, from this point of view, with the sole aim of satisfying his aesthetic claim to beauty".[101] Cosmetic surgery, for many years, was considered a practice merely motivated by vanity, or in any case viewed as futile, not essential.

The evolution of legislation and jurisprudence, and the broadening of the concept of health, has paved the way for the full legitimisation of cosmetic interventions: if health is identified with full psychophysical well-being,[102] the discomfort caused by a body that does not conform to one's wishes and aesthetics is sufficient reason to justify such interventions. Different legal solutions have been adopted: in the United Kingdom, cosmetic surgery has been regulated as medically necessary surgery and defined as a legitimate medical practice ('proper medical treatment').[103] In France, following the enactment of the 2002 Kouchner Law, consent procedures are detailed, additional guarantees on publicity have been introduced, and a period of 'reflection' is required, but the patient's self-determination remains the sole criterion for justification.[104] In Italy, interventions performed on healthy subjects are considered to be legitimate, to the extent these interventions are aimed

99 Tony Bennett, *Cuts and Criminality: Bodily Alteration in Legal Discourse* (Ashgate, 2015).

100 Renato Rolli and Nicola Posteraro, "Salute e chirurgia estetica: dialogo col diritto. Legittimazione e sua terapeuticità," *Judicium* (2013): 6.

101 Rolli and Posteraro, "Salute e chirurgia estetica."

102 see the Constitution of the World Health Organisation, where health is understood as "a state of complete physical, mental and social well-being and not merely the absence of disease or infirmity"),

103 Danielle Griffiths and Alexandra Mullock, "The Medical Exception and Cosmetic Surgery: Culpable Doctors and Harmful Enhancement?," in *The Legitimacy of Medical Treatment. What Role for the Medical Exception?*, eds. Sara Fovargue and Alexandra Mullock (Routledge, 2016), 105–23.

104 Melanie Latham, " 'If It Ain't Broke, Don't Fix It?': Scandals, 'Risk', and Cosmetic Surgery Regulation in the UK and France," *Medical Law Review* 22, no. 3 (2014): 384–408.

at alleviating suffering however caused and realising the well-being of the patient.[105]

The discrepancy between one's outward appearance and one's desired self-image may be at the origin of requests for aesthetic surgery and legitimate the subjective interest in undergoing surgical intervention. And just as it is not necessary for the person to explicitly motivate his or her request of aesthetic intervention, neither is the aesthetic result obtained open to scrutiny (except in cases of injury or other damage resulting from the operation). Each of us has a model of beauty to pursue. Each of us can assess our own body as being more or less beautiful and wish to shape it in one way or another: the ideal of beauty that cosmetic surgery guarantees (or promises) is entirely subjective. The law protects the right to personal well-being, that is, to feel good and perceive oneself as conforming to a certain ideal, and allows for interventions to adjust physical appearance to that ideal. Using the categories mentioned earlier, we could say that by recognising people's rational understanding of the beauty (aesthetics), the law protects affective and sensuous dimensions produced by a re-configuration of bodily appearance (*aesthesis*).

However, even in this context aesthetic ideals are not protected by law as an absolute, but valued together with other values, and in balance with them. The pursuit of a subjective ideal of beauty (or a culturally prevailing ideal of beauty),[106] and the freedom to modify one's body to correspond to this ideal, is likewise limited. If the legal system protects the subject's self-determination concerning decisions on one's own body, such freedom is limited by the need to protect public health, principles of medical ethics, specific aspects of the healthcare system, and more.[107]

As emphasised by many scholars, the constant appeal to culturally dominant models of beauty can also create negative effects, especially in the most vulnerable subjects, concerning individual differences and the sense of inadequacy that some subjects may feel.[108] In this perspective, it is still necessary

105 Cass. Civ. 25 November 1994, no. 10014, in *Foro italiano*, 1995, I, 2913. Mauro Bilancetti, *La responsabilità penale e civile del medico* (Cedam, 2010).

106 On this alternative see Kathy Davis, "Revisiting Feminist Debates on Cosmetic Surgery: Some Reflections on Suffering, Agency, and Embodied Difference," in *Cosmetic Surgery. A Feminist Primer*, eds. Cressida J. Heyes and Meredith Jones (Routledge, 2016), 35–47.

107 Onora O'Neill, "Paternalism and Partial Autonomy," *Journal of Medical Ethics* 10, no. 4 (1984): 173–78; onora O'Neill, *Autonomy and Trust in Bioethics* (Cambridge University Press, 2002); Mary Donnelly, *Healthcare Decision-Making and the Law: Autonomy, Capacity and the Limits of Liberalism* (Cambridge University Press, 2010); Fabio Macioce, "What Can We Do? A Philosophical Analysis of Individual Self-Determination," *Eidos* 16 (2012): 100–29.

108 Yves Saint James Aquino, "Is Ugliness a Pathology? An Ethical Critique of the Therapeuticalization of Cosmetic Surgery," *Bioethics* 34, no. 4 (2020): 431–41. Susan Bordo, "The Body and the Reproduction of Femininity," in *Gender/Body/Knowledge: Feminist Reconstructions of Being and Knowing*, eds. Alison Jagger and Susan Bordo (Rutgers University Press, 1989).

to raise the question of the limits of such interventions, without absolutising subjective autonomy and the desire to adapt one's appearance to a certain aesthetic ideal. Concerns have been raised by both the Nuffield Council on Bioethics and the Italian Committee for Bioethics. For instance, the Nuffield Council highlighted that "appearance ideals are a source of concern where they feed existing negative and discriminatory attitudes" with respect to factors such as age, gender, race, class, and disability,[109] and that "high standards of professional conduct and integrity" required for any medical practice might overlap with "commercial imperatives" in unclear ways.[110] Moreover, these concerns are particularly pressing when considering the exposure of children and young people to idealised body images: accordingly, the Nuffield Council recommends, on the one hand, that specific guidance on appearance-related discrimination is provided, and that "all children and young people have access to evidence-based resources on body image". On the other hand, it restates the already accepted principle that

> procedures designed to change physical appearance without any scope for functional benefit . . . should not be made available to anyone under the age of 18, regardless of their ability to consent to such treatments, and regardless of their parent's willingness to consent on their behalf;[111]

consequently, the access to these procedures should be regarded as exceptional, and in need of robust justification.

In the same vein, the Italian National Committee of Bioethics (CNB) recognises that the broadening of the concept of health makes it virtually impossible to determine clear-cut boundaries between cosmetic and therapeutic surgery but affirms that deontological duties require doctors to assess the proportionality and appropriateness of any intervention. In short, it is not enough that the person is properly informed, and willingly requests a particular intervention. Every surgical intervention, however small it may be, has risks that must be weighed against the benefits and expectations associated with the intervention. As a consequence, the guarantee of subjective self-determination, and the freedom to decide whether and how to modify

109 On these aspects see for instance Eugenia Kaw, "Medicalization of Racial Features: Asian American Women and Cosmetic Surgery," *Medical Anthropology Quarterly* 7, no. 1 (1993): 74–89; Ruth Holliday and Joanna Elfving-Hwang, "Gender, Globalization and Aesthetic Surgery in South Korea," *Body & Society* 18, no. 2 (2012): 58–81.

110 Nuffield Council on Bioethics, "Cosmetic Procedures: Ethical Issues," https://www.nuffieldbioethics.org/publications/cosmetic-procedures.

111 See the Sunbeds (Regulation) Act 2010 (covering England and Wales); and Tattooing of Minors Act 1969.

one's body to correspond to an ideal of beauty, must always be balanced against the protection of health.[112]

Greater concerns, of course, are at stake when the person undergoing treatment is a minor or is not able to give valid consent. The general principle in international and national law is that when health treatment is to be performed on minors or persons incapable of giving valid consent, such consent must be given by the parents or guardians.[113] Aesthetic surgery on minors is therefore possible, and consent must be given by the parents or guardians, with serious consideration being given to the wishes of the minors themselves when it comes to the so-called mature minors.

A far more challenging case is that of cosmetic surgery on people with Down syndrome. As is well-known, Down syndrome determines certain somatic features and morphological characteristics including a tongue that is more developed than normal, a flattened nasal bridge, a small chin, the presence of epicanthic folds (a fold on the upper eyelid), nuchal folds, a wide neck, and so on. Currently, some of these features can be corrected or modified surgically both for clinical purposes and to improve certain functions such as breathing or swallowing. However, surgery can also take on merely (or mainly) aesthetic purposes, and it might be requested by parents of children with Down syndrome to facilitate social acceptance and reduce the stigma that is still, unfortunately, attached to this condition.[114] In such cases, balancing the pursuit of a subjective (and socially induced) standard of beauty with medical standards and respect for human dignity is much more problematic. First, these requests usually concern minors, but aesthetic standards are set by parents and guardians; second, these requests pursue a legitimate and understandable interest by very questionable means. The stigma still affecting persons with Down syndrome should be tackled by correcting the culture of the social group, and the current canons of beauty, not the somatic features of the persons affected by this stigma.[115] Third, aesthetics and aesthesis are separated, if not opposed. The re-configuration of a body

112 The same Court of Cassation has, in fact, reiterated that 'on the subject of surgical treatment, for the patient to be able to consciously exercise his right, which the Constitutional Charter attributes to him, to choose whether or not to undergo the operation, a specific duty of information on the benefits and modalities of the operation, as well as on the foreseeable risks in the post-operative phase, falls on the sanitary person'; with the consequence that the omission of this duty, beyond the success of the planned operation 'does not exempt the sanitary person from responsibility . . . should a harmful event occur' (Cass. Civ, no. 9705/1997).

113 Oviedo Conv., Art. 6.

114 Rolf-Ruediger Olbrisch, "Plastic and Aesthetic Surgery on Children with Down's Syndrome," *Aesthetic Plastic Surgery* 9 (1985): 241–48.

115 Jill Aylott, "Should Children with Down's Syndrome Have Cosmetic Surgery?," *British Journal of Nursing* 8, no. 1 (1999): 33–38; Jean V. McHale, "Children, Cosmetic Surgery and Perfectionism: A Case for Legal Regulation?," in *Inspiring a Medico-Legal Revolution: Essays in Honour of Sheila McLean*, eds. Graeme T. Laurie and Pamela R. Ferguson (Ashgate Publishing, Ltd., 2015), ch. 12.

according to specific aesthetic criteria is performed on a subject that is not the one who experiences the affective and sensuous dimensions produced by such a re-configuration of bodily appearance.

This is one of the dark sides of beauty – which we will discuss in a later chapter – that should be carefully considered. Aesthetic values are powerful instruments, socially and politically, and this is why they can also be instruments of oppression and discrimination, especially when they are imposed as a canon, a criterion of recognition and social acceptance. In this sense, and rightly so, many scholars accurately emphasise the difference between interventions on persons with Down syndrome for therapeutic purposes (improving respiratory dynamics, nutrition, and speech), and merely cosmetic interventions. While the former must always be considered legitimate, the latter should be excluded as unnecessary for the person's health. Indeed, somatic aesthetic change can determine in the minor a sense of otherness concerning his or her image (hindering the process of self-identification) and the perception of being rejected by the social environment and especially by those who should take care of him or her.

This ambivalence of beauty must be revealed by law and ruled according to the necessary balance between human dignity, well-being, autonomy, and equality. In other words, the legal recognition of beauty and its value finds a limit in other values of equal standing, with which it must necessarily find a balance.

Chapter 5

The unfair beauty

Introduction

At the end of 2022, the writer and playwright Hanif Kureishi was admitted to a Roman hospital. Unable to write due to limb paralysis, he underwent months of therapy, during which he received numerous visitors who helped him by morally supporting him. Kureishi gave an account of this period in a Twitter diary, which he wrote through dictation. One day, he writes, he received a visit from a former student who grew up in Nigeria and was working on a novel set there. He only read the beginning of the book, because of the fatigue that reading implied in his condition: however, he says that when the author had written a considerable part of the book, she decided to show it not to a friend, a publisher, or an agent, but to a so-called 'sensitive reader'. She was worried about whether her work would be politically correct or considered offensive by anyone, and she was concerned about whether the book would be accused of sexism, racism, cultural appropriation, and so on. Critically and perhaps a little sarcastically, Kureishi published this comment:

> The writers I prefer, the ones I grew up with, are the wild ones, the demented ones, the rude ones who don't give a damn. I can give some names and will present a mere handful: Shakespeare, Dostoevsky, Plath, Rhys, Celine, Burroughs, Miller, Baldwin.

Kureishi's opinion is that it must be part of the writer's job to be offensive, or even blaspheme, to shock and turn the world upside down. Art – he continues –

> should not be safe or complacent; it should frighten, alarm and make us want to throw the book across the room. I don't want to live in an atmosphere of fear and inhibition where writers are afraid of expressing their true selves for fear of offending someone or other.[1]

1 "Hanif Kureishi (@Hanifkureishi) / X: 21 mag 2023," https://hanifkureishi.substack.com/p/rude.

DOI: 10.4324/9781003589426-5

These reflections by Kureishi, whether they can be shared or not, raise a series of important questions concerning the relationship between law and aesthetics. More specifically, these reflections by Kureishi raise the issue of censorship, or self-censorship, to which artists may be led for moral, political, or social reasons. It is well-known that the relationship between aesthetics and law may be conflicting or can be the source of social, moral, and political conflicts. While works of art may be opportunities to experience beauty, they can at the same time display elements or content that, morally or legally, people consider unfair for some reasons. If, for example, we consider racism morally and legally wrong, we could be upset by a work of art (a painting, a literary work, a performance, a theatrical representation) containing elements of racism. This is true for every possible form of injustice and for every depiction of what, in some respect, we consider to be an example of injustice.

Again, I argue that to fully understand the problems related to the 'conflict' between the aesthetic and legal dimensions, it is necessary to hold together a rational approach to aesthetics and one centred on *aesthesis*. In other words, moral criticism of aesthetics can concern the analysis of production and contents of works of literature, theatre, painting, or sculpture, trying to formulating both aesthetic and moral judgements on these aesthetic objects; at the same time, it is also possible and necessary to focus on *aesthesis*. In other words, it is necessary to consider how these objects affect people, and how people feel, see, hear, and experience these aesthetic objects: it is necessary to understand what perceptions arise in sentient bodies because of their experience.

Different aspects of such a complicated interweaving of aesthetic analysis and *aesthesis* come to the fore. Aesthetics can serve as emblem of socio-political goals that, from an external point of view, we consider unjust, harmful, unworthy, and so on. If, as we have said, art can be used to display a socio-political ideal, it is not surprising that it can also be used for political and legal ideals or ideologies that we consider unacceptable (as, for example, racist, colonialist, sexist, etc.). When art is used for political goals, and when works of art embody specific political values, these works are fatally exposed to a judgement that is no longer merely aesthetic but is inevitably a reflection on these same ends. The first problem, then, is to understand whether and to what extent art, which embodies political ideologies, is and should be immune to the judgements we can make on the political and moral level, about these political and legal dimensions. Generally speaking, we tend to separate these planes and to distinguish the aesthetic value of a work from the political and legal context for which it was created, and thus we tend to consider beauty as an independent value, separated from the moral, legal, or political content that a specific work was intended to celebrate. But this approach, as we will see, do not take *aesthesis* into consideration: the rational analysis of contents and ideals displayed is only one side of the coin, and the consideration of feelings, fears, anxieties aroused by that work remains on the background.

It is also possible that the contents of a work, while not being directly celebratory of a political vision or regime, are nevertheless deemed as offensive by many or some people, due to modes, forms, and content they consider unfair. This is the case most directly considered by Kureishi: if artists intentionally (or unintentionally) offend and awaken consciences, through words and images and modes, what is the legal relevance of these offences? On the one hand, it might be necessary for artists to depict what the mainstream culture considers unacceptable or offensive; on the other hand, the perceptions of sensate bodies are intrinsic to the experience of art: to what extent, then, do these offences not deserve consideration by social institutions and law?

Censorship, and its limitations, is only one aspect of the problem. The question, more in general, concerns the social attitude towards what we can call the *unjust beauty*, and what should be the legal translation of such attitude. Of course, we can introduce laborious distinctions, and specify that that work, that painting, that piece, does not (any longer) represent the sensibilities and values of those who display and enjoy them. This is what the Warner Bros. does, *si parva licet*, when it reminds us before a Tom and Jerry cartoon that "These animated shorts are products of their time. Some of them may depict some of the ethnic and racial prejudices that were commonplace in American society".[2] However, I argue that while this is a legitimate answer, it only considers the rational and conceptual side of the coin: this answer acknowledges the distance between the values or modes displayed by the work of art, and the values accepted by the political community at stake. It does affirm the distance, from a conceptual point of view. At the same time, it ignores the fact that these works, these expressions of beauty, are for some people seriously insulting and offensive, so much so to create pain, discomfort, anxiety, or other seriously negative emotions. If we do not take *aesthesis* into consideration, we simply refuse to place ourselves on the side of the victims, and ignore the suffering that certain words and images can still cause, just because deep down they do not affect us.

Art and morality: distinct and inseparable

It is not easy to disentangle the multiple dimensions that unite ethics and aesthetics and to distinguish, set boundaries, and separate the points of view from which it is legitimate to evaluate beauty, its content and its expressions. This problem is not new, indeed, and many reasonable answers have been given. Therefore, I consider useful to start from Thomas Aquinas, to give order to the many perspectives from which to address this issue. Not because the Aquinas was the first to address the issue: he takes up Aristotle's distinctions and observations on the point. But because he was the first to give a

2 https://www.warnerbros.com/tv/tom-and-jerry-1965-volume-4.

systematic answer, that is, to set the stage and address all the possible questions and sub-questions related to this problem. And of course, he did all this with a precision and depth of analysis that, even if one does not agree with all his conclusions, is truly impressive.[3]

Now, precisely in an effort to put things in order, St Thomas moves from Aristotle's distinction between acting and doing[4] to make it clear from the outset that aesthetics cannot be reduced to ethics, or vice versa. In short, he argues that any claim to confuse art and morality, to overlap them, to use the same categories and principles for both, is undue. Art and morality must be kept distinct because they belong to two different domains: art concerns the 'doing', is *recta ratio factibilium*, and its purpose is representing something; ethics concerns the *recta ratio agibilium*, and its objective is all human activity, not only a particular purpose.[5]

It is not just a question of level, a distinction between more general and more particular issues. It is a matter of recognising that art and ethics have different goals, and that these goals – to direct human life, on the one hand, and to depict something – are not reducible to one another. Therefore, St Thomas continues, even if we use the same term and the same category (that of goodness) to refer to the artist and the human being who acts, we are aiming at different things. We can say that someone is a good artist, and we can say that someone is a good person, but in the first case, we value the artist as an artist (*Artifex in quantum artifex*), in the second case the artist as a person (*Artifex in quantum homo*). Conversely, we can accuse someone of being a bad artist, that is, someone who commits a kind of artistic sin – sadly, countless movies, books, paintings, and songs are real sins, aesthetic monstrosities that continually bother our lives – or we can accuse him or her of being a bad person, without the first and second accusations being in any way intertwined.[6]

After this basic distinction, Thomas Aquinas proceeds by distinguishing three different levels on which the question of the relationship between the aesthetic and the moral good can be examined. These levels are not only plausible but are actually present in many confusing discussions concerning art, the moral value or disvalue of certain artworks, and so on. With great lucidity, then, Thomas holds that the question can be posed from the point of view of the subject who works (the artist), from the point of view of the object (the work), and the point of view of the action, that is, the activity by which the work is created.

3 Francesco Olgiati, "S. Tommaso e l'autonomia dell'arte," *Rivista di Filosofia Neo-Scolastica* 25, no. 4–5 (1933): 450–56.
4 Aristotle, *Nicomachean Ethics*, 1140 a, 2–5.
5 Thomas Aquinas, *Summa Theologiae*, I, q. 39, a. 8.
6 Unde ex primo peccato culpatur artifex in quantum artifex; sed ex secundo culpatur homo, in quantum homo: *Summa Theol.*, I-II, q. 21, a. 2, ad 2).

The first aspect is perhaps the easiest, and one whose solution directly depends on the basic distinction stated earlier. And it is an aspect on which there is (apparently) little debate, and a broad consensus. In other words, from the first point of view, we must distinguish the moral quality of the artist as a person from the evaluation of his or her work.[7] Our interest lies in the artist's creation of something beautiful, not in his or her being a good person. Despite some famous discussions, for example, regarding the anti-Semitism of Wilhelm Furtwängler, or of Céline, or concerning Heidegger and Schmitt, the moral evaluation of the person has no bearing on his/her work.

The second aspect is far more complex. The question is whether, and to what extent, the judgement concerning the artist's will and intention affects the evaluation of the work. From an ethical point of view, according to some, as we will see, this is not only possible but necessary: following Aristotle, when we evaluate the action performed by a subject, we also evaluate the intention with which that action was performed, the moral quality of the will as well as of the action itself.[8] According to St. Thomas, on the contrary, if this attitude is plausible in the moral sphere, it cannot be accepted in art, and it makes no sense. It does not make sense (*non pertinet*) to evaluate a work by asking what the subjective intention with which it was made is: aesthetics does only concern the "what" and the "how", not the "why".[9] Consequently, not only can art and ethics diverge but they can also conflict: art may well convey immoral content, according to the Aquinas, and notwithstanding this morally negative content, it may still deserve appreciation on an aesthetic level. Artistic value is about the *forma,* and the artist can therefore represent everything, even what is morally unworthy and merits appreciation on an aesthetic level as long as it is expressed perfectly, achieving the *splendor formae*[10] within the work.

The third profile relates to artistic activity per se, that is, the reasons why artists do what they do. Even in this case, St. Thomas argues, we must not confuse the *intrinsic* aim of art (the representation of something according to a criterion of formal perfection) and the *extrinsic* objective, which can certainly vary and be, in many respects, praiseworthy or despicable. Let us think, to give an example, of 'state art' or, in general, of all politically oriented artistic production aimed at glorifying a regime, a ruler, a certain worldview, an ideology, and so on. In all these cases, the judgement on the artist's reasons and motivations is placed on an extrinsic level, which, however relevant,

7 Ad artem non requiritur artifex bene operetur, sed quod bonum opus faciat (I-II, q. 57, a. 5, ad 1)

8 For an analysis of the relevance of intentions in Aristotle's ethics, see Anthony W. Price, "Choice and Action in Aristotle," *Phronesis* 61, no. 4 (2016): 435–62.

9 Non pertinet ad laudem artificis, in quantum artifex est, qua voluntate opus faciat, sed quale sit opus quod facit: *Summa Theol*, I-II, q. 57, a. 3.

10 Olgiati, "S. Tommaso e l'autonomia dell'arte," 452.

cannot be confused with the intrinsic judgement on the value of the work. Often, in literature, Leni Riefenstahl's 1935 documentary – *The Triumph of the Will* – is mentioned as a typical case study. Of course, on an extrinsic level, it is a propaganda film, a glorification of the nazi regime and the role of Germany as a great European power, and Hitler as the creator of that glory and inspirer of the German people: on this level, the artist's aims can be politically or morally judged. On an intrinsic level, however, the aims are different and can be traced back to the documentary depiction, which is aesthetically appreciable (according to the parameter of *splendor formae*), of the Nuremberg rally of the National Socialist German Workers' Party, held from 4 to 10 September 1934, and Adolf Hitler's speeches given on this occasion.

However, this distinction should not be interpreted as a radical separation. For St. Thomas, these three aspects are connected to each other. As Manderson rightly notes,[11] in Aquinas' thought beauty is that which the apprehension itself (*apprehensio ipsa*) pleases: accordingly, beauty does not involve a mere conceptual understanding or observation, or a passive nor a purely epistemic attitude, for it involves an *apprehensio*, a tension toward distance and an attempt to bridge it. Between the work of art on the one hand and the performer or observer on the other, there is a synthesis, in which the work has been truly grasped and remade, and in which the distinction between creator and user blurs. If this is so, these three levels must be considered jointly, and a focus on both aesthetics and *aesthesis* is necessary.

Moralism, aestheticism, and other ways of judging art

Thomas Aquinas does not dismiss the question of the relationship between ethics and aesthetics as irrelevant: these dimensions are distinct but not separate, because in human experience (the experience of embodied observers), the relationship between morality and art is very close. Artists are certainly not their work, but they express in their work their ideas and values. And so, according to Thomas, if the criteria of beauty are independent of that of morality, it is also true that the artist – like every human being – must be guided by ethics even when working as an artist. He or she who sculpts, paints, and narrates does not merely produce simple forms, but aims at affecting people as observers, interacting with them.

On a purely theoretical level, the form of a work might be distinguished from its content, but we can hardly do so on an existential level: a work of art moves, exalts, or urges us in some way, always *also* through the content it proposes, from which it can never be completely detached. This is why, according to a perspective that Thomas takes from Aristotle, a work that

11 Desmond Manderson, *Songs without Music: Aesthetic Dimensions of Law and Justice*, vol. 7 (University of California Press, 2000), 15.

represents something morally negative may be appreciable in terms of form, but since form and content are inseparably united, it ends up acquiring an immoral physiognomy. All the more so when, as is the case with propaganda or politically oriented art, its purpose is precisely that of soliciting adherence to values and ideals that – morally speaking – we may consider despicable. When an artwork becomes an opportunity for evil, an incentive to sin, an exaltation of morally negative values and ideas, writes St Thomas, it ends up being itself negative, at least from this point of view, even if it remains appreciable on a formal level. So much to justify, Aquinas continues, prohibitions and censures, precisely in order to avoid this solicitation to evil that the work would bring with it.[12]

Now, leaving aside, for a moment, the question of censorship – to which we will return – the perspective of Thomas Aquinas is an example of ethicism, an approach that considers moral judgement as pertinent to art, at least in terms of content. Ethicism, however, has different degrees: it can be moderate, like that of Thomas Aquinas, or it can be a form of strong moralism.[13] Strong moralism, for example, is typical of Tolstoy, who, after his conversion, abandoned the idea that the artist should only represent life without schemes and ideologies and became convinced that art should promote specific feelings and values: "the evolution of feelings takes place by means of art, replacing lower feelings, less kind and less needed for the good of humanity, by kinder feelings, more needed for that good. This is the purpose of art".[14] Examples, in his eyes, are works such as Friedrich Schiller's *The Masnadiers*, Victor Hugo's *Les Misérables*, Charles Dickens's novels, Harriet Beecher Stowe's *Uncle Tom's Cabin*, all works in which truth and positive feelings are conveyed by words. For radical moralism, art is not only judged by moral criteria but must also have a moral and pedagogical orientation: art must be a vehicle of love for one's neighbour, and it must – in practice – translate the precepts of morality into forms and feelings, that is, into forces capable of moving the soul of the work's user.[15] This is the reason why, for many readers, appreciating the Marquis de Sade's *Juliette* is highly difficult: however beautiful from a literary point of view, it is a novel that requires us to respond with admiration to a rape, a violent sexual intercourse against someone's will, something most people hold to be unequivocally wrong.

Radical moralism differs from moderate ethicism only in its extent, that is, concerning the limits within which moral judgement in the aesthetic realm

12 *Summa Theol.*, II-II, q. 169, a. 2, ad 4.

13 Matthew Kieran, "Art and Morality," in *The Oxford Handbook of Aesthetics*, ed. Jerrold Levinson (Oxford University Press, 2003), 451–70.

14 Lev Tolstoy, *What is Art?*, trans. Richard Pevear and Larissa Volokhonsky (Penguin, 1897/1995), 123.

15 Noël Carroll, "Art, Narrative, and Moral Understanding," in *Aesthetics and Ethics: Essays at the Intersection*, ed. Jerrold Levinson (Cambridge University Press, 1998), 126–60.

is legitimate. However, the basic assumption of these positions is the same: the content cannot be separated (in part, or at all) from the form, and the appreciation of a work is never only formal: it is always also relative to the feelings and passions that it arouses, and to the ideas and values it represents.[16] This is an idea that we find in Hume, in a well-known passage of the essay *On the Standard of Taste*: it is quite possible, Hume writes, that a work of art contains speculative errors, and certainly this does not detract from the aesthetic value of the work itself and its enjoyment. Quite different, according to Hume, is the case of works containing morally problematic elements, because it is much more difficult for the readers to disregard them and detach themselves from their own values and moral horizon.[17] In the same vein, we can certainly try not to consider the racist or sexist contents of a work, but this will require a considerable effort on our part, and a certain 'suspension' of judgement, because the more these contents clash with our convictions, the more difficult it will be for us to consider them irrelevant in the enjoyment of the work itself. And this depends on the fact that if, on a purely conceptual level, we can distinguish our moral convictions from the evaluation of the aesthetic qualities of a work, on the level of our affective and felt reality as sensate subject, we cannot make this separation: the work of art affects us; its force relates to the conditions of our sensory perception, besides our values or ideas.

At the opposite extreme, pure or radical aestheticism claims the autonomy of aesthetic judgement and the irrelevance of moral criteria in aesthetics. For some, aesthetic judgement must be limited to an internal assessment of the aesthetic qualities of the work, avoiding any reference to the moral characteristics or qualities of what is represented.[18] A proper consideration of people's sensory life (affects and aversions, how the world affects the body and is rooted in the body), the somatic and affective level, besides the conceptual level, fades away: here, the aesthetic assessment of art, and the rational

16 See, for example, Noël Carroll, "Moderate Moralism," *The British Journal of Aesthetics* 36, no. 3 (1996): 224; Mary Devereaux, "Beauty and Evil: The Case of Leni Riefenstahl's Triumph of the Will," in *Aesthetics and Ethics: Essays at the Intersection*, ed. Jerrold Levinson (Cambridge University Press, 1998); George Dickie, "The Myth of the Aesthetic Attitude," in *Aesthetics: A Critical Anthology*, ed. George Dickie, Richard Sclafani, and Ronald Roblin (St. Martin Press, 1989); Marcia Eaton, *Merit, Aesthetic and Ethical* (Oxford University Press, 2001); Berys Gaut, "The Ethical Criticism of art," in *Aesthetics and Ethics: Essays at the Intersection*, ed. Jerrold Levinson (Cambridge University Press, 1998); Matthew Kieran, "Art, Imagination, and the Cultivation of Morals," *Journal of Aesthetics and Art Criticism* 54 (1996): 337–51.

17 "They confound the sentiments of morality and alter the natural boundaries of vice and virtue. They are therefore eternal blemishes": David Hume, "Of the Standard of Taste," in *The Philosophy of Art: Readings Ancient and Modern*, eds. Alex Neill and Aaron Ridley (McGraw-Hill, 1995), 247.

18 Richard Posner, "Against Ethical Criticism," *Philosophy and Literature* 21 (1997): 1–27.

consideration of moral values, obliterates the relevance of aesthesis. A statement in the preface to *The Portrait of Dorian Gray* is often quoted in this regard: "There is no such thing as a moral or an immoral book. Books are well written or badly written. That is all".[19] Art, from this perspective, only admits an aesthetic judgement; it can only be discussed in aesthetic terms. Everything else, from its utility to its morality, is irrelevant. Pure aestheticism refuses to assign purposes to art other than art itself: art serves itself, and therefore there can be no external criterion for judging it, be it political, moral, economic, or religious. The content of the work, from this point of view, is indifferent, at least insofar as one wants to use it as a reference to judge the work's merit. It does not mean that art has no content; it just means that the content interests us only from an aesthetic point of view, and must rationally be distinguished from other aspects.

Even then, there is a more moderate version of this position, which is legitimate when the artist himself brings to the forefront the political meaning and the moral values represented in the work. It is very difficult, for example, to look at Picasso's *Guernica* without considering what it represents, without considering the political and moral significance of the work itself. Of course, one can appreciate its formal qualities and compositional choices, but the content – the judgement on the bombings, the war, Francoism, and the faults of the German and Italian air forces – inevitably comes to the fore, and it is very difficult to disregard it. Similarly, we cannot overlook the moral and political issues when we attend a performance of a Greek tragedy, because the author himself generally addressed his audience assuming an ethical and political reading of the work, and not simply an aesthetic appreciation.[20] As Carroll correctly writes, they "possess an ethical dimension, not adventitiously but constitutively".[21] Or, again, we cannot pretend that Ensor's or Grosz's expressionism did not presuppose a very strong political and moral critique of the society of their time, and we can hardly disregard an analysis of these profiles to understand and fully appreciate their work.

Moderate autonomism recognises that substantive issues that are related to the content of the work, and the resulting political or moral judgements, are legitimate, at least in many cases.[22] Artwork can be the place for representing and expressing ideas, values, principles, political and moral statements, and the judgement on these is certainly possible. However – here is the difference with moralism – such a work does not cease to be beautiful,

19 "The only excuse for making a useless thing is that one admires it intensely. All art is quite useless' (Oscar Wilde, *'Preface,' The Picture of Dorian Gray* (Penguin, 1982), 5.
20 Noël Carroll, "Art and Ethical Criticism. An Overview of Recent Directions of Research," *Ethics* 110, no. 2 (2000): 351 ff.
21 Carroll, "Art and Ethical Criticism," 357.
22 James C. Anderson and Jeffrey Dean, "Moderate Autonomism," *The British Journal of Aesthetics* 38, no. 2 (1998): 150–66.

or aesthetically appreciable, because of its moral merits or flaws. The moral limitations of a work are never reflected in its aesthetic value:[23] aesthetics and ethics remain separate domains, and people's perceptions and feelings, affections and aversions, as well as how a work of art strikes the observer's sensate body, are not seriously considered.

I argue that moderate moralism is an approach that can hold together a rational consideration of beauty and art, and the recognition that visual elements and sensations affect observers as sentient beings. This approach, precisely because it holds both of these aspects together, can be fruitfully used to understand the intertwining of ethics and aesthetics.

In *The Rape of Europa* (1560–62), Titian depicts the abduction of the young princess by Jupiter, with a swirling movement of waves, bodies, and winds, in one of the most famous paintings by this extraordinary artist. Yet, according to some, Titian would have 'eroticised' the rape: the event would be depicted in such a way as to give the idea of pleasure as a consequence of the violence imposed.[24] If we compare the painting with other depictions of the same subject, this observation is not so peregrine, even if inaccurate. Rembrandt, in fact, almost a century later, depicted Europa far more frightened and restless than Titian did, even though the incriminated painting depicts the abduction, not the rape (which instead takes place later, with Jupiter changed into an eagle). According to some, all these elements would convey the morally unacceptable idea that women, even if forced and victims of violence, can enjoy the abuse perpetrated against them, and that therefore their resistance is only apparent, at least sometimes.[25] At the same time, even assuming that this accusation is well-founded, Titian is Titian, and the painting can still be considered marvellous from an aesthetic point of view, even by those who blame him on a moral level: the most pertinent plane for appreciating art (or, at least, a large number of artworks) is completely independent of the moral or political one.[26]

I argue that both of these perspectives are correct, but partial. Both, while reaching opposite conclusions, evaluate Titian's painting exclusively from a conceptual point of view, either to consider its aesthetic value abstractly, or to highlight, equally abstractly, the idea of womanhood and sexuality that it portrays. Both the things are true. It is possible to argue that Europa's painting is beautiful, aesthetically speaking, as well as that it carries unacceptable patterns and values. However, the question remains as to how this painting affects the viewer, how it interacts with the perceptions of embodied

23 Carroll, "Moderate Moralism," 232.

24 Anne W. Eaton, "Where Ethics and Aesthetics Meet: Titian's Rape of Europa," *Hypatia* 18, no. 4 (2003): 159–88; Jane Nash, *Veiled Images: Titian's Mythological Paintings for Philip II* (Associated University Press, 1985).

25 Eaton, "Where Ethics and Aesthetics Meet," 162.

26 Carroll, "Art and Ethical Criticism," 374.

observers. If we place ourselves in this perspective, we can give more prominence to the position of those who argue that this painting arouses pain, discomfort, offence, without dismissing it as abstractly moralistic or nonsensical. At the same time, it is possible that people differently situated bodily or emotionally may find nothing bothersome or offensive in Titian's painting, being able to isolate its formal and compositional aspects. In any case, a position of moderate moralism allows these two approaches to be held together, without dismissing any of them as irrelevant.

Judging, passing down, educating

This necessary consideration of both aesthetics and *aesthesis*, that is, the relevance of both conceptual and perceptual approaches, the rational appreciation of art and the sense perception of subjects living in a social space, is useful to understand a further question: the social and educational value of aesthetic objects.

We already discussed how the *kalòn*, what is beautiful, noble, and admirable, not only arouses our appreciation but in some way motivates the person to virtuous actions. Beauty sharpens our gaze: it trains us to look at things with attention and care and to turn our gaze to find other beauty to contemplate and protect.[27] This is one of the reasons for the protection of cultural heritage: we protect our artistic heritage and the beauty that comes from the past because this heritage is deemed crucial for the human and spiritual progress of future generations. The idea of *traditio*, which we analysed in a previous chapter, is deeply entangled with this educational goal. The fact is, that if beauty has crucial political and moral value, and contributes to the moral growth of the individual and the social and political development of a community, the idea that the aesthetic and moral value of an artwork can be intertwined seems very reasonable. However, only by considering the relevance of both the rational appreciation of art and sense perception of subjects living in a social space this question can be appropriately discussed.

Martha Nussbaum[28] tries to go down this path to justify moderate ethicism. Indeed, Nussbaum believes that, at least as far as novels are concerned, we only find aesthetically pleasing those works that treat human beings as such, and not only as animals or objects. And this is a moral quality, such that in a novel "aesthetic interest and moral interest are not altogether unrelated".[29] According to Nussbaum, our relationship with literature and with the characters is also emotional: through their stories, and our emotional

27 Elaine Scarry, *On Beauty and Being Just* (Princeton University Press, 1999), 43–45, 65 ff.

28 Martha C. Nussbaum, "Exactly and Responsibly: A Defense of Ethical Criticism," *Philosophy and Literature* 22, no. 2 (1998): 343–65.

29 Nussbaum, "Exactly and Responsibly," 357.

involvement, we develop our moral sense. Literature offers us the possibility of better perceiving the dignity of others: art (especially fiction) directs our attention to specific situations, contexts, and people, and allows us to enter imaginatively into the stories and experiences of other individuals whose lives are narrated to us. It allows us, in other words, to develop the capacity to put ourselves in the other person's perspective, which is empathy, the capacity to *intuarsi* and *inmiarsi* (literally: to enter into you and me, reciprocally) that Dante mentions in Canto IX of Paradise[30] – that is the basis for our moral development and action.

There is, however, one aspect that ethicism – even that of Nussbaum – seems to overlook. Art and beauty can certainly contribute to the elaboration of a moral thought, or a political conscience, but they can do so by representing different models of real life, different perspectives, even from a negative point of view. Therefore, art can offer the opportunity to judge these models, which means comparing them and learning from them, but it also means criticising them, mocking them, appreciating them, and so on. Certain works of art may be morally negative or ambiguous since they represent ideals and social models that we today consider reprehensible in many respects; at the same time, these aesthetic objects can be praiseworthy precisely because they lead us to explore the meaning of our moral convictions, to verify how solid these convictions are, and they stimulate us to reflect on what we would otherwise take for granted.[31] Admitting the legitimacy of a moral judgement on art does not mean denying value to works that propose morally questionable content, even in the perspective of moral and social development: aesthetic objects and artefacts can play a positive social role even when they represent something we condemn or despise. The moral significance of art does not lie in its ability to persuade us to choose a particular lifestyle or ethical ideal that we consider better than others. Rather, it lies in affecting our senses as much as stimulating our reflection, moving and disgusting us and at the same time proposing concepts and ideas. This is why they can remind us that some moral choices are urgent but painful, that some circumstances call for an ethical or political stance, that some of these choices are complex and humanly demanding, and so on.

In short, the moral value of a work may come unexpectedly, and perhaps precisely from a work's ability to undermine our convictions or force us to deepen them.[32] A work deserves our moral appreciation when it makes us

30 Dante, *Paradiso*, IX, 81.

31 Christopher Hamilton, "Art and Moral Education," in *Art and Morality*, eds. José Luis and Bermúdez Sebastian Gardner (Routledge, 2003), 37–55.

32 Matthew Kieran, "Forbidden Knowledge: The Challenge of Immoralism," in *Art and Morality*, eds. José Luis Bermúdez and Sebastian Gardner (Routledge, 2003), 56–73; see also Matthew Kieran, "Art, Morality and Ethics: On the (Im)Moral Character of Art Works and Inter-Relations to Artistic Value," *Philosophy Compass*, no. 1–2 (2006): 129–43, 134 ff.

reflect, but also when it shakes us out of our torpor; when it confronts us with the urgency of certain choices and moral dilemmas, or when it destabilises us and throws us in a state of crisis. The double track of aesthetics and *aesthesis* is always necessary, also (and perhaps even more urgently) concerning works that, from the point of view of content, we might judge to be immoral. The question of the legitimacy of moral judgement cannot be reduced to the evaluation of the narrative or visual contents of a work: whether the contents are good or bad, positive or negative, is one thing; whether they produce certain consequences, or give the impetus for certain decisions or actions, is another.

The fact that the character of Michael Corleone, in *The Godfather*, is morally negative, as negative is the whole code of honour and value system of the mafia, obviously takes nothing away from the aesthetic value of Francis Ford Coppola's film. Above all, the negative judgement on the mafia and its ethical horizon does not exclude that those contents, Corleone's character, and the way of representing him, provide the opportunity for morally relevant reflections and evaluations, as well as for reflections elaborated from the distance between the theoretical and the existential level. We can certainly feel sympathy for Michael Corleone, or Hannibal Lecter, or find them fascinating in any case, just as we can admire Achilles, even when – or notwithstanding his tying the body of defeated Hector to his chariot and dragging it around the walls of Troy. And we can do so because the fictional context of artwork allows us to engage in an imaginative activity which in real life we would consider immoral, without sharing its contents. There is an aesthetic distance between us and what the work portrays, and we can derive pleasure from works that we consider morally problematic. On the contrary, we can get from the enjoyment of these works some morally positive indications, since such works can drive us to deepen our understanding of the values at stake.[33] We can read *Lolita*, and sympathise or otherwise empathise with Hubert, without approving of a sexual relationship between an adult man and a 12-year-old girl. On the contrary, the fictional horizon allows us to explore – better than the chronicle of an actual event would – the complexity of the moral issues at stake, the narrowness of ideological judgements, the difficulty in defining the concepts of autonomy and consent, and so on.

Offensive beauty

The necessity of this double track is even more urgent concerning those contents and works that some people consider to be not merely objectionable, but plainly offensive. Certain aesthetic objects, notoriously, can be deemed to be harmful or offensive to dignity and/or discriminatory: here, the question no longer concerns a moral judgement, but a possible harm resulting from

33 Kieran, "Art, Morality and Ethics," 136.

the work, even irrespective of the artist's intentions or the object of the representation. Where this happens, the problem ceases to be exclusively theoretical and becomes fully social and legal, and concerns the balance between the freedom of expression and other fundamental rights.

However, if one approaches this problem from an exclusively epistemological perspective, some important aspects are not captured: I argue that taking subjective perceptions into account, and focusing on *aesthesis*, can help us understand these issues, and foster reasonable solutions. In other words, it is possible – and quite common – to discuss whether and to what extent moral and political judgements are legitimate when referring to aesthetic objects or performances, or to what extent these objects or performances are consistent with the respect for human rights and freedoms that are protected by national and international laws. However, both of these questions are placed on a theoretical level, that is, merely concerning the rational understanding of specific aesthetic objects, a rational assessment and balancing of rights, and a rational assessment of any harm. Such analyses do not adequately consider the other side of the coin: namely, as we have said, that aesthetics is not only about a rational appreciation of art and a definition of beauty, but also (as *aesthesis*) about sensate perceptions, and people's immersion in a social space that is affected by what takes root in the gaze. For this reason, I argue it is necessary to take into account not only a rational balancing of rights, but also people's emotions, sensations, affections, and aversions. It seems to me that, from this perspective, Feinberg's principle of offence may be a good way to legally translate this approach.

A few examples can help illustrate this diversity of plans and the need to take both approaches into account. For instance, we can think of the difference between our enjoyment of a painting by Caravaggio, a sculpture by Benvenuto Cellini, the aforementioned *Triumph of the Will*, and a work by Gauguin. In the first two cases, we are dealing with works produced by artists who, in their lives, committed morally reprehensible crimes and actions (murder, violence, rape), which are in no way reflected in their works. I can enjoy Cellini's *Perseus* in Florence without being concerned about, as he himself recalls in *Vita* (his autobiography), his existence being marked by crimes and violence.[34] When Oscar Wilde read the *Vita* of Cellini, he dubbed him the 'supreme rogue' of the Renaissance, whose existence is united by the splendour of his artistic triumphs and the shame of his boasting, his misogyny, and the crimes he committed. Cellini was notorious in the Victorian age for being the only Italian Renaissance artist tried and convicted for committing repeated acts of sodomy with Fernando, a young man working as

34 Benvenuto Cellini, *Vita* (Bur, 2014).

an apprentice in his workshop in Florence.[35] But even today, reading his autobiography from a different moral horizon, we cannot fail to be struck by the nonchalance with which he writes about murders and violence, thefts and brawls, and even the rape of his maid-lover Caterina (whom he calls the *"ribaldella puttana"* or *"iscellerata puttanella"*, ribald and infamous whore), who had denounced him for sodomy, also in revenge for being fired. In short, a life that may perhaps fascinate like a novel, but which is certainly marked by morally questionable actions. And yet, moral judgement on these aspects (although possible) is completely irrelevant to the understanding and appreciation of his work, which makes him one of the greatest artists of the Italian Renaissance.

In the case of Riefenstahl's film, as has been said, we are faced with a work whose very content, and the manifest intention of the author, is aimed at glorifying the nazi regime. It is possible, also here, albeit with more difficulty compared to the previously cited case, to keep the two aspects separate, and appreciate the documentary on an aesthetic level and for its cinematic technique, and we can at the same time despise the exaltation of Hitler as the charismatic leader of the German people, or the rhetoric of strength and power that is imbued into every scene. In short, we can distinguish (following Aquinas) the extrinsic purpose of the film, that is, the glorification of the regime and Hitlerism, from the intrinsic purpose of the work as a documentary, that is, the narration through images of parades, speeches, and audiences, and consequently differentiate judgements and levels of enjoyment. In other words, although here the work is imbued with morally problematic aspects and issues, the distinction of levels is quite straightforward, so much so that each may be completely indifferent to the other.

The case of Gauguin is much more nuanced. It is nuanced because the artist's private morality is not at stake, nor can it be said that his works explicitly and consciously convey a political or moral message, or that they explicitly represent models and values that we might disapprove of. In short, the problem with Gauguin's works does not lie in the fact that he abandoned his wife and children to go to Tahiti to paint, nor in the fact that in Tahiti he had relations with 13-year-old girls and infected them with syphilis, that he used them as sexual objects before he used them as models, nor even in the compositional choices and themes of his works. The problem raised by Gauguin's works, and not by chance the subject of repeated debates[36] at exhibitions and museums, lies in the fact that the women against whom these actions were committed are precisely those, or many of those, portrayed in

35 Margaret Gallucci, *Benvenuto Cellini: Sexuality, Masculinity, and Artistic Identity in Renaissance Italy* (Springer, 2016).

36 Rod Edmond, ed., *Representing the South Pacific: Colonial Discourse from Cook to Gauguin* (Cambridge University Press, 1997).

his paintings. And it lies above all in the fact that these actions are not simply the consequence of a personal choice: rather, they are the expression of a colonial culture that treats non-Western populations as objects of conquest, as free territories for the action and predation of the Western white man, and the women of such countries as sexual objects devoid of will and dignity.[37] A painting by Caravaggio has no bearing on the violence committed by its author; it does not represent it, it does not make it relevant, and it does not need to be interpreted in the light of Michelangelo Merisi's lifestyle and personal choices. Conversely, even if Gauguin's art does not celebrate a colonialist and patriarchal cultural model, it cannot be fully understood without also considering this aspect. That such paintings are, and remain, marvellous does not detract from the relevance of this issue: in particular, it does not detract from the fact that for some people, even today, Gauguin's art may be felt as offensive, not because it celebrates a political and cultural system whose negative effects are still alive and relevant today, but because viewers are struck – and may legitimately feel unease and resentment – by the seemingly innocent depiction of victims of sexual abuses and colonial exploitation.[38]

This leap forward, whereby a work is not only objectionable on a moral or political level but can be deemed offensive precisely because of the content it represents, shifts the question from the theoretical level to the experience of people, and how they are affected by some works. It is not a question of whether and how we can use moral and political criteria to judge a work, nor what relevance such judgements have to the more general understanding of the work itself. It is a question of what response to give to people who feel offended by such works: and since these works are generally exposed to public enjoyment, if not even publicly celebrated and proposed as formative content and common heritage, the question of the offence becomes an equally public question, both legally and politically.

However, it is well-known that the concept of offence is extremely elusive (far more so than that of harm). We know that we can be offended if someone does not greet us, of course, but no one would ever consider this unpleasant feeling of neglect or rudeness as something legally or politically relevant. This is because the concept of offence is very broad, and denotes different actions, on different planes, and with different levels of intensity.[39] Additionally, we can use it to denote an action (the act of insulting, for instance), as well as

37 Erich Hatala Matthes, *Drawing the Line: What to Do with the Work of Immoral Artists from Museums to the Movies* (Oxford University Press, 2021), 72.

38 Norma Broude, ed., *Gauguin's Challenge: New Perspectives After Postmodernism* (USA: Bloomsbury Publishing, 2018); Elizabeth C. Childs, "Taking Back Teha'amana: Feminist Interventions in Gauguin's Legacy," in *Gauguin's Challenge: New Perspectives After Postmodernism* (USA: Bloomsbury Publishing, 2018), 229.

39 Larry Alexander, "Harm, Offense, and Morality," *Canadian Journal of Law & Jurisprudence* 7, no. 2 (1994): 199–216.

the result of this action (the feeling that follows the action). Also, we can use the term 'offence' to denote an action that is morally reprehensible, legally relevant, politically negative, and so on: we deem offensive whatever disgusts us, for example, but we use the same concept in criminal law with different meanings. It denotes the person who is the holder of a legal right that is protected by the criminal legislation which has been breached by an act that constitutes an offence under national law (the *offended* party), as well as a specific action that is legally relevant (the insult, the action, or expression that damages the dignity of another person, undermining their reputation or their self-esteem). Each of these offences produces different consequences: sometimes only reprobation, sometimes social stigmatisation, and, in the most serious cases, a criminal sanction. However, as Young correctly states, if one is physically injured, robbed, or cheated, one is harmed (independently from his or her state of mind), while if this person is offended, one *feels* some emotions he or she dislikes: disgust, outrage, upset, concern, or else.[40]

Joel Feinberg is one of the scholars who has most and best explored the problem of what an offence is, how it can be distinguished from harm, and with what consequences.[41] In his theory, Feinberg tries to expand the area of what deserves to be the object of prevention, beyond mere harm;[42] the principle of harm places indeed the threshold of what is legally relevant very high, excluding those negative actions towards others, which do not cause any harm in a narrow sense: offences. Offences lie, for Feinberg, within this intermediate territory, in which the action produces a negative effect (the offence), but no harm; and yet the effect of the action is negative and unpleasant enough to justify a demand for protection, even at the cost of restricting the freedom of others.[43]

40 James O. Young, "Profound Offense and Cultural Appropriation," *The Journal of Aesthetics and Art Criticism* 63, no. 2 (2005): 135–46.

41 Joel Feinberg, *The Moral Limits of the Criminal Law, Vol. II: Offense to Others* (Oxford University Press, 1984–1988).

42 Feinberg first tries to provide a better definition of the so-called *harm* principle, which from J. S. Mill onwards constitutes one of the fundamental paradigms of liberal culture. In Mill's formulation (*On Liberty*, reprint in J. S. Mill, *Utilitarianism, On Liberty and Considerations on Representative Government* (Dent, 1993)) this principle states that the only reason why individual liberty can be legitimately limited is to prevent harm to others ('the only purpose for which power can be rightfully exercised over any member of a civilised community, against his will, is to prevent harm to others': Mill, *On Liberty*, ch. 1, par. 9). Many authors have considered this principle to be excessively vague: what is harm, how can it be prevented, and who are the recipients of these acceptable limitations? (Arthur Ripstein, "Beyond the Harm Principle," *Philosophy & Public Affairs* 34, no. 3 (2006): 215–45).

43 There are [some] experiences that are harmless in themselves yet so unpleasant that we can rightly demand legal protection from them even at the cost of other persons' liberties': Feinberg, *Offense to Others*, 10.

In what sense, then, does an offence produce a sufficiently negative or unpleasant result? And when is that result negative enough to justify a restriction of freedom? Many activities produce negative or unpleasant feelings in us, ranging from disgust to embarrassment, from anxiety to frustration, from humiliation to fear. Such feelings may be motivated by intentional deeds or performances that affect our moral convictions, religious values, and feelings of love for our country, but they may also depend on how they affect people's belonging to ethnic groups, their gender identities, or sexual orientations, as well as other factors people perceive to be relevant to their dignity and identity. What is legally puzzling is that these feelings, affections, and emotions are legitimate but also highly subjective, insofar as the same actions may be highly offensive to some people, and irrelevant to others, if not downright amusing (think, for instance, of the *Charlie Hebdo* cartoons, highly offensive to many, and amusing or ironic to others).[44]

The offence principle, in short, is a slippery criterion: Feinberg's attempt, therefore, is to provide a definition that is sufficiently precise to be used in a court, thereby answering the demand for justice that the harm principle leaves unaddressed. In this sense, writes Feinberg, offence does not always have the same value, nor does it always have a *legal* value: there are offences to which we must respond in other ways, or which we must tolerate, not being serious enough to justify a limitation of the freedom of others (to speak, to write, to paint, to sing, and, through these means of expression, to offend).[45]

The offence, according to Feinberg, becomes more or less relevant due to a number of factors: first of all, its extent, that is, the intensity and duration of the feeling of repugnance aroused, and the extent to which this repugnance could have been foreseen by the perpetrator of the offending action. In addition to this, the ease with which people who disapprove of the content of the offending action can avoid such activities is also relevant: it is not the same thing if an anti-Islamic satiric cartoon is drawn on posters put up around town, or if it is published in a newspaper that I may not buy or read. Finally, it is also relevant whether or not the offended person has voluntarily taken the risk of being offended (for example, by going to an exhibition where works that he/she finds offensive are displayed).[46] At the same time, it is necessary to consider – taking the side of the offender – the social utility of the action performed (e.g. whether the offence is conveyed by means of a newspaper article, by works exhibited at an art exhibition, or whether it is an advertisement for a pair of shoes), and the availability of alternatives of

44 Brian Trench, "Charlie Hebdo, Islamophobia and Freedoms of the Press," *Studies: An Irish Quarterly Review* 105, no. 418 (2016): 183–91.

45 Robert Amdur, "Harm, Offence, and the Limits of Liberty," *Harvard Law Review* 98, no. 8 (1985): 1946–59.

46 Feinberg, *Offense to Others*, 26.

time and place that may reduce the degree of offensiveness (a particularly contested work may be exhibited on the street in front of a museum, but it could also be exhibited inside the museum itself). Finally, the intention of the perpetrator is also relevant, as well as the general context in which the action takes place (an anti-Christian satire show has a different offensiveness in Paris compared to a small and very pious community).

Within this framework, some practices, expressions, or artworks can cause significant offence, whose effects are not strong enough to limit the freedom of others. This is the case of works or performances that offend religious symbols, or display abused and degraded bodies: these aesthetic acts do not produce a direct offence, at least to the extent to which people are not directly and necessarily exposed to the offending message. Since people may look away, ignore the action, or not listen to it, these are offences that Feinberg qualifies as relating merely to the knowledge of the action:[47] they are offences that do not produce an actual victim but are outrageous to people's moral sensibilities. I can choose whether or not to visit Serrano's exhibition in which the *Piss Christ* (a photograph of a crucifix immersed in the artist's urine) is on display, even if my moral sensibility as a Christian could be offended by the mere knowledge of such an exhibition. The intensity of these offences, for Feinberg, is not serious enough to justify any restrictions to the freedom of others: for example, Serrano's freedom to exhibit his work.

In other cases, on the other hand, offences are so profound and so intense, or so intensely perceived by some subjects, as to make the restriction of others' freedom justifiable.[48] These are those offences that Feinberg calls performative utterances, that is, all those manifestations of thought that – in fact – are the verbal or visual equivalent of a punch in the face. They are expressions that, because of the context in which they are uttered or acted upon, the persons to whom they are addressed, and the intentions of the person acting or speaking, become harassment, and deserve to be restricted by law, or even sanctioned.[49] In short, the intensity depends on the specific circumstances of the offending action, not on an abstract consideration of the content of the work: it is not the same thing, to take up the previous example, exhibiting the *Piss Christ* in a museum (where those who do not want to see it may choose not to enter) or to use Serrano's photograph as the symbolic image of the municipality's initiatives for Christmas. Similarly, if an aesthetic act or fact is perceived as being offensive by a minority, or a particularly vulnerable group, the consideration of feelings, anxieties, or fears perceived by

47 Feinberg relates them to the "bare knowledge": Feinberg, *Offense to Others*, 60.

48 John Gardner, "Hart and Feinberg on Responsibility," in *The Legacy of H. L. A. Hart: Legal, Political, and Moral Philosophy*, eds. Matthew H. Kramer et al. (Oxford, 2008; online ed., Oxford Academic, January 1, 2009).

49 Amdur, "Harm, Offense, and the Limits of Liberty," 1954.

people belonging to it should be more intense. An offence against people with disabilities, a religious minority, or an ethnic group with a history of discrimination and marginalisation (the Roma or Sinti, for example) is certainly more serious and less tolerable than an offence that offends the moral sensibilities of the majority, or of a social group with no specific vulnerable traits.

What is a vulnerable group, or a particularly vulnerable group, is itself not an easy question and, consequently, a much debated one.[50] In the perspective of this analysis, it suffices to say that even in the absence of an all-encompassing definition of a vulnerable group, the European Court of Human Rights has developed a substantial case law based on a casuistic assessment of the conditions of vulnerability that are experienced by different groups of people.[51] Accordingly, the Court recognised conditions of vulnerability either through an inductive approach, whereby specific circumstances are considered indicative of a condition of vulnerability common to a group or category of people, or through a deductive approach, whereby specific categories of people are in principle recognised as vulnerable, and therefore deserving of specific and higher standards of protection by public institutions. Therefore, while vulnerability is an intrinsic trait of human beings, the Court recognises that the modalities and characteristics of vulnerability may vary considerably due to the individual membership of a certain group, or specific conditions of vulnerability that are common to other people: the Roma, persons with mental disabilities, asylum seekers, persons with HIV are examples of particularly vulnerable groups by virtue of the specific difficulties they are faced with. This is because, as the Court stated for example about the Roma minority,[52] social, political, and legal factors make this group, in itself, particularly vulnerable, and consequently the individuals belonging to it.

Particularly vulnerable groups, in other words, have a special need for protection, due to specific circumstances and factors affecting their life. This is the reason why, when vulnerable people or groups are at stake, it is necessary to proceed with contextual analysis, to consider all the elements that define the framework within which this offence takes place. It is necessary to

50 Fabio Macioce, *The Politics of Vulnerable Groups: Implications for Philosophy, Law, and Political Theory* (Springer Nature, 2022); Fabio Macioce, "The Enabling Value of Group Vulnerability," *Contemporary Political Theory* 22, no. 2 (2023): 209–29.

51 Samantha Besson, "La vulnérabilité et la structure des droits de l'homme. L'exemple de la jurisprudence de la Cour européenne des droits de l'homme," in *La vulnérabilité par les juges en Europe*, ed. L. Burgorgue-Larsen (Éditions Pedone, 2014), 59–85.

52 *D. H. and others v the Czech Republic (GC)*, App. no. 57325/00; see also *Chapman v the United Kingdom*, App. no. 27238/95, no. 181: "the vulnerable position of Roma/Gypsies means that special consideration should be given to their needs and their different lifestyle both in the relevant regulatory framework and in reaching decisions in particular cases". For a comment see Ivona Truscan, "Considerations of Vulnerability: From Principles to Action in the Case Law of the European Court of Human Rights," *Retfærd: Nordic Journal of Law and Justice* 142, no. 3 (2013): 64–83.

assess the intensity of the offence, that is, how severely the artwork affects people. It is also necessary to consider the place and time of the performance and the possibility of evading contact with it. Finally, if people offended by that specific artistic form or representation belong to a particularly vulnerable group, the level of protection afforded them must be higher than the standard, and restrictions imposed on the freedom of others may be justifiable, that would not be legitimate in other cases. In all other cases, even if the offence to one's feelings and moral or religious convictions may be unpleasant, it is not sufficient to justify a compression of a fundamental right, or the freedom to exhibit and enjoy works of art.

Aesthetics in the public sphere: when offence becomes public

The relevance of both approaches, and the need to take into consideration both the rational and conceptual plane, and that of perceptions and sensations, is even more evident when entering public space. This is because certain aesthetic dimensions of public space are, on the one hand, intentionally oriented to communicate a message, to convey values and ideals, to represent a certain idea of power. On the other, they affect the gaze, arouse feelings, and shape the space in which subjects act, feel, and live.

Memorials and monument, for instance, are public emblems of a community's collective memory.[53] They serve to honour, celebrate, and shape the public space, as well as to mark public space through the affirmation of that memory, and of the values it expresses: as Matthews and Wall write, "Sovereignty has to be staged", thereby signalling a division between ruler and ruled, or giving substance to notions such as people and community.[54] It is not by chance that iconoclastic and destructive actions against monuments always follow the fall of a regime, the very regime that previously stages itself through those monuments. For, indeed, if statues are made to remain, the collective memory they are meant to celebrate tends to change, fatally, over time. The permanence of bronze, or marble, which is used precisely to overcome the impermanence of human life, is contradicted by historical change, changing regimes, different ways of thinking, and interpreting community ties over the years: when the sociocultural landscape changes, it leads to a different evaluation of the narratives these monuments encapsulate.[55]

53 Peter Goodrich, *Legal Emblems and the Art of Law: Obiter Depicta as the Vision of Governance* (Cambridge University Press, 2014).

54 Illan Wall and Daniel Matthews, "Sovereignty and the Persistence of the Aesthetic," *The Modern Law Review* 87, no. 6 (2024): 1399.

55 Joseph Leo Koerner, "On monuments," *Res: Anthropology and Aesthetics* 67, no. 1 (2017): 5–20.

Not always do monuments catch the eye, becoming part of the urban furniture, like fountains, trees, and all the other objects of use or decoration that are in our cities, and they attract indifferent gazes. Robert Musil noted this a century ago when he wrote: "Monuments possess all sorts of qualities. The most important is somewhat contradictory: what strikes one most about monuments is that one doesn't notice them. There is nothing in the world as invisible as monuments".[56] However, monuments and memorials have a specific political and/or moral intentionality. They are instruments for the shaping of public space, which are erected to celebrate someone or something, and thus, to build a collective memory in the present and for the future.

Tearing down a monument, therefore, has this purpose: it serves to challenge, or deny, the permanence of this political intentionality. What that monument stood for and its significance no longer has any value or must even be disowned today. With an expression that is not entirely correct, such actions are often referred to as examples of a *damnatio memoriae*, showing that the practice of pulling down monuments or effigies was already present in imperial Rome.[57] In fact, as has been correctly noted,[58] *damnatio* is a label we use today to indicate a set of practices, even very different ones, aimed at depriving the memory of some individual or family of the public praise of their essence and standing (*substantia et dignitas*):[59] these measures could range from the elimination of images (on statues, but also friezes and coins), to the deletion of the name on inscriptions, to the destruction of a house, to the prohibition for family members to perpetuate the name of the person. After Caligula's death, the busts and statues that portrayed him were first disfigured and then thrown into the Tiber,[60] in a gesture that was itself despicable, because it was reminiscent of that intended for the corpses of criminals or slaves who died in the arena. Or, in a less iconoclastic logic, some statues were re-configured, and their features modified so that they could be converted into the depiction of other subjects (Augustus, for instance) whose memory still deserved to be preserved.[61] As the Polish poet Stanislaw Lec said, "When smashing monuments, save the pedestals – they always come in handy".[62]

56 Robert Musil, "Monuments," in *Selected Writings*, ed. and trans. B. Pike (New York: Continuum, 1986), 320.
57 Valérie Huet, "Images et" damnatio memoriae," *Cahiers du Centre Gustave Glotz* (2004): 237–53.
58 Edoardo Bianchi, "Il senato e la "damnatio memoriae" da Caligola a Domiziano," *Politica Antica* 1 (2014): 33–54.
59 D. 11.7.2.6; 35.1.27.
60 Harriet I. Flower, *The Art of Forgetting. Disgrace and Oblivion in Roman Political Culture* (Chapel Hill, 2006), 152.
61 Bianchi, *Il senato e la "damnatio memoriae*, 35.
62 Stanislaw Jerzy Lec, *Unkempt thoughts*, trans. Jacek Gałązka and Clifton Fadiman (Minerva Press, 1962).

Every revolution, therefore, produces rubble, not only as remnants of the struggle but precisely as the negation of a past that deserves to be destroyed as much politically as physically.[63] And if that past has been enshrined in a stone, that stone must be destroyed and removed. The statues of the kings of Judea beheaded during the French Revolution, and now on display at the Museum of Cluny, bear witness to precisely this: it is not enough to behead the king in the flesh (Louis XVI), and his court, one must behead every effigy of royalty, even if they are the statues displayed on the façade of Notre Dame, and if they are kings of a distant past.

Three positions generally crystallise on these issues. On the one hand, some are in favour of preserving 'contested' monuments at all costs, in the name of a historical perspective: the past cannot be denied or erased, even in the traces it has left in the urban fabric, in toponyms, in the conformation of places. The transmission of memory, even the memory of errors, is what can prevent such errors from being repeated.[64] Removing a monument is both illusory and dangerous, because it conveys the idea that the past can be hidden or erased and deprives the community of the opportunity to remember and learn from its mistakes. Those who believe that contested monuments should or can be removed, on the contrary, are motivated by the idea that monuments are a means of conveying political messages. When these messages are wrong or appear to be at odds with the community's reference values in the present, they should be removed precisely to publicly and politically affirm the seriousness of an error that is not to be repeated in the future.[65] One can indeed learn from past mistakes, but there are many ways to do this, and it is certainly not necessary to use monuments that hurt and offend a part of the community for this purpose.[66]

Finally, an intermediate position, which in my opinion is very reasonable, is argued by those who believe that contested monuments should be re-signified, or re-contextualised. By intervening with explanatory plaques, or additions and modifications, monuments can at the same time be left in their context without conveying a politically negative or offensive meaning. A monument can, if modified, dishonour a person or a political ideology; it can be altered, in short, in such a way as to allow people to remain in contact

63 Aleida Assmann, "(In) Visible Monuments. What Makes Monuments Controversial?" in *Contested Urban Spaces: Monuments, Traces, and Decentered Memories*, eds. U. Capdepón and S. Dornhof (Springer, 2022), 23–44.

64 Jeffrey Blustein, *Forgiveness and Remembrance* (Oxford University Press, 2014); Avishai Margalit, *The Ethics of Memory* (Harvard University Press, 2009).

65 Johannes Schulz, "Must Rhodes Fall? The Significance of Commemoration in the Struggle for Relations of Respect," *Journal of Political Philosophy* 27, no. 2 (2019): 166–86.

66 Travis Timmerman, "A Case for Removing Confederate Monuments," in *Ethics Left and Right: The Moral Issues that Divide Us*, ed. B. Fisher (Oxford University Press, 2020), 513–22.

with the past that the monument was intended to celebrate, but by changing its meaning, its symbolic and performative significance.[67]

In my opinion, the second and third perspectives are applicable in all cases involving memorials, those monuments that are purely or mainly commemorative. These are monuments less problematic from our standpoint since they are works that have a prevalent political significance: they are political speech acts.[68] We can think of the statue of General Lee in Virginia, strongly contested by those who feel offended by the celebration of a 'hero' of the Confederate and slaveholding states, especially in the context of the Black Lives Matter movement.[69] From a similar perspective, we might consider the cancellation of any reference to Peter Stuyvesant in New York City (naming of streets and gardens, statues) because of his anti-Semitism. Again, we can consider the statue of Roosevelt placed in front of the Museum of Natural History, depicting the president on horseback, flanked by a Native American and an Afro-descendant: the statue is offensive as expressive of patriarchal values, an idea of white supremacism, and colonialism, on the one hand, but the depiction of some ethnic groups or communities as inferior to others, and subjugated, is an experience that can generate anxiety, despondency, sadness, or anger, on the other.[70] The examples could be multiplied. In all these cases, as has been said, we are faced with works that can be contested on a theoretical level, as celebrating values or political projects people despise, as well as offensive on a perceptual level.

If a community no longer recognises itself in a *traditio*, or even finds the contents of that *traditio* offensive, there is no reason to preserve it; even when the community is internally divided. Indeed, the very fact that a community is divided on the value to be accorded to actions of the past, and that part of the community does not recognise itself in them or finds the celebrations of that past insulting, is a good reason to say that there is no *traditio* worth preserving. On that past, in short, precisely because it is divisive, the community can no longer build its future. In such cases, therefore, the choice (and it seems to me that this is really a matter of political decision) is between removal and re-signification, depending on what in that specific context is deemed most suitable to heal the offence caused by the monument.

67 Dan Demetriou and Ajume Wingo, "The Ethics of Racist Monuments," in *Palgrave Handbook of Philosophy and Public Policy*, ed. D. Boonin (Palgrave, 2018), 341–55.

68 Geoffrey Scarre, "How Memorials Speak to Us," in *Philosophical Perspectives on Ruins, Monuments, and Memorials*, eds. J. Bicknell, J. Judkins, and C. Korsmeyer (Routledge, 2019), 21–33.

69 Dave Beech and Mel Jordan, "Toppling Statues, Affective Publics and the Lessons of the Black Lives Matter Movement," *Art & the Public Sphere* 10, no. 1 (2021): 3–15.

70 Arianne Shahvisi, "Colonial Monuments as Slurring Speech Acts," *Journal of Philosophy of Education* 55, no. 3 (2021): 453–68.

In Italy and Germany, the question of contested monuments is particularly complex, relating to the monumental and architectural legacy of the fascist and nazi regimes. Even more thorny is – today – the problem in Italy, because most of German buildings or monuments, such as the Braunes Haus, the national headquarters of the nazi party in Munich, or the Neue Reichskanzlei and the Führerbunker in the ministerial gardens in Berlin, were seriously damaged by Allied bombing, and then demolished and removed immediately after the war. Hitler's own body was burnt and buried (and then – perhaps – exhumed and thrown into a river). In Italy, on the contrary, the architectural and monumental memory of the fascist regime is more present and cumbersome, so that Mussolini's body, which was buried in Predappio, still attracts small (but growing) crowds of nostalgics.

It is not just a question of numbers and quantity. The problem underlying discussions of fascist monuments in Italy stems from the difficult reconciliation between the recognition of the formal value of fascist-era architecture and monuments (often splendid examples of Italian modernism and rationalism), and their necessary interpretation as expression and celebration of the regime's politics. Architectural beauty and celebration of violence and racist colonialism coexist in a way that is truly impossible to deny. Of course, not all the works of the fascist period are politically qualified. If we take one of the symbols of Piacentini's monumentalism, the so-called Square Colosseum in Rome (the Palace of Italian Civilisation and Labour), we can certainly perceive the links with the regime, either in the reference to the Roman empire, or in the quotation of Mussolini carved on the façade ("un popolo di poeti di artisti di eroi di santi di pensatori di scienziati di navigatori di trasmigratori": a people of poets, artists, heroes, saints, thinkers, scientists, navigators, aviators), but these links are not explicit, or less obvious, or such as to represent a limited offence to the contemporary conscience. Thus, in the same way, we can praise the Sapienza University Campus, the Museum of Roman Civilisation, the FAO building, and many others, without the values they intended to exalt being explicit and immediately offensive.

Other works, on the contrary, convey an inextricable union between formal beauty and political violence: two very significant examples are the Foro Italico in Rome or the Casa Littoria (now the building hosts financial offices) in Bolzano. It is not possible, for anyone passing through the Foro Italico (to go to the Olympic stadium, for example), not to see the great obelisk that dominates the area, an enormous monolith of Carrara marble 18 metres high, with the inscription 'Mussolini Dux' engraved on the front. And it is impossible not to notice, in what is one of the busiest areas of Rome, the bas-reliefs, the inscriptions, and the mosaics, celebrating the colonial and war exploits of the fascist regime. A similar problem is raised by the Casa Littoria in Bolzano, on the front of which stands an enormous bas-relief by Hans Piffrader (57 panels by 36 metres in length) depicting Mussolini on horseback, in the act of the Roman salute, and illustrating the 'triumph of fascism'.

In cases like these, I am convinced that Feinberg's principle of offence does apply: the effect of the artistic action is negative and unpleasant enough to justify a demand for protection. Both the Foro Italico and the Casa Littoria in Bolzano are performative actions, political speech acts that celebrate the regime, as well as its military and political actions. Therefore, they are messages that Italian people cannot but reject (at least, if they want to be faithful to those values that the Constitution has sanctioned as fundamental for Italian republican identity). This does not mean, however, removing or destroying those monuments. It is possible to reconcile the protection of beauty and artistic heritage with the protection of people from offences they find intolerable. In Bolzano, for example, the provincial administration entrusted the artists Arnold Holzknecht and Michele Bernardi to re-signify the monument, under the supervision of a technical commission. Thus, in contrast to the exaltation of the glories of Fascism and the phrase "Believe, obey, fight" on the bas-relief, a luminous inscription was placed in the centre of the frieze, with a quotation from Hannah Arendt translated into three languages: "No one has the right to obey",[71] as well as a series of explanatory panels to guide the public in understanding the intervention.

Interventions of this kind, in my opinion, are very appreciable, and suitable to respond to the offence. Without denying the past, such interventions make the events and personalities of that past understandable to the observer. They make explicit the contrast between the values promoted by the artwork and those that we consider to be the foundations of the identity of the political community. At the same time, such interventions preserve beauty and make it still enjoyable, because they separate the extrinsic aspect of the work (the glorification of fascism) from its intrinsic value as an artwork. Finally, they are interventions by which a community actively reflects on its past, and comes to terms with it: the fact that they are promoted by the local administration, that are entrusted to artists, and carried out in conjunction with commissions of experts ensures that the political value of the intervention on the work is retained alongside the artistic and historical value.

71 "Kein Mensch hat das Recht zu gehorchen": Hannah Arendt quoting Kant in a famous radio interview on the Eichmann trial, aired on November 9, 1964, in Südwestrundfunk (SWR). A full transcript is published in Hannah Arendt, "Hannah Arendt im Gespräch mit Joachim Fest. Eine Rundfunksendung aus dem Jahr 1964," *HannahArendt.Net* 3, no. 1 (2007), https://doi.org/10.57773/hanet.v3i1.114.

Chapter 6

The dark side of beauty

Ugliness and beauty: the inseparable opponents

The relationship between aesthetics and law, as well as the aesthetics of law, is often understood, implicitly, in a positive sense. Often, in other words, when discussing the aesthetics of law, there is a tendency to interpret this issue in a positive sense, and to put the issue of beauty centre stage. Whether it is the beauty of law, or the protection of cultural and artistic heritage, or the difficult legal definition of art, aesthetics tends to take on a positive meaning.

However, ugliness is also present in the legal dimension, and over the centuries legal systems provided answers to the multiple questions it raised: as we will see, these answers have often taken the tones of exclusion and marginalisation. The relationship between law and ugliness, in short, is less inspirational and uplifting than the one with beauty: it is a relationship where law demonstrates – with some exceptions, of course – its violent and exclusionary side.

Over-simplistic interpretations, again, are to be avoided. The legal relevance of such negative aesthetics[1] cannot be interpreted as a mirror image of issues related to beauty: and this is because, first of all, it is not possible to draw a clear-cut separation between beauty and ugliness, between positive and negative aesthetics. Of course, the understanding of beauty as order and justice may correspond to a concept of ugliness as a source of disorder and injustice, and law undoubtedly should tend towards one and reject the other. Against what Hugo said in the preface to Cromwell, according to which 'Le beau n'a qu'un type; le laid en a mille', the reduction of beauty to formal symmetry and fullest harmony is a simplification. Beauty, as much as ugliness, is a detail of a complex set that escapes the beholder and constantly shows new and incomplete aspects. Both ugliness and beauty are multiple and varied, and they cannot be understood as an inverted image of the other. In Hegel, the forms of ugliness constitute a wide range of figures that reveal cowardice

1 William S. Allen, *Aesthetics of Negativity: Blanchot, Adorno, and Autonomy* (Fordham University Press, 2016).

DOI: 10.4324/9781003589426-6

and vulgarity and refer to the hybrid, the terrible, death, illness, and fear, but also a whole world of negativity and pain that cannot be redeemed on the level of art, removed, or transfigured.[2] Accordingly, and starting from a Hegelian perspective, Karl Rosenkranz noted that the ugly has a value *per se*: it serves to enhance the sense and understanding of beauty. Within its analysis of the forms of the ugliness, Rosenkranz distinguishes between the absence of form (amorphousness, asymmetry, disharmony), incorrectness, disfigurement, and deformity; however, ugliness is never the negative correlate of beauty, but a moment of an inevitable dialectic. The beauty, without the need to confront ugliness and overcome it, becomes intolerably boring, "as long as it remains at the level of sheer correctness and does not make it to a means of soulful manifestation".[3] Ugliness transgresses measure, distinction, and harmony, but by denying these dimensions it allows beauty to fully reassert them.

The fact that ugliness cannot be reduced to the opposite of beauty has already been argued by Plato,[4] where the question of ugliness and beauty is examined from an ontological point of view. According to Plato, beauty has an ontological consistency; it 'is' in the proper sense. Ugliness does not, it is not, there is no idea of Ugliness in the Realm of Ideas. This could be interpreted as a mirror-like situation (Beauty 'is', Ugliness 'is not'), but this is not so, or at least not entirely: both the beauty and ugliness we observe in the world exist, as shadows, and as expressions within the physical world of the Realm of Ideas. Therefore, ugliness, which is not, does exist, not only as a degradation of something beautiful.[5] Similarly, Aristotle draws a complex picture, by pointing out that the beautiful and the ugly can also coexist: when we represent something ugly in a proper and good manner, for example. In this sense, Homer's verses describing the ugliness of Thersites are beautiful, even though their object and purpose is the description of ugliness.[6] Since classical thought, beauty and ugliness are not mere alternatives so that when one is there, the other is missing: they can coexist, both in the same thing (which can manifest imperfect beauty) and in the representations of things themselves.

This coexistence of beauty and ugliness is even more evident within Christianity. On the one hand, the understanding of reality as the fruit of creation could not but accentuate the Platonic model, whereby everything that 'is'

2 Gabriele Scaramuzza, *Il brutto nell'arte* (Il Tripode, 1995), 64.
3 Karl Rosenkranz, *Aesthetics of Ugliness. A Critical Edition*, trans. Andrei Pop and Mechtild Widrich (Bloomsbury Academic, 2015), 90.
4 Umberto Eco, *Storia della bruttezza* (Bompiani, 2018), 19 ff.
5 Plato, *Parmenides*, 130 c-d.
6 Aristotle, *Poetics*, 1448b: What happens in human experience proves this, for we enjoy looking at accurate likenesses of things which are themselves painful to see, obscene beasts, for instance, and corpses. (cfr. *Aristotle: In 23 Volumes*, trans. W. H. Fyfe (Harvard University Press, 1933).

displays in itself the idea of beauty: in Christian theology, the idea of the *pankalìa* (the beauty of the whole creation) is a necessary consequence of the idea of a divine creation out of love, and therefore of creation as an expression of the divine *lògos*, order, and justice. Of course, reality has been corrupted by the original sin, but not so much so that its beauty can be denied: even if we observe something ugly, we perceive it as a corruption of a previous good. And therefore, however ugly the reality may be, insofar as it exists it always allows us to refer, at least as a reference, to a dimension of beauty.[7]

Even what is obscure possesses some light, Augustine would say, and even things that appear disordered and degraded to us are so ordered in the universe of nature, that to those wisely considering, they have their turns not unbecomingly.[8] Even monsters, or what we consider monstrous, acquire from this perspective a certain undeniable beauty: since everything comes from God, and everything was created by God's love, we can and must find some beauty in everything. We are the ones who fail to grasp the beauty in what appears ugly to us, but this depends on the partiality of our perspective, on our inability to see it. If something were simply and utterly ugly, it would not even exist.[9] Everything that exists has been created according to the divine plan, everything has its place within it, and however degraded or disordered a thing may be, it will still be worthy of consideration and appreciation, at least a little.[10] As Eco rightly argues,[11] even the devil, whom Christian tradition and Western iconography always tend to depict as hideous (and he necessarily is, being the archetype of the fall and degradation with respect to God's creation), cannot be entirely and only ugly. If Dante's devil has bat wings, weeps out of six eyes, and drools over three chins,[12] Milton's Satan

7 Francis J. Caponi, "Beauty, Justice, and Damnation in Thomas Aquinas," *Pro ecclesia* 19, no. 4 (2010): 396.

8 Augustine, *De Natura Boni Contra Manichaeos Liber Unus*, 16: "Quae tamen etiam privationes rerum sic ordinantur in universitate naturae, ut sapienter considerantibus non indecenter vices suas habeant".

9 Augustine, *De Natura Boni*, 17 "Non ergo mala est, in quantum natura est, ulla natura; sed cuique naturae non est malum nisi minui bono. Quod si minuendo absumeretur, sicut nullum bonum, ita nulla natura relinqueretur".

10 In *De civitate Dei*, St Augustine writes that since God has created all beings, He knows where and when each thing ought to be, or to have been created, because He sees the similarities and diversities which can contribute to the beauty of the whole. But He who cannot see the whole is offended by the deformity of the part, because he is blind to that which balances it, and to which it belongs (Deus enim creator est omnium, qui ubi et quando creari quid oporteat vel oportuerit, ipse novit, sciens universitatis pulchritudinem quarum partium vel similitudine vel diversitate contexat. Sed qui totum inspicere non potest, tamquam deformitate partis offenditur, quoniam cui congruat et quo referatur ignorant).

11 Eco, *Storia della bruttezza*, 179 ff.

12 Dante, *Inferno*, XXXIV, 54–55.

retains an undeniable pride, and Goethe's Mephistopheles is nevertheless an elegant and respectable gentleman.[13]

Probably, the place where the coexistence of beauty and ugliness is most evident, in Christian culture, is the person of Christ. The scourged and crucified Christ is, at the same time, ugly (in his flagellated and wounded body) and beautiful (because of the splendour of the salvation he attains through his death). Grünewald's crucifix for the altar in Isenheim, just to mention one of the most atrocious representations of Christ's *wounded suffering*, covered in sores and twisted by pain, can only be understood in this light. He is Isaiah's Man of Sorrows: "He had no majestic bearing to catch our eye, no beauty to draw us to him. He was spurned and avoided by men, a man of suffering, knowing pain, Like one from whom you turn your face".[14] Christ is the one who is mocked and humiliated (think also of Beato Angelico's *The Mocking of Christ*, where Jesus is spat on by one of his persecutors), but he is also the one who guides and saves human beings: indeed, it is precisely those wounds and sores which procure our salvation, and it is therefore through those horrible wounds that the beauty of the glory and promise of salvation is expressed.

Much of the Christian tradition confirms this inextricable union between beauty and suffering, or between the ugliness of wounds and sores, and the beauty of faith and salvation. Mantegna's Saint Sebastian, and that even more sexualised by de Ribera in the Capodimonte Museum, are a stunning visual testimony to this. But it is the very perspective of *vanitas vanitatum*, from Qoèlet onwards, that shows the inner corruption of all earthly beauty, and unites the death and decay of the flesh with the beauty and happiness of mundane life: from the terrifying crypt of the Capuchin friars in Palermo to Bruegel's *Triumph of Death*, Christian aesthetics continually mixes the macabre and the beautiful, the horror of death and suffering with the exaltation of creation.

As this horizon of faith fades, the realms of ugliness and beauty begin to separate. What is ugly, at most, can be interesting (so it is in Swift, who describes monsters and deformities without any anguish, but also without any openness to the beauty of creation that might be concealed in them), or fascinating, but it does not seem in any way intertwined with what is beautiful. From the Renaissance onwards, thanks to the discoveries of new lands and new peoples, the category of the portentous seems to replace that of the monstrous, and ugliness gives way to the *curiositas*.[15] The gaze towards ugliness is that of the scientist: and it is certainly a less fearful, less horrified gaze, but it is also detached: it is a gaze that does not care to grasp the little

13 Eco, *Storia della bruttezza*, 182.
14 Isaiah 53:2–3.
15 Eco, *Storia della bruttezza*, 241.

bit of beauty that every creature must necessarily display. The exhibition of the monstrous also begins in this era, with profound cultural and social consequences, contributing to the exclusion of ugliness from the social context. As the object of curiosity, deformity becomes interesting, exciting, and exhibited as strangeness or absurdity. As the object of experiments, it is, precisely, objectified.

However, if the Renaissance tends to exalt this distinction by emphasising a cognitive and rational approach to aesthetics, Romanticism will go in an opposite direction. The category of the sublime takes centre stage: Vico had already used the sublime to mark the limit of the empirical against Descartes' rational enlightenment, thereby embracing the obscurity of history and human vicissitudes. The disembodied Cartesian reason is unable to capture the complexity of human existence, while the wondrous and the astonishing enable "the perception of an alterity transcending one's state."[16]

The category of the *Sublime* shifts the focus from the object of the gaze (which can be ugly, horrendous, terrible) to the effects it produces on the beholder, the impact of the hideous, and the formless on the beholder. Schopenhauer writes that our inadequacy, our struggle with nature, and our broken will are made manifest when we look at a stormy sea, at the clouds that bring the hurricane, or at the waves that beat impetuously on the cliff.[17] The Sublime does express at the same time our limitations and our moral greatness, the infinite and the finite, and the individual and the universal: its effect lies precisely in the shaking, in the upheaval of the beholder's soul. The sublime once again opens up space for an aesthetic (and not only scientific) contemplation of ugliness: Burke, in his *Enquiry into the Origin of our Ideas of the Sublime and Beautiful*,[18] links the idea of terror and horror to the concept of the sublime, and begins to propose the idea of the sublime as a category distinct, but not opposed, to that of beauty and ugliness. Kant, in the *Critique of the Power of Judgment*, will move in a not-too-different direction. Here the sublime (das Erhabene) is not reduced to an emotion or psychological impact on the onlooker, but becomes a critical feeling: it means experiencing what shakes the ordinary exercise of our capacities. While the beauty is connected to the ideas of limitation and form, the sublime refers to those of limitlessness and formlessness.[19] The sublime arouses the feeling of

16 Giuseppe Mazzotta, *The New Map of the World: The Poetic Philosophy of Giambattista Vico* (Princeton University Press, 2014), 105.

17 Arthur Schopenhauer, *The World as will and Representation* (Courier Corporation, 2012), III, 39.

18 Edmund Burke, *A Philosophical Enquiry into the Origin of Our Ideas of the Sublime and Beautiful* (Columbia University Press, 1958).

19 Serena Feloj, *Il sublime nel pensiero di Kant* (Morcelliana, 2012); Daniela Angelucci, "From the Sublime to the Monstrous. Two Interpretations of Kant," *Con-textos Kantianos: International Journal of Philosophy* 15 (2022): 287–96.

simultaneous attraction and repulsion, astonishment and respect, and attests to the capacity of reason to understand such greatness and power even starting from the human condition of limitation and weakness. As Sequeri rightly points out, the ambivalence of the sublime within the realm of the symbolic prompts the orientation of the "surplus and power" of the *affective* toward transcendence.[20]

The interest in the category of sublime sheds light on the effects that the contact with infinite produces on sensate bodies: when the reason and its claim to certainty, totality, and systematic knowledge fail, the sublime points to that which exceeds representation.[21] To a certain extent, the sublime drives from aesthetics to *aesthesis*. As Sherwin notes, the sublime puts us "in touch" (by virtue of our embodied nature) with that which is other than mind: or, with Lévinas' words, that which is otherwise than being.[22] This is something worth noting: the category of the sublime, in other words, puts the importance of *aesthesis* on centre stage: and this is particularly relevant to our analysis of the relationship between law and ugliness, as we shall see. Just as the theme of the sublime foregrounds the perspective of embodied subjects, the problem of the legal relevance of ugliness cannot be understood by adopting a merely aesthetic approach, but requires considering, at the same time, the relevance of *aesthesis*.

The identification of beauty with whatever is orderly, pacified, measured, and proportionate is a classical theme, as well as the opposite tendency to equate what is ugly with what is (rationally understood as) disordered, conflicting, inordinate, deformed, lacking in proportion, and inappropriate. However, how emotions and feelings shape social relationships is equally important in this perspective. Feelings of outrage, revulsion, as well as fears and emotions such as disgust, revulsion, and horror have often been used to exclude and marginalise, or otherwise reinforce exclusionary tendencies of nonconforming individuals and groups.[23] In other words, this kind of negative *aesthesis* is crucial to understanding some policies of oppression and marginalisation, as these policies have found such negative affections to be a crucial resource and support.[24]

20 Pierangelo Sequeri, *Il sensibile e l'inatteso. Lezioni di estetica teologica* (Queriniana, 2016), 195 ff.
21 Sequeri, *Il sensibile e l'inatteso*, 126 ff.
22 Richard K. Sherwin, "Sublime Jurisprudence: On the Ethical Education of the Legal Imagination in Our Time," *Chicago-Kent Law Review* 83, no. 3 (2008): 1157–96.
23 Mary Douglas, *Purity and Danger: An Analysis of the Concepts of Pollution and Taboo* (Routledge and Kegan Paul, 1966); Julia Kristeva, *Pouvoirs de l'horreur* (Ed. du Seuil, 1980), Leon S. Roudiez, trans., *Powers of Horror: An Essay On Abjection* (Columbia University Press, 1982); Sianne Ngai, *Ugly Feelings* (Harvard University Press, 2007).
24 Tobin Siebers, *Disability Aesthetic* (University of Michigan Press, 2010), 1.

As Siebers rightly argued, ugliness can be understood as a "social location complexly embodied."[25] Ugliness is a receptacle for sociocultural feelings and attitudes, thereby producing relevant political, social, and existential consequences: when a body is labelled or understood as 'ugly', a series of social, legal, and political processes are activated explicitly or implicitly, with the goal of excluding or marginalising subjects. Processes of social and political exclusions have often used a double track, either by exploiting emotions such as fear and disgust or by translating an aesthetic of ugliness, disorder, and disproportionality into legal norms. Ugliness has been, from a legal and political perspective, a sort of receptacle for everything that did and does not correspond to the reference standard for respectability and dignity, depending on the time and place.[26] Thus, from time to time, what was considered irrational, disordered, but also merely discordant, excessive, or irregular, was construed as ugly, as well as what was deformed, marginal, excessive, and disproportionate: aesthetic and legal categories have become intertwined, thereby consolidating processes of exclusion and oppression. What cannot be reduced to a standard that is at the same time aesthetic and ethical-political is marginalised within the realm of ugliness.

At the same time, ugliness becomes a sort of political and legal threat: it ridicules and deprives of the necessary seriousness and respect, breaks harmony, undermines the social order, mocks authority and calls it into question, and confuses things and plans that are good to be separate.[27] The fact that ugliness is threatening and disruptive (or, better, that it is perceived as such), while beauty is deserving and appreciable, means that ugliness must be excluded and limited, fought against and anaesthetised. In his *Aesthetic Theory*, Adorno sees in the reference to beauty the sign of an elitist, exclusionary, and oppressive cultural attitude, precisely because of this continuous struggle against the siege of ugliness: it is the very image of beauty as a single and differentiated something arising from "the emancipation from the fear of the overpowering wholeness and undifferentiatedness of nature", and from the attempt to "making itself impervious" to the presence of the ugly.[28] The beauty, writes Adorno, establishes a sphere of untouchability, and opposition to what simply exists. Moreover, this opposition generates fear and violent responses: it produces repression, for example against the underclass, the people who bear the stigma of manual and alienated labour.

Ugliness so becomes a category of opposition (or, again, it can be perceived as such): it gains a subversive value, of contestation of an order that needs

25 Tobin Siebers, *Disability Theory* (University of Michigan Press, 2008), 14.

26 Greta Olson, *Criminals as Animals from Shakespeare to Lombroso*, vol. 8 (Walter de Gruyter, 2013).

27 Nina Athanassoglou-Kallmyer, "Ugliness," in *On the Politics of Ugliness*, eds. S. Rodrigues and E. Przybylo (Palgrave, 2018), 31.

28 Theodor W. Adorno, *Aesthetic Theory* (Athlon Press, 1997), 50 ff.

to be overthrown and revolted.[29] In *Rabelais and His World*, for example, Mikhail Bakhtin[30] uses the model of the medieval carnival and the category of the grotesque (which is one of the multiple forms of ugliness) precisely as a symbol of the rejection of dominant forces and political and cultural oppression, and as a revolt against the repressive ideology of the state by popular forces and 'low' culture. Humour, the grotesque, parody, deformation, and the disruption of harmony and form are all strategies of resistance to the norm: a norm that is both aesthetic, legal, and political, at least insofar as it conveys models of order and measure that hold and support each other. A similar idea was also argued by Marcuse, according to whom repression would stimulate images of liberation, and the creative process stimulates resistance: aesthetics is a space of freedom against propaganda and forces us to reconsider nature and culture against mainstream narratives.[31]

Accordingly, ugliness is used politically and legally as a criterion for exclusion and oppression, in a variable interweaving with other categories: gender, race, class, age, ability, sexuality, and body measurements and proportions.[32] The political mechanisms of oppression, in short, operate at the intersection of these categories and use ugliness as a strategy for exclusion, a stigma that justifies racist, ableist, or ageist policies, as well as all other forms of social and cultural marginalisation. Ugliness becomes a sign of marginalisation, as well as the justification of the necessity to exclude. Those who carry the stigma of ugliness deserve to be excluded from full social integration, the full enjoyment of the privileges (and rights) enjoyed by the elite, by people who, on the contrary, embody the aesthetic and political canon, what is beautiful, appropriate, functioning, performing, worthy, and decent. One caveat must be stressed: ugliness is a stigma, a label attached to a person or a group of people by other people, those who have the power to decide what is beautiful and worthy and what is not, what deserves to be looked at and appreciated

29 Many academic and non-academic works are devoted to the generative and oppositional potential of ugliness, highlighting its racist, sexist, and colonial trajectories or premises. Among the many, see Stefanie Snider, "On the Limitations of the Rhetoric of Beauty: Embracing Ugliness in Contemporary Fat Visual Representations," in *On the Politics of Ugliness*, eds. S. Rodrigues and E. Przybylo (Palgrave, 2018), 337 ff.; Maylee Rollins, "The Ugliness Movement: Riot Grrrl's Use of Ugliness as Feminist Subversion," *The Purdue Historian* 11, no. 1 (2023): 7.

30 Michail M. Bakhtin, *Rabelais and His World*, trans. H. Iswolsky (Indiana University Press, 1984).

31 Herbert Marcuse, *The Aesthetic Dimension* (Beacon Press, 1978); see also Carol Becker, "Herbert Marcuse and the Subversive Potential of Art," in *The Subversive Imagination: Artists, Society, and Social Responsibility*, ed. Carol Becker (Routledge, 1994), 113–29; Antonio Negri, *Art and Multitude: Nine Letters on Art, Followed by Metamorphoses: Art and Immaterial Labour*, trans. Ed Emery (Polity Press, 2012), 119–20.

32 Athanassoglou-Kallmyer, "Ugliness," 281.

and what does not.[33] In other words, ugliness and beauty are not inherent properties of persons or things: ugliness is a product of disabling social practices and injustice, and of legal choices – as we will see – about what is worthy of being seen and what is not. However, as such, ugliness also becomes the object of practices of contestation and resistance, in a dialectic between exclusion and contestation whose effects are still visible today.[34]

The process of labelling, and the consequent marginalisation of practices and persons who are labelled as 'ugly', has taken on variable forms, and variable names, from a legal point of view. However, all these forms are united by the direct or indirect legal relevance of the aesthetic dimension, in a sort of reverse kalokagathìa.[35] In other words, law takes up processes of social and cultural labelling and marginalisation, based on which certain practices or persons are deemed unsightly, and gives them a legal status, by transforming the ugly into something illegal. This is a crucial issue: what is at stake are not mere processes of criminalisation, through which we qualify as crimes some behaviours that on a moral and social level are deemed blameworthy. In these cases, the law internalises aesthetic judgements and affections, and uses them to justify policies of criminalisation, discrimination, or exclusion.

The forms of exclusion: the obscene

The semantic and sociocultural sphere of ugliness is very vast (ugliness can express itself in many different ways, as we know). However, the intertwining of aesthetic devaluation and negative sentiment of revulsion is particularly evident in the norms regulating the obscene. In fact, within the regulations that sanction or criminalise the obscene it is possible to note both a negative rational judgement, relating to concepts and values such as public morality or decency, and an emotionally negative reaction to images or behaviours that arouse aversion, scandal, resentment, or otherwise.

On a purely lexical level, what is considered obscene seriously offends the sense of decency, especially when it relates to the sphere of sexuality, and by extension it can indicate what is foul, filthy, or repugnant. In a figurative and hyperbolic sense, it can also indicate that which we consider significantly ugly, or lacking in taste, so much to constitute an offence to our aesthetic sense (and thus we say that someone dresses obscenely, or writes obscenely, etc.),[36] and what is morally wrong or disgusting according to accepted standards. Obscene, then, is whatever arouses a strong emotional reaction,

33 Howard S. Becker, *Outsiders. Studies in the Sociology of Deviance* (Free Press, 1973).

34 Ela Przybylo and Sara Rodrigues, "Introduction: On the Politics of Ugliness," in *On the Politics of Ugliness* (Palgrave, 2018), 17.

35 Ingomar Weiler, "Inverted Kalokagathia," *Slavery & Abolition: A Journal of Slave and Post-Slave Studies* 23, no. 2 (2002): 9–28.

36 Cambridge English Dictionary.

revulsion or disgust that motivates the individual and political will to exclude that same image or action from the realm of the visible. We do not want to see what disgusts us; we want it to remain hidden or not to be perceptible in any way, just as we do not want to see that which gives us a wide range of unpleasant feelings: discomfort, shame, nausea, disgust, annoyance, embarrassment, and so on.

Of particular interest – and very closely linked to the category of the obscene – is the feeling of disgust: according to some, this feeling is linked in a particular way to the idea of *contact*, and therefore to the perception of a risk of trespass between what is outside of us (and which we would like to remain outside) and our bodily sphere:[37] not by chance, it seems to be linked to the three most tactile senses, namely touch, smell, and taste, and therefore to the fear of being contaminated by what is outside of us. In this vein, it is linked to the idea of decay, disease, and death (which would explain the disgust for such natural things as excrement and corpses).[38] In any case, disgust seems to be linked to the fear of contagion: we are disgusted by what we fear may contaminate us and threatens to cross the protective boundaries we have drawn around us, physically or psychologically, threatening our physical or moral integrity.[39] And just as disgust drives us, physically, not to ingest something or get close to the source of that feeling, so we tend on a cultural and social level to exclude and distance ourselves from whatever is a source of disgust, in a collective effort to isolate and protect individuals from contagion.

However, disgust is a risky feeling, especially when it is used as a basis for regulatory and political choices. As an emotion, disgust is both difficult to rationalise and has a negative orientation: it does not push us to improve something or to operate constructively, but simply to put a safe distance between us and what disgusts us.[40] In fact, it serves to exclude, marginalise, and conceal, not to build. Indeed, it can lead to oppression and discrimination, to the marginalisation of people and groups: this happens when one human group is identified as "less human" than the others, living on a threshold between civilised society and the animal dimension. And it is precisely when certain groups are identified in this sense that they are used – by excluding them – to emphasise the dignity and value of others, namely us. The Jews, women, homosexuals, the so-called untouchables and *pariahs*, people of an inferior class, as well as those belonging to an ethnic or religious minority,

37 David Haekwon Kim, "Mortal Feelings: A Theory of Revulsion and the Intimacy of Agency" (PhD diss., Syracuse University, 2001).

38 Matthew Kieran, "On Obscenity: The Thrill and Repulsion of the Morally Prohibited," *Philosophy and Phenomenological Research* 64, no. 1 (2002): 31–55.

39 Martha C. Nussbaum, *Hiding from Humanity: Disgust, Shame, and the Law* (Princeton University Press, 2009), 93–94.

40 Nussbaum, *Hiding from Humanity*, 105.

all these groups have been imagined and marginalised as contaminating and defiling elements, both physically and socially.[41]

Now, if the obscene arouses disgust, it is not surprising that a dynamic of disgust-exclusion is at the basis of so many rules relating to behaviour and acts deemed obscene. As Vincenzo Manzini – one of the main scholars of European penal enlightenment – wrote, pornography is obscene because it is

> the filthy pleasure of the immature or degenerate and the filthy speculation of intellectual lechers, it is a deadly moral toxin that degrades feelings and the intellect, even physically degrading the person, with the habit of artificial erotic excitement and the consequent acquisition of vices.[42]

The feeling of repulsion towards what is considered obscene is rooted in the conviction that it is something 'toxic', that it 'debases' and degrades; and it is for this reason that such actions or images must be banned, prohibited, hidden, and outlawed.

Examples of legislation on obscenity are many, and confirm this exclusionary tendency.[43] The U.S. Federal Law On Obscenity[44] considers, among other illicit actions and facts, the possession with intent to sell, and sale of, obscene matter on Federal property, mailing indecent matter on wrappers or envelopes, broadcasting obscene language, distributing obscene material by cable or subscription television, etc. Within this framework, the U.S. Supreme Court affirmed that judges and juries must establish whether the matter is obscene: the test has been provided in *Miller v. California*[45] and other subsequent cases, and aims to determine whether the average person believes that the material, taken as a whole, appeals to "prurient interests" (which is exemplified as an erotic, lewd, abnormal, unhealthy, degrading, shameful, or morbid interest in nudity, sex, or excretion); if this person believes that the material depicts or describes sexual conduct in a patently offensive manner; and if the subject matter, as a whole, lacks serious literary, artistic, political, or scientific value.

41 Nussbaum, *Hiding from Humanity*, 107–8.

42 Manzini, *Trattato di diritto penale italiano* (UTET, 1936), 389 (translation mine).

43 Kevin W. Saunders, "Obscenity Laws in the United States, Canada, and Europe," in *The Wiley Blackwell Encyclopedia of Gender and Sexuality Studies* (John Wiley & Sons, 2016), 1–5.

44 18 U.S.C. § 1460 and ff.

45 *Miller v California*, 413 U.S. 15, 24–25 (1973).

In the UK, the 1959 Obscene Publications Act provides a definition of obscenity (Section 1) according to which

> an article shall be deemed to be obscene if its effect or (where the article comprises two or more distinct items) the effect of any one of its items is, if taken as a whole, such as to tend to deprave and corrupt persons who are likely, having regard to all relevant circumstances, to read, see or hear the matter contained or embodied in it.

In this vein, to deprave means "to make morally bad, to pervert, to debase or to corrupt morally. To corrupt means to render morally unsound or rotten, to destroy the moral purity or chastity, to pervert or ruin good quality, to debase, to defile".[46]

In France, protection against obscenity is achieved through the prosecution of offences to public decency. The former French Criminal Code of 1810 punished the public indecency under Article 330, stating that "Toute personne qui aura commis un outrage public à la pudeur sera punie d'un emprisonnement de trois mois à deux ans, et d'une amende de 500 F à 15 000 F".[47] This law was enforced between 1810 and 1994 and has now been replaced by a new provision condemning "sexual exhibition". Obscenity is now limited to what we might call sexual harassment, named by the French Code "exhibition sexuelle et du harcèlement sexuel" (Articles 222–32 à 222–33).

In Italy, Article 529 of the Criminal Code states that acts and objects are considered to be obscene if, according to common feeling, offend decency. However, Section 2 specifies that a work of art or science shall never be considered obscene unless, for a reason other than that of study, it is offered for sale, sold, or otherwise procured to a person under the age of 18 years.[48] The obscene is, therefore, that which offends decency, and is negative in two respects: it is not compatible with the normal understanding of decency shared by people, and it is not contained in a work of art or science, because in that case the social value of these areas of knowledge "purifies" or de-contaminates the obscene act or image.[49]

The legal category of obscene intersects both rational judgement and emotional reaction to some aesthetic objects: it concerns whatever offends the

46 *R v Penguin Books Ltd* [1961] Crim. LR 176, at 177.

47 Any person who commits public indecency will be punished by imprisonment of three months to two years, and a fine of 500 F to 15,000 F.

48 Art. 529 C.P. "Agli effetti della legge penale, si considerano osceni gli atti e gli oggetti che, secondo il comune sentimento, offendono il pudore. Non si considera oscena l'opera d'arte o l'opera di scienza, salvo che, per motivo diverso da quello di studio, sia offerta in vendita, venduta o comunque procurata a persona minore degli anni diciotto".

49 Silvia Rodeschini, "Osceno all'italiana: tracce per una storia del concetto," *Gender/Sexuality/Italy* 9 (2022): 12.

public understanding of decency and arouses disgust, thereby deserving to be excluded from what is worthy to be seen or is acceptable to be touched. This does not mean that it is clear what decency is, and where the threshold is set by current moral standards. On the contrary, this standard is culturally variable and lies at the intersection of law and morality:[50] it changes with changing sensibilities and widespread culture. Additionally, much of what offends the sense of decency has been – historically – linked to the sexual sphere, but it need not be so: decency can also be offended by violence, or by vulgarity, or by a combination of these factors.[51] Whatever they may be, some behaviours and images, in some societies, arouse feelings of revulsion strong enough to motivate their removal from what deserves to be seen: these objects, actions, or people, for different cultural or historical reasons, affect that aesthetic and moral sensibility that in each context is crystallised as mainstream.

In this sense, the obscene is the object of processes of exclusion for three reasons or three types of reasons:[52] first, since it arouses revulsion and disgust, or because it is understood as an offence to feelings that deserve to be protected. This is the perspective analysed by Nussbaum, who links the rejection of the obscene to the feeling of the danger of contamination, and the disgust that ensues. Second, it is excluded because it proposes immoral and unacceptable content (and therefore it goes against those values and that anthropology that a specific society intends to promote). One can think, here, to both Mill, who linked the necessary exclusion of the obscene to the need to protect the moral standards of the majority, thereby setting the boundaries of the tolerable,[53] and the moralism of Lord Devlin. Devlin's idea, expressed in connection with the discussion on the decriminalisation of homosexuality, was that every society has an interest, and the right, to defend itself from internal fragmentation, and thus an interest in promoting certain values (e.g. monogamy), and making them compulsory even for those who disagree.[54] Obscenity, in both cases, is deemed conceptually incompatible with values and interests that society intends to promote. Third, obscenity may be prohibited because it is considered a sin, that is, an action that distances people from God, Truth, and Right.

What emerges, in all these possible strategies to ban obscenity from society, is that the ban against obscenity is justified either on conceptual grounds,

50 Michele Mangini, "Atti osceni e danno morale," *D&Q Diritto e Questioni Pubbliche* 10 (2010): 386.

51 Mangini, "Atti osceni e danno morale," 391.

52 Mangini, "Atti osceni e danno morale," 394 ff.

53 Leonard W. Sumner, *The Hateful and the Obscene: Studies in the Limits of Free Expression* (University of Toronto Press, 2004).

54 Patrick Devlin, *The Enforcement of Morals* (Oxford University Press, 1965/1996); Ronald Dworkin, "Lord Devlin and the Enforcement of Morals," *The Yale Law Journal* 75, no. 6 (1966): 989 ff.

that is, on the basis of rational justification (however contestable), or because of feelings of disgust or revulsion that the obscene object arouses in situated and sensate observers. In both cases, even if the underlying legal interest varies, the intention to exclude and marginalise what is considered obscene does not change. Whether it is a question of protecting the sense of decency or protecting the morals of the majority or society itself from disintegration, it does not change the fact that obscene behaviour is excluded, denied, and cancelled. There is – as Nussbaum noted about disgust – no positive drive, no attempt to build a better society, and no impulse for change. Even beyond what we may think of obscene acts and images (i.e., whether they are truly obscene, or not), it is striking that when faced with ugliness as obscenity, the solution provided by the law is one of pure and simple negation, a mere attempt to reaffirm the boundaries and exclude from the horizon of the visible what is considered offensive.[55]

The debate on pornography is an interesting example of this exclusionary orientation of law and sheds light on it. From what we might call a 'conservative' perspective, pornography has been identified with the obscene, and as such represented a threat to the maintenance of shared moral values, or to society itself insofar as it encourages promiscuous and deviant behaviours. Pornography should be criminalised because of the effects it would have on society as a whole, and on the people who enjoy it.[56] On the contrary, from a liberal perspective, pornography should not be restricted, whatever the value or disvalue of the published images, simply because it does not produce any harm to others. Therefore, it should be considered covered by the freedom of expression, and deserving legal protection, however objectionable it may be.[57]

These two positions, which I have summarised here in a few lines, have animated endless debates,[58] outside and inside courtrooms and parliaments, and are united by the same perspective: both discuss the legitimacy of a ban, and the necessary or illegitimate exclusion of pornography from what deserves to be watched, in a purely negative approach. Either we ban pornography (because we consider it harmful, offensive, and so on) or we do not (because it is covered by the freedom of expression), what is at stake is in any case the question of prohibition and exclusion. It is only thanks to the contribution of feminism that this narrow horizon has been opened

55 Phoebe C. Godfrey, "Law and the Regulation of the Obscene," in *Handbook of the New Sexuality Studies*, eds. S. Seidman, N. Fischer, and C. Meeks (Routledge, 2007), 372–80.

56 Devlin, *The Enforcement of Morals*; Michael Sandel, "Morality and the Liberal Ideal," *New Republic* 190 (1984): 15–17.

57 Ronald Dworkin, "Do We Have a Right to Pornography?," in *A Matter of Principle*, ed. Ronald Dworkin (Harvard University Press, 1985), 353.

58 Andrew Altman and Lori Watson, *Debating Pornography* (Oxford University Press, 2018); Mari Mikkola, *Pornography: A Philosophical Introduction* (Oxford University Press, 2019).

up, and that the question of obscenity and exclusion has been – at least in part – unhinged. Feminist scholars began to shift the debate from the aesthetic and moral sphere (that is, the definition of the obscene, and the limits of freedom of expression) to the political and social realm: what really matters in pornography is not the outrage on a moral horizon, but the exploitation and oppression of women that pornography displays.[59] In contrast to merely erotic content, pornography tends to depict women as objects of use and sexual exploitation for male pleasure, reflecting mechanisms of domination, oppression, and subordination that are characteristic of society as a whole, at all levels. In this sense, the feminist critique of pornography is neither focused on the definition of obscenity, nor on the question of depiction of sexuality: rather, what matters is the link between that representation of sexual acts and the patriarchal structure of society, which makes women objects also in the sexual sphere. Consequently, the point of feminist critique is not the compatibility of pornography with a moral order that society wants to protect, or with the fundamental freedoms and rights: the objective is the critique of the entire system of social relations, and the attempt to reformulate them on new and egalitarian bases. In other words: the problem is not whether pornography is obscene or not, an offence to our sense of decency or not, and aesthetically disgusting or not; the problem is that pornography reflects a system of power that needs to be undermined, and changed, a way of 'seeing' women as objects of use, but which has nothing to do with aesthetics, so much as with justice and power relations in society.

It does not seem to me, however, that the feminist perspective has become the mainstream. On the contrary, the legal debate on obscenity is still internal to an aesthetic horizon: the issue of porn and its freedom is still that of deciding whether and to what extent it is unpleasant, whether and how much it offends our feelings of decency and decorum, and whether it is consistent with certain values and fundamental freedoms. Therefore, such a debate is still very much focused on what deserves to be seen, what does not, and what must be excluded from the realm of the visible or deserves to be displayed in the public sphere. Unfortunately, such debate leaves largely unaddressed the system of power and oppression that produces that kind of pornography which makes women mere objects of pleasure, and often of a violent pleasure.

Decency and decorum

The disabling and exclusionary aspect of some approaches to aesthetics emerges with particular evidence in the legal use of the category of *decorum*.

59 Nadine Strossen, "The convergence of feminist and civil liberties principles in the pornography debate," *New York University Law Review* 62 (1987): 201; Catharine A. MacKinnon, *Only Words* (Harper Collins, 1995).

Decorum is an elusive category: originally used in the context of rhetoric, to designate the appropriateness of style to subject,[60] it is gradually being applied in the sphere of social relations to indicate what is appropriate to a certain thing or person, and what is appropriate to it because of its position, nature, role, function, and so on. What is decorous, or decent, therefore befits the social status of a person, or the nature and function of a thing or place; in other words it affirms its dignity and value. Through the concept of decorum a kind of social aesthetics is hence developed[61] to define whether people behave, speak, or dress decently or indecently, depending on whether what they do, say, or wear suits the place they live in, their role, the context, the people they interact with, and so on. It is interesting to note, at first, that in the semantic field of decorum some aspects typical of a rationalistic and conceptual approach to aesthetics emerge: these aspects are certainly not the only ones, for as we shall see, the way in which certain behaviours affect observers and arouse emotions and feelings is also relevant in this field. However, with an aesthetic perspective, law understands decorum as that which expresses order and proportion, similar to Cicero's analogy between the harmony of the body and the appropriateness of one's conduct:

> For, as physical beauty with harmonious symmetry of the limbs engages the attention and delights the eye, for the very reason that all the parts combine in harmony and grace, so this propriety, which shines out in our conduct, engages the approbation of our fellow-men by the order, consistency, and self-control it imposes upon every word and deed. We should, therefore, in our dealings with people show what I may almost call reverence toward all men – not only toward the men who are the best, but toward others as well.[62]

In this vein, it is not surprising that the law values decorum in many circumstances. For example, the Italian Civil Code mentions individual decorum when it awards compensation for non-economic damages coming from insult, and from the loss of reputation. Although no longer a criminal offence,[63] the law protects the 'honour or decorum' of a person, that is, the respect or regard due to each individual.[64] More frequently, the law takes decorum into account when it concerns urban aesthetics and the protection of some

60 Jan D. Müller, *Decorum. Konzepte von Angemessenheit in der Theorie der Rhetorik von den Sophisten bis zur Renaissance* (De Gruyter, 2011).

61 Elisabetta Di Stefano, "Decorum. An Ancient Idea for Everyday Aesthetics?," *ESPES* 10, no. 2 (2021): 25–38.

62 Cicero, *De Officiis, I, 28, 98–99*, trans. W. Miller (New York: William Heinemann Ltd, G. P. Putnam's Son, 1928), 101 ff.

63 See the Law no. 67/2014.

64 Corte Suprema di Cassazione, sent. no. 34599/2008.

accepted aesthetic standards in single communities and places. Many examples are possible, such as norms intended to restrict the number and placement of billboards along the streets or highways,[65] measures providing for the distinction between historic and non-historic districts, or natural reserves and protected areas, with different architectural standards targeted based on aesthetic criteria as 'appropriate' or not, and broader policies for planning the space of cities according to standards of proportion, regularity, symmetry, and applying them to the roads, squares, and buildings.[66] Additionally, we can also consider the importance of professional decorum, which, for example, requires those practising the legal profession to observe the duties of fairness, honesty, and dignity even outside their professional activity, safeguarding their reputation and the very image of the profession. In this case, the image of professional dignity and the appropriateness of conduct and communications are protected because of the subject's belonging to a broader category, and the compliance with practices that are deemed appropriate to the dignity of the group itself.

This connection between decorum, functions, and the social prestige of people and roles has ancient roots: Vitruvius considered decorum to be a crucial category alongside *ordinatio* (order), *dispositio* (arrangement), *eurythmia* (proportion), *symmetria* (symmetry), and *distributio* (distribution). Thus, Vitruvius recommended to architects that a building and what is inside it should be 'appropriate'. The form must be appropriate to the content, and single architectural elements must fit into the whole, also with reference to the natural environment. Last but not least, decorative spaces must adapt to the needs of their users.[67] Similarly, Leon Battista Alberti takes decorum as a criterion concerning the amount and type of ornaments for different buildings, taking into account their functions and the social prestige of those who worked or lived there: thus, decorum doesn't concern decorations and ornaments of buildings but the aptness or fitness to purpose, on the one hand, and the social prestige and function, on the other.[68] Since the 1537 design of Piazza del Campidoglio by Michelangelo, the idea of planning and rationalising the space of cities to make it (including buildings, squares, gardens, and monuments) more appropriate gained increasing relevance and triumphed in

65 Emily Talen, *City Rules: How Regulations Affect Urban Form* (Island Press, 2012); Frederick R. Steiner, Kent Butler, and American Planning Association, *Planning and Urban Design Standards* (John Wiley & Sons, 2012).

66 Pierre Merlin and Françoise Choay, *Dictionnaire de l'urbanisme et de l'aménagement* (Presses Universitaires de France, 1988).

67 Vitruvius, *Ten Books on Architecture*, ed. Ingrid Rowland, illust. Thomas Noble Howe (Cambridge: Cambridge University Press, 1999), 1, 2, 5–7.

68 Leon Battista Alberti, *On the Art of Building in Ten Books*, trans. J. Rykwert, N. Leach, and R. Tavernor (The MIT Press, 1988), V, 3, 121–22; Di Stefano, "Decorum. An Ancient Idea for Everyday Aesthetics?," 32.

the nineteenth century. Thanks to Baron Hausmann, these ideas of remodeling the urban space were combined with objectives of welfare, hygiene, and social control, and made Paris a model of urban planning for the next century.[69]

However, when applied to cities, these ideas of appropriateness, decorum, and beautification can have, as a counterpart, exclusionary and marginalising effects: the appreciation of what is appropriate to a certain social function or status implies, conversely, the devaluation of what is inappropriate and unfit. In modern times, this discriminatory orientation has marked since the 70s securitarian approaches to urban policies: the idea that patterns of community and interpersonal interaction (the way people behave and act outside the private sphere) are correlated with some 'physical' signs observable in the territory began to thrive. Some visible elements present in the urban territory, such as abandoned or burnt buildings, unkempt property, and vandalism, but also the mere presence of idle youths roaming the streets, can convey to community members a sense of social disorder, and the idea of a territory that is fertile for criminal activities and in any case not safe:[70] in a sort of aesthesis of disorder and decay, the sight of certain objects or behaviours affects negatively and produces feelings of abandonment, discouragement, anxiety, or even fear. Such a correlation was translated in past decades into specific policies, spreading outside academic circles as the 'broken window theory'. The underlying idea of this theory is that urban decay is not simply unsightly, but capable of conveying the perception of abandonment and neglect, and the idea that legal and social order are somehow suspended. Beyond a devaluation on the theoretical and aesthetic level of what is contrary to order and inappropriate, what is against decorum affects the senses of people situated within the social space, and generates negative and feelings of revulsion. If a broken window is left as it is, those passing by the building may think that no one cares about it, and so they may start throwing litter, which would accumulate, generating further decay and neglect. Soon, that area will be perceived as unhealthy, ugly, unpleasant, and progressively abandoned (because people prefer to spend their time in more pleasant areas), and it will become the perfect framework for criminal activity, a sort of no-man's-land where everything is permitted and disorder mutates into crime.[71]

69 David Harvey, *Paris, Capital of Modernity* (Routledge, 2004); Antoni Remesar, "New Urban Decorum? City Aesthetics To and Fro," in *Aesthetic Energy of the City. Experiencing Urban Art and Space,* eds. A. Gralińska-Toborek and W. Kazimierska-Jerzyk (Łódź University Press, 2016).

70 Albert Hunter, "Symbols of Incivility: Social Disorder and Fear of Crime in Urban Neighbourhoods" (Annual Meeting of the American Criminological Society, Dallas, 1978).

71 George L. Kelling and James Q. Wilson, "Broken Windows," *Atlantic Monthly* 249, no. 3 (1982): 29–38.

As mentioned, this theory achieved considerable success and attention outside the academic debate and became the reference for security policies using the struggle against decay for social and economic purposes. The most famous example has certainly been the policy of the mayor of New York, Rudolph Giuliani, who in 1994 inaugurated a 'Zero Tolerance' programme focused on the link between public safety and urban decorum.[72] Not only were the police forces increased but they were also deployed for a capillary control of the streets: the target was no longer, and not only, traditional and typical criminal activities, but everything that conveyed an idea of decay and inappropriateness. Beggars and panhandlers, homeless people, street artists and taggers have been prosecuted and criminalised, as well as "squeegee men", people who cleaned car windows at traffic lights forcefully demanding a tip. Anyone or anything that displays the idea of disorder and illegality, even minor incivilities, or that expresses an inappropriate (i.e., properly speaking, indecorous) use of public space, is criminalised.[73] None of the problems underlying these behaviours, such as social exclusion, poverty, unemployment, and domestic violence, are addressed: the core of these policies is not to tackle social problems, but the use of decorum and aesthetics as tools for policies aimed at social control.

Rudolph Giuliani inspired other cities and administrations, also thanks to his alleged successes in terms of security and prevention of crime.[74] Tony Blair's government in 1998 introduced the Crime and Disorder Act, where the so-called ASBOs, or Anti-Social Behaviour Orders, are enforced.[75] The ASBO is similar to other security measures provided for by many European legal systems, which are intended to target the behaviour of persons considered socially dangerous, and where the rhetoric of crime prevention merges with authoritarianism, communitarianism, and re-moralisation. However, in the British case, these measures were linked to a broad range of hypotheses, which included, alongside more explicitly criminal behaviours, conduct such as abandoning cars, drunkenness, begging, littering, vandalism, defecating or urinating in a public place, and even simply spitting on the ground.

The Italian case is interesting because zero-tolerance policies took an explicitly aesthetic approach, especially when enforced by the authorities of touristic cities, or when concerned with touristic areas. City administrations explicitly used the argument of decorum to justify measures aimed at

72 Maurice Punch, *Zero Tolerance Policing* (Bristol, 2007; online ed., Policy Press Scholarship Online, March 22, 2012), accessed February 4, 2024, https://doi.org/10.1332/policypress/9781847420558.001.0001.

73 Alessandro De Giorgi, *Zero tolleranza. Strategia e pratiche della società di controllo* (Derive-Approdi, 2000).

74 Alison Mountz and Winifred Curran, "Policing in Drag: Giuliani Goes Global with the Illusion of Control," *Geoforum* 40, no. 6 (2009): 1033–40.

75 John Muncie, "Institutionalized Intolerance: Youth Justice and the 1998 Crime and Disorder Act," *Critical Social Policy* 19, no. 2 (1999): 147–75.

social control and preventing criminal phenomena.[76] For instance, mayor ordinances targeted prostitution (which, although not illicit, is considered indecorous), vandalism, and begging, in the same perspective being enforced by administrations on both sides of the Atlantic.

As Pitch rightly notes,[77] a decent city is a city where misery and marginality are unseen, where germs and bacteria-carrying contagion are identified in people belonging to minorities (such as Roma and Sinti), beggars, squeegee men, street vendors, and prostitutes, as well as in the proliferation of 'ethnic' food shops. Decent cities sweep the dust under the carpet, with the aggravating factor that the dust is made of people, and often vulnerable people. So, for example, prostitution on call, or via the web, is perfectly accepted, because it is not visible, and because it is socially decent, expensive, and aimed at targeting affluent and respectable males. It is street prostitution that is not seemly, because it offends the gaze of decent citizens and tourists and is mostly practised by migrant exploited women: the focus of zero-tolerance policies is the visibility of prostitution, not the condition of the exploitation, or the provision of work, social integration, and a stay permit. What matters is that they do not get in the way and our decent gaze.

A similar approach is taken with regard to (so-called) 'nomads', or those referred to by this nonsensical term in local ordinances: they also are considered to offend our aesthetic standard of respectability and decency. They offend our sense of decorum when they engage in begging, or rummage through rubbish bins to retrieve ferrous materials, and so we ghettoise them – in many cities – in 'camps', in semi-peripheral areas where they are tolerated because they are invisible, and to the extent the poor sanitary conditions in which they live are not visible. To be more precise, they are only partially tolerated, because city administrations sometimes decide that the camps must be cleared, and eviction operations are carried out in a manner that has been judged at odds with human rights standards.[78] In both Rome and Milan, the evictions were carried out without any warning, any guarantee of people's rights, any consideration of people's times and needs, any protection for the property rights of these same people, and with a veritable 'deportation' of residents to other places on the city's outskirts (i.e., far from the eyes and thoughts of respectable citizens and tourists), resulting in the loss of opportunities for work, education, and relationships.[79]

76 Cittalia/Anci, *Oltre le ordinanze. I sindaci e la sicurezza urbana*, Seconda edizione (Roma, 2009); Carmen Pisanello, "Europa di quarzo. L'immagine di Europa fra decoro e Security State," *Iconocrazia* 11 (2017): 1–9.

77 Tamar Pitch, *Contro il decoro. L'uso politico della pubblica decenza* (Laterza, 2013), ch. 3.14 Kindle.

78 Report of Council of Europe Commissioner for Human Rights Thomas Hammarberg, following his visit to Italy on 26 and 27 May 2011, CommDH(2011)26, 7 September 2011.

79 Pitch, *Contro il decoro*, ch. 5.11 ff.

People targeted by zero-tolerance policies offend the sense of decency shared by the majority of the population, or the part of the population that is in positions of privilege: they are sometimes perceived as harassing by their very attitude or posture. In Florence in 2009, the (left-wing) mayor issued an ordinance in which these 'bothering' activities were listed in detail: among them, those invasive and insistent active behaviours, also practised with the use of tools to distract attention (for instance, by subjects dressed in a white tunic and headgear whose face is disguised in white wax which makes it impossible to identify their precise somatic features and has a disturbing emotional impact); the begging carried out with the use of animals, simulating a state of necessity and provoking an unmotivated feeling of pity along with a progressive loss of urban decorum and perception of individual sense of security; the begging carried out with the use of musical instruments such as accordions, mandolins, guitars with which the patrons of bars and restaurants are approached in a repeated and annoying manner, producing a progressive decrease in the sense of security and the quality of urban decorum.[80]

Decorum, in short, is used as a tool to exclude the indecorous from our visual space, a means to exclude what is perceived as ugly or disturbing or degraded from the horizon of the visible, by law. And as it happens with the category of obscene, even in this case the law takes a merely negative perspective: whatever is indecorous must be erased, hidden, ghettoised, or marginalised. Not by chance, central areas of cities, as well as tourist areas, are the main subject of these policies, where economic factors bolster the need for such an aesthetic approach. These policies do not deal with the factors underlying situations of decay, be they poverty, unemployment, the housing crisis, or anything else: they simply concern what is allowed to be seen, and what is not.

The unpleasant

In 1881, in Chicago, the City Code stated that

> Any person who is diseased, maimed, mutilated, or in any way deformed, so as to be an unsightly or disgusting object, or an improper person to be allowed in or on the streets, highways, thoroughfares, or public places in this city, shall not therein or thereon expose himself to public view, under the penalty of a fine of $1 for each offense.[81]

Regulations of this kind had also appeared earlier, in other cities, as scattered references within more general measures against begging; in San Francisco,

80 Ord. no. 00814, 26 November 2009.

81 Chicago City Code 1881: see Susan Schweik, *The Ugly Laws: Disability in Public* (New York University Press, 2009), 9.

for instance, as early as 1867, an ordinance prohibited street begging and prevented certain individuals from showing themselves in the streets and public places. Specifically, it prohibited

> Any person who is diseased, mutilated, or in any way deformed so as to be an unsightly or disgusting object, or a person unfit to show himself in the streets, highways, thoroughfares, or public places of the city or county of San Francisco, shall not expose himself in any manner to the public view.[82]

While unfair treatment of persons due to their ugliness as perceived or assessed by others has been studied in social sciences, focusing on lookism, heightism, sizeism, appearance discrimination, and beauty bias,[83] the legal translation of these attitudes is largely unaddressed. The 'ugly laws' or 'unsightly beggar ordinances' spread in the United States and some European countries towards the end of the nineteenth century and operated as devices of social exclusion and victimisation based on alleged 'ugliness': they were legal instruments that in various ways, and with a different scope, excluded the access of certain subjects to public spaces on the basis of the *unpleasant* and contaminating effect that their bodies would have on these spaces.[84] Different and non-normative bodies were at stake, and any manifestations of otherness with respect to a standard order, decorum, and proportion that was set by subjects with greater power and resources. These bodies belonged to poor people, immigrants, people with illnesses or disabilities, injured workers, and people of colour, who were excluded from the sphere of the 'visible' and from the horizon of what could be looked at because they were dirty, disabled, deformed, sick, smelly, or simply unsightly. Ugly laws are striking examples of how the objective of excluding what is perceived as a threat by dominant classes arises from the intersection between an aesthetic category (ugliness) with ableist, racist, classist, and colonialist ideologies. People who are targeted by these laws are marginalised and (often) criminalised not for what they do, how they behave, or what they say, but for their bodies, for the unpleasant sight of bodies reduced to ugly objects.[85] As Schweik rightly pointed out, ugly laws highlight the persistent link between disability and poverty, and the complex intertwining of economic interests, social policies,

82 "To Prohibit Street Begging, and to Restrain Certain Persons from Appearing in Streets and Public Places" (Order no. 783. 1867), sec. 3.

83 For an overview, see Bjørn Hofmann, "Aesthetic Injustice," *Journal of Business Ethics* 189, no. 2 (2024): 217–29.

84 Schweik, *The Ugly Laws*.

85 Nöel Carroll, "Ethnicity, Race, and Monstrosity: The Rhetorics of Horror and Humour," in *Beauty Matters*, ed. Peg Zeglin Brand (Bloomington, Indianapolis: Indiana University Press, 2000), 52.

and the construction of the public imagination, at work in the identification of what is ugly and deserving of being hidden.[86]

Ugly laws are a perfect normative image of the concept of *abjection*. That which is abject, wrote Julia Kristeva, provokes a rejection, a "révolte de l'être contre ce qui le menace et qui lui paraît venir d'un dehors ou d'un dedans exorbitant, jeté à côté du possible, du tolérable, du pensable. C'est là, tout près mais inassimilable ".[87] The abject is not acceptable because it is not within the boundary of the rules, it is not within the territory that the rules of decency – established by those who have the power to draw the line – define as worthy and decent. Therefore, the abject, the dif-form, is an intrinsic otherness: its diversity is embodied in its flesh, in a body that cannot be cared for, and must be hidden and made non-visible, so that it does not upset the stability of civilised and ordered societies. For this reason, what is most disturbing is not the dying body, or the explicitly criminal action, but that which lies in an intermediate zone, and casts doubt on the clear-cut distinction between good and bad people. Again, Kristeva writes that " Ce n'est donc pas l'absence de propreté ou de santé qui rend abject, mais ce qui perturbe une identité, un système, un ordre".[88]

It is interesting, however, that ugly laws have often taken on the language of assistance and charity. Bodies that do not deserve to enter the public sphere are unsightly, and must be punished if they do not respect the prohibitions imposed by ugly laws, on the one hand, but they can be 'managed' by public and private institutions of assistance, on the other. These institutions have always been present in Europe thanks to religious orders, and at the end of the nineteenth century they began to spread in many US states and cities. Once these institutions of care were in place, the task of dealing with bodies that 'must not be seen' was no longer entrusted to prisons, but was entrusted to them, being indeed morally legitimised from the perspective of care and assistance.[89] Private and public institutions provide care and assistance, without doubt, and deserve appreciation: religious orders provided for centuries care for people abandoned by every other social institution (including families) and excluded from the community. However, from the perspective of our analysis, it is important to notice that legal provisions concerning people with non-normative bodies and behaviour have in no way provided support for such initiatives, with the purpose of social inclusion: from the point of view of ugly laws, what matters is only that these people are made not visible, hidden from the gaze of others, taken away from the public sphere. The fact that this exclusion is reached through the (forced) inclusion in hospices and

86 Schweik, *The Ugly Laws*, 63.
87 Kristeva, *Pouvoirs de l'horreur*, 18.
88 Kristeva, *Pouvoirs de l'horreur*, 21.
89 Schweik, *The Ugly Laws*, 26.

institutions only makes it more acceptable and justifiable in terms of image but does not change its marginalising effect.

The great confinement of vagabonds and paupers is one of the many examples of the power exerted on bodies, by that biopolitics which demands, first and foremost, correction and isolation.[90] Disciplinary power is exercised over the imprisoned, healing policies and social therapies are experimented with, and the "power of the Norm appears through the disciplines. . . . The Normal is established as a principle of coercion";[91] thus, a power is applied on ugly bodies to make them invisible insofar as they differ from the aesthetic and moral canons, and a discipline that subjects them to treatments, examinations, practices of transformation and moralisation, and so on. Contemporary societies implemented institutions to isolate and segregate, expressly alternative to prisons (i.e., either you are placed in an institution of care, or you go to prison) to 'cure' people who infringe the rules on vagrancy or display their ugliness, and promote internalisation of these mechanisms of power.[92] Marginalised people internalise the standards of ugly laws because these laws, in addition to providing penalties and containment measures for ugly bodies, promote mechanisms of self-correction and self-control: the whole community is invited, with a typical mechanism of general prevention, to exercise control over their bodies and habits, because everyone is asked to conform to those criteria of dignity and appropriateness that are, at the same time, morally and aesthetically justified.[93]

It should be pointed out, however, that ugliness is never, or almost never, thematised as an autonomous element: even in the context of ugly laws it is used from an intersectional perspective. The object of these laws rarely concerns people with ugly bodies *tout court*, but people with ugly bodies who are at the same time poor, ethnically diverse, addicted to alcohol, or too old, and so on. Disability and mutilation, for example, were well tolerated in the late nineteenth century if they were mitigated by belonging to a high social class, or a job and income. On the other hand, working injuries or war mutilations were frequent, and they could be considered with a benevolent or even admiring gaze, if referred to persons who, by class or status, were considered respectable. Ugliness does not operate in isolation, but functions in relation to other categories: it is poor, sick, or racialised ugliness that is unsightly and deserves to be confined.

Examples of this self-interested tolerance are freak shows. These shows were quite common between the end of the nineteenth century and the first

90 Michel Foucault, *Discipline and Punish. The Birth of the Prison*, trans. A. Sheridan (Vintage Books, Random House, 1995), 121.
91 Foucault, *Discipline and Punish*, 184.
92 Michael Hardt and Antonio Negri, *Empire* (Harvard University Press, 2001).
93 Schweik, *The Ugly Laws*, 65.

half of the twentieth century, continuing in new forms the tradition of 'cabinets of curiosities' and collections of oddities and monstrosities that had been multiplying since the sixteenth century, intended for the excitement and the amusement of the public.[94] Freaks are perturbing elements. They represent what Freud describes as distressing (*unheimlich*) because they are beyond reason, as that which "belongs to the realm of the frightening, of what evokes fear and dread engenders anguish and horror", and "arouses fear in general".[95] And so conjoined twins, bearded women, people with mutilated limbs, exceptionally tall or short people, people with a condition of microcephaly, albinos, and many others are exposed to the public's amused and curious gaze, both to tickle such a curiosity and to indirectly confirm the normality of others, the beholders.

All these characters and shows embody anxieties and fantasies of a community by making them commercial, producing income, and acting as fetishes for entertainment and education (i.e., for two socially appreciable purposes): therefore, they consolidate the awareness of one's normality and dignity in their paying spectators. As Garland Thomson argues, the elaborate staging of specific bodily eccentricities resulted in the confirmation of a clear division between 'normal' and 'abnormal', between healthy and dignified people, on the one hand, and freaks, on the other.[96] The display of non-conventional bodies for the benefit of the public's morbid gaze effectively marks the opposition between those who are entitled to recognition of their full dignity as human beings and those who are excluded from that humanity because of their 'ab-normality', their being outside the norm.[97] Iris Marion Young correctly emphasised the connection between all forms of group oppression, such as racism, homophobia, ableism, and sexism, and ideas or assumptions about the ugliness, awfulness, or abnormality of bodies. The dominant culture determines who belongs to the group of the normal and who does not, who embodies reason and who represents ugliness.[98] From this perspective, the exposure of freaks is internal to the statement of the normality of those who share power and privileges, because it justifies oppression and discrimination as the necessary prevention of what is inadequate, unworthy, sick, and disturbing.

From a legal point of view, the issue of freak shows has often been examined with reference to the question of consent, opposing those who consider

94 Robert Bogdan, *Freak Show: Presenting Human Oddities for Amusement and Profit* (Chicago University Press, 1988).

95 Sigmund Freud, *The Uncanny*, trans. D. Mclintock (Penguin Books, 2003), 123.

96 Rosemarie Garland Thomson, ed., *Freakery: Cultural Spectacles of the Extraordinary Body* (New York University Press, 1996), 10.

97 Brunella Casalini, "Disporre in autonomia del proprio corpo disabile," *il Mulino, Rivista trimestrale di cultura e di politica* 4 (2017): 580–87.

98 Iris M. Young, *Justice and the Politics of Difference* (Princeton University Press, 1990), 124.

the person's consent irrelevant due to their absolute right to honour and dignity, and those who recognise the full autonomy of the people involved and consider the employment contract agreements they signed valid, having as their object precisely the exhibition of their bodies.[99] Specific performances have also been discussed by legal scholars and bioethicists: the *dwarf throw*, a kind of competition that involves throwing a person with dwarfism, often through a window or a hoop of fire, is an example. The French Council of State, in a well-known ruling in 1995, upheld the decision of the mayor of Morsang-sur-Orge to prohibit this performance and to prohibit an attraction that "jeopardizes" the necessary respect for human dignity.[100] Here, however, another aspect is relevant, namely the legal regime of shows that are precisely based on what other rules, in other contexts, prohibit: the display of unsightliness.

The attitude of the law towards freak shows reflects the oppressive and discriminatory approach we have already discussed. Beyond good intentions, the legislation assumes that a social stigma is the consequence of non-conventional bodies, rather than the normalising and oppressive gaze of those taking part in the shows. When law provides bans for these performances, it is because legislators believe that people performing these shows do not have the capacity to make decisions, or because of the fear that such performances can corrupt public morality. Even when the exploitation of these persons comes to the fore, it is still assumed that they – as disabled or people with unconventional bodies – do not have the capacity to express their consent.[101] Moreover, it is typical of the language of freak shows to refer to these people as 'monsters', or 'unnatural' phenomena. The circus stage, or theatre stage, is the only place where bodily deformity can be exhibited, the only place in public space where disability and non-conforming corporeity are allowed to enter. As Bernardini recalls, numerous rulings of Western Courts dealt with freak shows, always starting from an interpretation of disability or non-conformity as pathology, and thus functioning as devices of exclusion.[102]

The exhibition of non-conventional bodies is only a limited and exceptional visibility of the unsightly, and is functional as an exception to reaffirm the rule, which is the normality of aesthetically appreciable and decent bodies. From this point of view, regulations concerning freak shows produced

99 Brigham A. Fordham, "Dangerous Bodies: Freak Shows, Expression, and Exploitation," *UCLA Entertainment Law Review* 14, no. 2 (2007): 218.

100 "interdire une attraction qui porte atteinte au respect de la dignité de la personne humaine" (Conseil d'Etat, Assemblée, du 27 octobre 1995, 136727).

101 Fordham, "Dangerous Bodies," 228.

102 Maria Giulia Bernardini, *Disabilità, giustizia, diritto. Itinerari tra filosofia del diritto e Disability Studies* (Giappichelli, 2016), 181; si veda anche *World Fair Freaks and Attractions v Hodges*, 267 So. 2d 817 (Fla. 1972).

exclusion, denying disabled individuals the possibility of affirming their will, and reinforcing marginalisation.[103]

The deviant

An aesthetic approach to social science is also behind one of the most notorious and violent forms of criminalisation of deviance and social marginality. I am referring to the idea that physiognomy (i.e., by definition, an aesthetic understanding of the human being) can be used as a marker of criminality, and therefore as a contributing factor to justify preventive measures of exclusion, deterrence, and coercion.

Physiognomy has ancient roots. The already-mentioned example of Thersites, in Homer, is significant of the opinion the body can be read as a map in order to investigate positive or negative moral tendencies of a person; however, in Pseudo-Aristotle the fundamental connection of body and soul is drawn from a list of physical and aesthetic elements and signs.[104] The basis of the physiognomic understanding is the analysis of body parts and their conformation, of the body as a whole, or even of the bearing and gait: movements, gestures of the body, colours of eyes and skin, the characteristic expression of the face, the growth of the hair, the smoothness of the skin, the voice, the single parts of the body, and the physique as a whole. All these elements, in some way, can give information concerning a person's character and, thus, concerning his or her possible behaviour. Since this first treatise, physiognomy has not ceased to be present in Western culture, at different levels.

Of course, the reading of body traits and forms has not always been considered predictive of certain behaviours and characters. One may think, for example, of Leonardo's theory of the *movements of the soul*, with which modern and rationalist physiognomy took its first steps, and used painting as its expressive medium.[105] In Leonardo's thought, movements of the soul are not linked to the body in a direct and deterministic manner: it is true, writes Leonardo, that the signs of faces partly show the nature of men, their vices and complexions . . . but this is a "fallacious physiognomy and palmistry" that has no scientific foundation.[106] What Leonardo and the physiognomy of his time are interested in is the expressive dynamics of emotions, and how

103 Bernardini, *Disabilità, giustizia, diritto*, 182.

104 Marke Ahonen, "Ancient Physiognomy," in *Sourcebook for the History of the Philosophy of Mind: Philosophical Psychology from Plato to Kant*, eds. S. Knuuttila and J. Sihvola (Springer, 2014), 623–31.

105 Flavio Caroli, *Storia della fisiognomica. Arte e psicologia da Leonardo a Freud* (Electa, 2012); Piers D. G. Britton, "The Signs of Faces: Leonardo on Physiognomic Science and the 'Four Universal States of Man'," *Renaissance Studies* 16, no. 2 (2002): 143–62.

106 Leonardo, *Treatise on Painting*, no. 288 (my translation).

feelings can condition our bodies, our appearance, or our movements.[107] Indeed, it is precisely this approach that will form the foundation of his studies of anatomy, and of his marvellous painting skills. The sixteenth century, not surprisingly, has also been the moment when Western culture began to scientifically analyse madness, and to give it a powerful visual representation. From Sebastian Brant's *Narrenschiff* – of 1494 – to Dürer's *Melancolia*, from Leonardo's "Head of a Screaming Man", to Hieronymus Bosch's *Ship of Fools* or *The Cure of Folly*, as well as Erasmus' *Praise of Folly* of 1509, madness enters European visual space and imagination in a powerful way,[108] and the idea of a link between psychic interiority and body begins to take root, as well as between inner and outer disorder, between (what we would call) psychology and physiology.

However, it was a long time before physiognomy could be used by the social sciences, and not only by artists and intellectuals. In the works of Giovan Battista Della Porta – in 1586 – physiognomy is presented as a tool for understanding individual drives and inclinations: the "segni che sono fissi nel corpo" (signs that are fixed in the body) reveal people's natural inclinations and character, and conversely, inner drives are imprinted in physiognomy as visible signs of interiority ("accidenti che trasmutano i segni"). Physiognomy, on this basis, begins to have a predictive and regulatory orientation.[109] In a way, Leonardo's perspective is inverted: it is no longer a question of understanding which expressions and physiology are linked to certain characters and drives: rather, *through* the analysis of the body one could understand which attitudes, behaviours, and characters the person tends to develop.

The classic zoomorphic references (whereby there is a typology of man-sheep, man-lion, man-ox, and so on, depending on the similarity between the somatic features of the two species) begin to emerge as a literary and aesthetic *tòpos*.[110] After Della Porta's works, the drawings and works of Charles Le Brun, as well as La Fontaine's and La Rochefoucauld's fables, gained a wide resonance: however, the whole Western culture between the sixteenth and seventeenth century began to shed light on the relationship between body and soul, and the way in which the impulses of the soul shape

107 Caroli, *Storia della fisiognomica*, 15.

108 Michel Foucault, *History of Madness* (Routledge, 2013), 20–21. See also Andrew Scull, *Madness in Civilization: A Cultural History of Insanity, from the Bible to Freud, from the Madhouse to Modern Medicine* (Princeton University Press, 2015).

109 "Il nome della Fisonomia vien da physin, che vuol dir 'natura', e gnome, 'regola'; quasi volesse dir legge o regola di Natura che con certa regola, norma et ordine di natura si conosce da tal forma di corpo, si conosce tal passion dell'anima" (The name of Physiomy comes from physin, which means 'nature', and gnome, 'rule'; as if to say law or rule of Nature that with a certain rule, norm and order of nature is known from such form of body, such passion of soul): Giovan Battista Della Porta, *Della fisionomia dell'uomo libri sei*, ed. Alfonso Paolella (Edizioni Scientifiche Italiane, 2013), 96.

110 Olson, *Criminals as Animals from Shakespeare to Lombroso*, 40.

and deform bodies, faces, and expressions. The art of this century continues to work on Leonardo's teachings on the motions of the soul, it exalts them, takes them to extremes, and puts them at the basis of an extraordinary series of works. From the child bitten by a lizard by Caravaggio to *The Beaneater* by Annibale Carracci, from Rembrandt (in many works, from its marvellous self-portraits to the *Adoration of the Magi*) to Velasquez, from Vermeer to Bernini and his Saint Teresa in ecstasy, the soul and passions burst onto the scene and deform bodies and faces, giving rise to an extraordinary visual treatise on physiognomy.[111]

Zoomorphism also carries considerable weight in the work of Lavater, who in the following century contributed significantly to the success of physiognomy, and had a strong influence on artists like Goethe and Füssli. Above all, in Lavater the social traits of physiognomy, which are of particular interest to us here, are accentuated, and its darker traits come to the scene. As one of Lavater's contemporary commentators noted, the social use of physiognomy can produce dramatic consequences: if physiognomy one day becomes what Lavater expects – writes Lichtenberg – children will be hanged before they have performed feats deserving of the gallows.[112]

It was only in the seventeenth century, however, that all these seeds began to bear fruits and produce social consequences. Within the framework of scientific positivism, physiognomy and the new-born phrenology (the study of the parts and functions of the brain) are placed at the service of criminology, a science that is also new, whose social aims are consistent with the scientific treatment of deviance that begins to occupy centre stage. This union produces non-trivial results: the purely epistemic orientation of physiognomy, thanks to which the physiological effects of the 'motions of the soul' are noted and discussed, tends to be inverted, bringing to the scene objectives of criminal policy, and using the study of physiology and mimicry in a predictive function: that is, trying to determine which crimes or deviant actions can be inductively drawn from the observation of faces and bodies. As usual, it is not the perfectly ordered and measured body that captures the attention of scholars, but the deformed body, what is unconventional, abnormal, disproportionate, and unpleasant. The ugly body, in any case.

The criminological use of physiognomy stems from a correctional culture (think, for example, in Germany, of the thought of Franz von List),[113] in which punishment is understood as a technique aimed at personality modification. Such a culture shaped purposes of re-socialisation, intimidation, or neutralisation, on the basis of a classification of subjects into criminal 'types': the adaptable, the occasional, the unadaptable. In other words, criminal law

111 Caroli, *Storia della fisiognomica,* 81 ff.
112 Georg C. Lichtemberg, *Osservazioni e pensieri* (Albani, 2020), 164.
113 Franz Von Liszt, *Der Zweckgedanke im Strafrecht* (Pfeil, 1882).

doesn't focus on the crime, but on the person of the criminal. The object of punishment is not a deviant and unlawful behaviour, but the subjects themselves, by reason of their internal malignity or innate dangerousness.[114] The idea is that the criminal is an anthropologically inferior and degenerate subject, a danger from which society must defend itself with technically appropriate measures. And so, depending on the *type* of person and his or her nature, preventive or neutralising measures are implemented: these interventions are the natural consequence of a deterministic approach, in which criminal subjects are deprived of freedom, being entirely determined by their deviant nature.

Within this criminological approach,[115] physiognomy is understood by some as a formidable predictive tool. Cesare Lombroso – but, alongside him, authors such as Enrico Ferri and Raffaele Garofalo – argues a deterministic understanding of the human being, in which criminal behaviour can be detected inductively from the *stigmata* that character imprints on the body. By welding together with Spencer's ideas on society as a 'social organism', and Darwin's ideas on natural selection and the struggle for existence, criminal positivism lays the foundations for a medical-scientific treatment of deviance, in which subjects who bear the signs of social dangerousness on their body are treated in a technically appropriate manner, rendering them inoffensive, interning them, and eliminating them.[116]

In his most famous work, *The Criminal Man*, the notion of 'atavism' (i.e., the idea that the criminal subject shows somatic and behavioural traits that belong to a backward stage of development) and physiognomy are used by Lombroso to interpret the criminal phenomenon,[117] through an anthropological analysis that is attentive to physical traits that are different and divergent from a hypothetical normality. The *thief by tendency*, for example, is an individual with a small skull, a receding nose, and thick eyebrows; criminals have, in general, jug ears, thick hair, thin beards, pronounced sinuses, protruding chins, and broad cheekbones.[118] Lombroso's book analyses, with a scientific approach, the "Anthropometry and Physiognomy of

114 Luigi Ferrajoli, *Diritto e ragione. Teoria del garantismo penale* (Laterza, 1989), 254.

115 Nicole Rafter, "Cesare Lombroso and the Origins of Criminology: Rethinking Criminological Tradition," in *The Essential Criminology reader*, eds. S. Henry and M. M. Lanier (Routledge, 2018), 33–42; Mary Gibson, "Cesare Lombroso, Prison Science, and Penal Policy," in *The Cesare Lombroso Handbook*, eds. P. Knepper and P. Jørgen Ystehede (Routledge, 2013), 30–46.

116 Ferrajoli, *Diritto e ragione*, 255.

117 Paolo Marchetti, "Le 'sentinelle del male'. L'invenzione ottocentesca del criminale nemico della società tra naturalismo giuridico e normativismo psichiatrico," *Quaderni fiorentini per la storia del pensiero giuridico moderno* 38, no. 2 (2009): 1009–80; Paolo Marchetti, "The mark of Cain. The Search of the Criminal Man between Medicine and Law," *Giornale di Storia Costituzionale* 21 (2011): 15.

118 Cesare Lombroso, *L'uomo delinquente'* (Fratelli Bocca, 1927), (Eng. Ed.: C. Lombroso, *Criminal Man*, trans. M. Gibson, N. H. Rafter, and M. Seymour (Duke University Press, 2006), 53.

832 Criminals", and offers reflections on craniometry, cerebral, skeletal and visceral anomalies, body anomalies, and the "Physiognomy of Criminals". In so-called "born criminals", their bodies display "low, sloping foreheads, overdeveloped sinuses, frequent occurrence of the median occipital fossetta, overdevelopment of the jaw and cheekbones, prognathism, oblique and large eye sockets, dark skin, thick and curly head hair", and so on.[119] On the contrary, the mandible in criminals has superiority in weight, width, length of its branches, and general robustness in comparison with "normal" people.[120] Lombroso's analyses sound discriminatory and racist, but are meticulous and precise, focused on the detection of cranial and bony anomalies, of dissimilarities of various kinds and nature relating to the dimensions of the frontal sinuses, temples, jaw, and so on. The measurements of the nose, the eyes, the ear, the shape of the lips, the teeth, everything is measured and assessed, and everything contributes to defining a physiognomy of the criminal centred on dissimilarity and abnormality.[121]

If physiognomy is, at least in principle, aesthetically neutral (i.e., somatic features are interpreted as revealing character regardless of their aesthetic value), in the criminological perspective this discipline takes on an evaluative orientation, along the normality-abnormality axis. Given a physiological and aesthetic standard, unconventional bodies come to the scene: it is the crooked nose, the small skull, the excessively high or low stature, or the floppy ears that are discussed and examined. In short, everything that deviates from a canon that is both statistical and aesthetic captures the attention of scientists and criminologists. The normally conformed skull, or the proportionate and harmonious body, does not attract attention. It is the dissimilar, the abnormal, the deformed, the disproportionate (what deviates from an aesthetic standard) that is indicative of the natural propensity to crime. And it is therefore such an aesthetic judgement that justifies exclusionary treatment, to an even radical extent: people who are born criminal, who are criminal by nature, must be rehabilitated and educated to live within society. If this is not possible, they must be rendered harmless, or eliminated.

Therefore, the law reveals its exclusionary character towards ugliness, in all its violence, in the criminological perspective of Lombroso and the positive school of criminal law. Suffice it to think of proposals such as deportation for petty thieves, vagrants, and habitual offenders,[122] or the proposal of forced hospitalisation for those caught repeatedly in a state of drunkenness or squandering their property.[123] Fortunately, Lombroso's doctrine does not

119 Lombroso, *Criminal Man*, 222.
120 Lombroso, *Criminal Man*, 32–35.
121 David Horn, *The Criminal Body: Lombroso and the Anatomy of Deviance* (Routledge, 2015).
122 Raffaele Garofalo, *Criminologia* (Fratelli Bocca, 1891), 254.
123 Lombroso, *Criminal Man*, 356.

represent the mainstream of contemporary legal culture. But this does not mean that it has not conditioned contemporary legal systems, for example in security measures, those measures applicable to subjects considered, for various reasons, to be socially dangerous, and which precisely have the purpose of preventing the commission of future crimes, rather than punishing criminal behaviour that has already been committed. If these measures, in contemporary Penal Codes, echo the perpetrator-centred model rather than the fact-centred model, and represent police measures applied based on presumed dangerousness,[124] the positivist approach, linking physiognomy to criminal policy, has definitively disappeared.

Conclusion

The exploration of the relationship between aesthetics, ugliness, and the law reveals a necessary interplay between rational and conceptual approaches, on the one hand, and the experience of sensate bodies, on the other. Both beauty and ugliness, while often conceptualised as opposites, function as shifting and overlapping constructs that are employed to include, exclude, regulate, thereby working as systemic factors for oppression and privilege. Accordingly, the discourse on ugliness and law requires to consider both these approaches, thereby understanding how law impacts on lived experiences, particularly for those who inhabit bodies or identities labelled as 'ugly' or 'deviant'.

As we have seen, feelings and perceptions rooted in the embodied experiences of sensate beholders – what we have called "*aesthesis*" – interact with social, legal, and political frameworks. Feelings such as disgust, horror, or fear often drive the social and legal exclusion of specific groups or individuals, shaping legal norms around obscenity, decorum, and public visibility. For instance, laws targeting obscenity or urban decorum implement such negative *aesthesis*, giving legal substance to (also) people's emotional responses to some behaviors and practices: these laws reinforce processes of marginalisation and exclusion, drawing the line between what can enter the public sphere and what must be excluded, between what can be seen and what must not be seen. Moreover, these policies do not deal with the factors underlying situations of decay, be they poverty, unemployment, the housing crisis, or anything else: they simply concern what is allowed to be seen, and what is not.

However, the analysis also revealed the subversive potential of ugliness. Whether through the grotesque in Bakhtin's carnivalesque or feminist critiques of pornography, ugliness serves as a site of resistance against oppressive legal and social systems. It challenges the binary alternative between

124 Ferrajoli, *Diritto e ragione*, 812–13.

normal and deviant, acceptable and obscene, and reveal the contingent and politically constructed nature of these categories.

By embracing this nuanced interplay, legal systems and societies can move towards a more inclusive framework that values difference and complexity rather than suppressing it. Such an approach opens the possibility for reimagining legal aesthetics in transformative ways, inviting legal scholars to unveil exclusionary practices and fully implement principles that celebrate pluralism and the multiplicity of human experience. In doing so, the law would not merely regulate the visible and the acceptable but would engage with the richness of diversity: by recognising the intertwined roles of rationality and sensate experience, we could provide a foundation for addressing historical exclusions and creating spaces where all individuals, regardless of perceived conformity to aesthetic or social standards, are afforded dignity, visibility, and participation.

Index

FSC
www.fsc.org
MIX
Papier | Fördert gute Waldnutzung
FSC® C083411

Kolibri 360 GmbH
Ferdinand-Jühlke-Straße 7
99095 Erfurt, Deutschland
produktsicherheit@kolibri360.de